Kerry E Jacobs

Honorable
Intentions

A Southern Saga

An Edmond Book

This is a work of fiction. The events described are imaginary. The setting and characters are fictitious and not intended to represent specific places or persons.

Any connection between personalities and institutions is merely fictitious and unfathomable.

HONORABLE INTENTIONS
A Southern Saga

An Edmond Book

PRINTING HISTORY
2nd Edition 2010

ISBN: 9798859804689

Printed in the United States of America

10 9 8 7 6 5 4 3 2 1

Acknowledgments

Many thanks to supportive friends and family who not only endured the time it took to write this first work but who gave creative ideas as to publishing. Thanks to my kids David, Timothy, Anna, Jonathan, and Joseph, and their mother Candy, who allowed me the time to study and write. I am also grateful to Ben and Joann Johnston, Jon and Carolyn Jacobs, Jeff and Donna Jacobs, Steve Jacobs, Cindy Jacobs, and some of my encouraging friends at work, Bill German, Mitch Fenick, Beverly Seanor, Susan Loflin and Mike Holtzman. Thanks in particular go to Doug and Barbara Hewes for their critical support.

Much appreciation goes to Mary Reinink and Jon Jacobs who were fair but efficient editors!

Gratitude goes to Sharon S. McDonald of Illinois State University for historical accuracy concerning Andrew Jackson Smith's history.

A special thanks to Robert Whitlow, author of The List, The Trial and other clever works, for giving me writing tips.

A note about Honey Hill. The area where the historical battle took place is not generally open to the public. A historical plaque rests not far from where the battle took place. The owners request that persons interested in visiting call them first to gain permission.

Kerry E Jacobs

June 3, 2010

To Wilda and Jake

Honorable Intentions

A Southern Saga

Prologue

November 30, 1864
Honey Hill, SC

Hellish fire spewed from seven cannon atop a ridge called Honey Hill. Thousands of musket balls cut down northern troops headed up Grahamville Road, a highway in South Carolina which passed between the two 20 foot tall mounds constituting the southern position. Stationed along the top of the two hundred-foot long hills, a small contingency of southern troops held the advantage. The Yankees, five thousand strong, were intent on passing through the Honey Hill structure and destroying the Grahamville Railroad, the only supply line keeping Charleston and Savannah alive.

Screams of pain contrasted with a southern war cry of pungent victory as the Northerner's advance proved ineffective. Without warning a black Yankee regiment charged the plank-less bridge in front of the southern marksmen lying crouched down by a small creek in front of Honey Hill. Abruptly a barrage of double cannon fire and musket balls wiped out most of the regiment. Scalding death accompanied a haunting silence, which was soon broken by cries of mercy.

"Follow your colors!" a heavyset general with a thick beard and thin eyes rallied his troops ready to take the day. He galloped his horse in the midst of another advancing regiment. As he barked out his orders, a musket ball stuck his hand. Nearly falling from his bucking steed, he steadied his horse and fired his pistol across the swamp. All around him men were picked off by another barrage of musket balls. The lone rider led another charge.

A musket ball pierced the man's ankle while cannon-shot struck his chest. The brave soldier was whisked off his steed and hit the ground hard. A fellow officer rushed to the scene dodging musket balls and explosions which churned the earthworks around him. As he rescued his superior, a musket ball hit the general in the square of the back. His companion dragged him over numerous dead to safety.

In proud defiance, a small group of Southerners advanced beyond the barrier of trees and swamp but was violently repelled by northern bayonets. A hand to hand confrontation ensued.

One pot-bellied southerner, apparently out of ammunition, screamed as he swung a musket over his head. A northern sergeant struck the farmer in the shoulder with his bayonet with such force that it broke his shoulder and cut a bloody groove down his chest. The seemingly in slow motion, rose to his feet, hit and killed the soldier with his fists, jerked the bayonet out of his gaping wound and yelled a defiant "forward boys!" In utter shock he lost all his strength and collapsed.

Another more distinguished farmer brandished two pistols killing a number of the northern "aggressors". But a musket ball coming from the Confederate side struck the middle of his skull and he lay dead upon the field. The man behind him smiled, his gun smoking from just having been fired. Instantly, he himself was shot in the head and crumpled down in the creek.

History would record that more Northerners were killed than Southerners on that cool November day. The advantage of an elevated southern position proved too much for the Yankee invasion. The railroad was saved which extended the fading life of the South.

1

Present Day

Monday morning came too early for Jeffrey Carter. Helen Reddy's 'I am Woman, hear me roar' boomed across the speaker of his alarm clock. He respectfully pressed the snooze button and rolled over for another five minutes.

He lived in a two-tenant dwelling in downtown Charleston. One of his goals was to keep from disturbing the elderly man downstairs, which was a little difficult because the man never seemed to leave his residence. His other aspiration was to arrive at work on time, at least once a week. Unfortunately the warmer-than-usual late October sunlight beaming into his room and the fact that he had stayed up too late at a party on the Isle of Palms served to dispel his honorable intentions.

Five feet, nine inches tall, brown-haired, blue-eyed Jeff was still single, a fact that was due to his distrust of women. He had been disillusioned in high school when he caught his girl, Margaret Whinser, a junior, smooching with the quarterback of the varsity team. Yes, it was the quarterback's fault, he well understood. But it still left an emotional mark.

Work started promptly at 8:30 AM. An inventory control clerk for Eppy Electronics, he knew he was destined for greater things. After all, he had a prestigious degree in physical education.

Teaching for three years at a middle school near the city had proven more dangerous than enjoyable.

Man, he was late! It was 8:46. He sat up and swiveled to the side of the bed, put his blue slippers and bathrobe on and went to the dresser. Looking in the mirror, he scratched his face and belly and let out a burp.

"I gotta get a new life."

No time for a shower. The water heater was slow. He told his landlord many times that it needed fixing but was subsequently asked if he needed directions to the 'Y'.

After getting dressed, nuking some coffee and wolfing down some half-burnt toast, he ran out to his red 1978 Chevette.

Jeff's apartment was one of the long, thin houses that had been built parallel to others along Logan Street. There was only space for parking. His yard looked like a dry wasteland overhung with dense pine trees that never let in any sunlight.

After a few false starts, his car revved to life and he sped off towards North Charleston.

It was a twelve-minute drive to work. He passed the old Navy Base and, as always, noticed some prostitutes standing on both sides of the road trying to attract whatever business they could in the early morning hours.

As he turned into the parking lot he saw Jim Singleton, his assistant manager, clumsily hanging a sign Jeff was supposed to have hung that morning.

"Now more grief!" Jeff mumbled as he parked his car in a space by the highway.

"Glad you could make it today, Mr. Carter."

"Sorry I'm late today."

"Today? Try all last week, Carter. Too much more of this and I'll make some needed improvements around here, starting with better personnel!"

Someone in a small, black Accord drove up just in time to interrupt their not so gregarious conversation and a good-looking, well-figured blonde got out. Mr. Singleton nearly fell off the ladder gazing at this beauty as she walked to the door.

"Uh, be careful, Mr. Singleton. Hangin' signs can be very dangerous. Need any help?"

"Just you get inside and get to work before I..."

Jeff rushed through the door.

"Good morning, Jeff."

"Hi, Cindy."

The very attractive-but-married female was twenty-six and had adopted Jeff as her special project. He was the current subject of her matchmaking enterprise.

"So did you go out this weekend, Jeff?"

He shrugged his shoulders.

"I just wish you would date some of the girls I know."

"I go out ... and often. I know how to party just like the best of them."

"Sure, you do, but you always go alone or with Patrick here."

A young man in his early twenties with sandy blonde hair walked up and gave Jeff a high-five.

"What's shakin', dude?   Missed you Saturday," Patrick said.

"How was the game?"

"Went OK. We scored big time, but they got one in just at the last minute. Maybe next time we'll do some serious damage. How was your weekend?"

"Weekend went great. I didn't meet any egotistical women," he said as he smiled and winked at the secretary.

"Pardon me, Cindy, I know you're different. What a gal, fewww!" he jabbed Patrick in the ribs.

"Jeff, you know she's right. When are you going to meet some high quality female types?"

"Who needs 'em? Ahhh, the sovereign male, free as a bird, in command of his existence. That's the life for me," Jeff said rubbing his hands through his hair.

Cindy rolled her eyes and turned to address some envelopes.

He was kidding himself. He was thirty-two and loneliness sometimes proved a sullen, merciless enemy.

"Did you get a load of Mr. Singleton outside? I think he's definitely got it in for you, man."

"Yes," Jeff continued motioning to the front door, "I saw the old gray hawk, but as fortune would have it, Cindy grabbed his attention just in time."

"Well, I still think you'd better cool it for a while. You're this close to hittin' the trail."

"OK, OK, I'll simmer down. It's just so much fun getting different reactions from the old dude."

"What's all the chatter?" a rough voice came from down the hall. A heavyset man with a mustache and smiling eyes interrupted the conversation.

"The floor ready, Jeff?"

"Just getting to it, Mr. Brown. See ya, Patrick, Cindy," Jeff said as he headed to the back warehouse to retrieve merchandise for the floor.

Mr. Brown had served a full stint in the Marines. According to Jeff, he was one of the best managers he had ever had. He was strict when he needed to be and understanding most of the time. But he didn't like a lot of standing around chit-chatting during working hours. Jeff and he had hit it off right away. When he was hired, the first thing he did was to sweep the back of the store. A Marine really respected cleanliness and liked him ever since.

The rest of the day Jeff tried to stay out of Singleton's way, but being in such a small store, avoiding him was difficult. Singleton was a trip, but sometimes Jeff honestly felt that he was challenging him to succeed. He would say, "So, Mr. Carter, when are you going to apply for a salesman's position?"

But then the old man would add a little sarcasm, "Don't have the guts, huh? Well, I know that not punching a time clock and working for commission calls for a little more confidence than you're used to, but someday, maybe you'll have the intestinal fortitude."

Luckily for Eppy Electronics it turned out to be a busy day. Patrick, one of the best salesmen there, sold a lot of merchandise.

Jon Hudson, the only African American on board, stood six feet two inches tall and wore a large, puffy Afro and stylish clothing. Everyone was always complementing him on how well dressed he was. He sold a large screen television and clicked his heels at the commission.

Lewis Jones, a country boy from Tennessee, had a drawl that was unabashedly distinct especially when he spoke with his deep resounding tone. Of course his blonde hair, handsome jaw line and stout physique attracted most of the women who came in the place.

Then there was Brady Combstock, the Nintendo freak of the sales team. It was believed that he had every game available, legally or not. He would often take calls from friends that had nothing to do with company business, a fact that on more than one occasion had almost gotten him fired.

Monday and Tuesday were brisk. Customers were coming in to put gifts on layaway for the holidays. For Jeff however, the days all rolled together. He was living for the weekends especially when the manager gave him a Saturday off.

On Wednesday Mr. Brown reported that a VCR and Camcorder were missing from the cage in the back. Per company policy, everyone in non-management positions was scheduled for a lie detector test. All of the salesmen, Jeff and Cindy passed successfully. However, Mr. Brown, not having been able to discover who the thief was, left work early. He hated dishonesty. He wanted to be able to trust his crew.

Jeff's Thursday morning attempt to impress Mr. Singleton by coming to work early turned to naught when he found that Singleton had taken the day off. Jeff's disappointment turned into glee when he realized that he could enjoy a whole day without the old man's badgering.

Friday came and Jeff was eager for the weekend. Singleton relentlessly pushed Jeff throughout the day. Jeff had been carrying all the equipment from the warehouse to the sales floor, researching prices on the computer, trying to field questions about fixing car stereos he knew nothing about and carrying items out to the customers' cars.

On Friday nights when the last customer left, the employees broke out the beers and discussed the successes of the week. Mr. Brown liked this team-building exercise. After thirty minutes Patrick asked, "You gonna go to your lake house this weekend, Mr. Brown?"

"This Sunday everyone's invited. It's supposed to be 75 in the shade. Weird weather we're having. My new house is almost built.

You'll have to come and see it. New stereo jacks and phone plugs in every room. We'll be skiing out on the lake if you wanna come. Who's gonna be there? I need to plan for food and drinks."

Everyone except Jeff agreed to come.

"I really appreciate it, Mr. Brown, but I gotta help my aunt and uncle."

"They own that old plantation West of the Ashley, right?"

"Yes sir, all 157 acres. That old house was built before the Civil War-"

"Oh, please; spare us the details."

"Jim..." Mr. Brown shook his head to curtail any arguments.

"You go up there every month, Jeff? Don't your aunt and uncle have children to help them out?"

"No, Lewis. Their only son died last year. He was robbed at gun point in Statesboro, Georgia."

There was a short silence in the room.

"The hoodlums were represented by some expensive lawyers from Charleston and got off on a technicality. Anyway, ever since my mom and dad died, my aunt and uncle have always treated me, well, like a son. I know, it's weird, but," glancing at his watch and then at Mr. Singleton he said, "Hey, at least I'm wanted. See ya!"

There were muffled chuckles as Jeff quickly exited the building. He drove to his aunt and uncle's where he spent the night.

2

She never knew a simple breakfast. When her nephew visited, there would be plenty of eggs, bacon, grits, and those delicious southern biscuits made from scratch. The aroma of fresh bacon filled the house and Jeff was soon downstairs in his pajamas.

"Good morning, Jeff. How'd you sleep?" his aunt greeted him at the kitchen door with a hug. His uncle was sitting at the table reading the sports section.

"Pretty well, Aunt Bessie. Hey Uncle Jim. What's cookin'?"

"You know your aunt. Can't leave well enough alone. I have some of those Eggo's or whatever they're called, but she wants to cook everything from scratch. Not that I'm complaining, dear," the older man said as he glanced over at his wife and rubbed his stomach.

"You want to eat out on the porch? It's nice and cool."

"Sure, let's," Jim said as Jeff and he went over to the stove to have their plates filled with great country cooking. They walked upstairs, sauntered down the hallway, walked out onto the back screened-in porch and sat down. Bessie brought some coffee and orange juice.

When Jeff asked for a little syrup to put on his eggs, his uncle gave him a strange look.

"What do you think French toast is? Syrup-on-eggs, with bread. It's just that I done et' the brade 'fore I got to the ay-eggs!"

It was such a peaceful day with the birds making melodic concertos in the wind swept trees. A gentle breeze made for a comfortable setting.

Jim, Bessie and Jeff talked over old times in Douglas, Georgia where Jeff grew up.

Cousins sharing a big water melon in the backyard, his parents, aunt and uncle sitting on the white metal lawn chairs talking about current events, young Jeff helping his folks gather pecans from the sixteen pecan trees located in their backyard, all brought back peaceful thoughts of the past.

His aunt laughed.

"I remember those trees. After you spent your whole day working in the yard, your parents would have you jump in the car and take the bags of nuts to the local market. And what did you do with your wages again?"

"I would take my fifty cents across the dirt road to the country store and buy a ten-cent coke and a five-cent twelve-inch candy cane!"

Playing in the piles of leaves brought back memories of the aroma of Georgia living. His parents were gone now. His mother had succumbed to leukemia fourteen years previous. He was only eighteen at the time. Eight years later, his father died of lung cancer and he found himself in need of close family which his aunt and uncle readily supplied.

Southerby Royale, Jim and Bessie's plantation, held plenty of work for the couple through the years. They tried to keep the grand old plantation house and farm in good condition. But the house with the horse stables located down the hill became a more difficult match for them in their declining years.

"I can't help but admire how well-built this place is," Jeff commented between sips of coffee.

"Yessir, this old place was around ever since 1838. It's been through a lot. The Great Fire of 1861, a major cyclone of 1885 and our largest ever-recorded earthquake of 1886 had destroyed much of Charleston, but this old place has escaped those calamities," Jim said as he stepped inside to get some more coffee.

As he finished the last of his home-made biscuit covered with plenty of butter and grape jelly, Jeff asked, "Aunt Bessie, how are ya'll doing these days? Has Uncle Jim gotten better about taking it easy?"

"You know your uncle. He wouldn't slow down if he were taking his last breath. He's worked so hard for so long, it would almost kill him to -"

"Oh, Mamma," Jim said as he stepped onto the porch. "Don't you go fillin' the boy's head with worryin'. I just do the work a man's supposed to do. I'm as tough as an ox. Right, Jeff?"

Jeff just shook his head and smiled. Drinking the last bit of coffee, he got up from the table, went down to the kitchen, took his dishes to the sink and gave Bessie a hug.

"I'll be out in the south field," Jeff said as he headed out the front door.

"I'll meet you out there in a minute after I get my gloves."

It took Jeff seven minutes to reach the southwest range where he began what would be a long workday out in the hot sun. After a few minutes, Jim greeted him with a smile. He was wearing dingy overalls, an Atlanta Braves baseball cap and rugged brown work gloves. He carried a heavy ax and a fiberglass yellow-handled shovel. Sweat beaded on his face from the short jaunt from the main plantation house.

"Uncle Jim, you're working too hard. When are you going to retire?"

"'Retire' is not a word in my vocabulary. Besides, the day I quit working on this place, they'll probably wanna take it and sell it for development. Then I'd end up in some old folks home being given baths by strangers, not having anyone to talk to and waiting for hours for someone to take me to the bathroom. No, I'm gonna work till I caint'."

The weather was perfect. The subtle breeze gave them some relief from the daunting sunlight. Jim and Jeff worked for the better part of the morning, often taking water breaks at a nearby well.

Jim tipped a cup to his mouth. He breathed rapidly. He was not a man to approach a task lightly but threw great effort into his work. Maybe he could teach his young nephew a strong work ethic, something he thought to have been missing in society.

Looking at the grand, two story house in the distance, he commented, "Yessir, I bet there were many a majestic party in that house. I can just imagine how our relatives enjoyed inviting their society friends from Charleston over for social occasions. Those horse and buggy days must've been mighty fine!"

"It's a beautiful house, for sure. I think it's great how it's been kept in the family. Did one of your relatives build it or was it purchased from someone else?"

The old man took his cap off and scratched his head while spitting some of the tobacco out of his mouth.

"Oh, Thomas Carter. I thought I'd already told you about him and his wife Harriet. They had moved over here from Macon, Georgia. Thomas was interested in the shipping business and with all those wharves in Charleston, he wanted to make his fortune on the seas."

"Now I remember. He built this plantation from the ground up with the help of some of the neighbors, right? They had a barn-raising thing?   But I thought you told me he harvested cotton for a living?"

Jim Carter grinned, "Yeah, Thomas found out how hard it was to work for whom he called 'cranky old supervisors' on the dock.   I guess he discovered he was his own man and could do better by taking a risk by sharecropping. So he earned his fortune by harvesting cotton and building his plantation. It was their dream, both Thomas and Harriet's, to have the biggest, fanciest mansion in the county. And I 'spect they done just that."

"But how could he afford the land? Did he buy all 157 acres?"

"The land wasn't near as expensive as it is now. The government wanted people to move in and increase the economy so sections of land were sold at auctions at one of the public markets on Vendue Range downtown. So after many a year of hard work and determination, old Thomas' dream came true and here we are to enjoy it all. Too bad the place looks so run down now."

He took another sip of water and placed the cup on the well.

"You ready to get back to it, Jeff?"

"Sure, one more sip ..."

As he turned towards the well Jeff thought he noticed someone across the way. He looked again, but shook his head and followed his uncle back to the fields.

3

Returning to work Monday was always difficult after such an enjoyable weekend. Getting away from the hustle of the city and out in the country air was medicinal. Nonetheless he had determined that he would try to smooth things out with Mr. Singleton.

Hanging signs again, Singleton looked down at Jeff as he got out of his car.

"Whoa! Mr. Carter. It's only 8:15. Is there a fire?   Are you getting an extra paycheck of which I am not cognizant?   Have you been summoned to answer for the stolen goods of last week? What with this miraculous event I think I am entitled to early retirement or at least a trip to Cancun!"

"Mr. Singleton, with all due respect, ki... - keep up the good work, sir," Jeff said, trying to be as copiously congenial as he could.

After entering the building and greeting everyone, he went to the back and arranged some of the stereos and other sound equipment in layaway. He was moving a heavy box of glass shelves when it slipped from his fingers and crashed to the floor.

"Oh, crud! How am I ever gonna pay for this mess?   Mr. Brown's gonna kill me. Jeeze!"

He had no other recourse but to explain it to the boss. Wanting to get it over with he briskly walked towards the front office. On the way he passed Mr. Singleton.

"Are we keeping busy?"

"Yes sir. Sure thing. I just need to see Mr. Brown about something, OK?"

"What's wrong, Carter?"

Singleton could spot an obvious nervousness and seldom-present cordiality from is subordinate.

"Nothing. Everything's cool."

Mr. Singleton rushed to the back of the store.

Before Jeff reached Mr. Brown's office, he heard his superior pitching a fit. People all over the store could hear it. Singleton came stomping down the hallway.

"Carter, get your butt back here, boy!"

Cindy and Mr. Brown ran to the warehouse and saw Jim Singleton leaning over an opened box of splintered glass.

"Look at this mess, will you! Bill, you've gotta get rid of this kid before he breaks everything in the store!"

"What happened?"

Patrick and Jeff arrived at the scene.

"Your wonder boy here just managed to obliterate seventy-five dollars of fine glass. What's next, is he going to demolish a computer or set the store on fire?"

"Just a minute, Mr. Singleton," Patrick chimed in. "Ever since Jeff came to work for us, you've been on his case. The floor wasn't clean enough. He couldn't bring your merchandise fast enough. He never measured up to your standards. With all due respect, lighten up, will ya?"

"Need I remind you to whom you are speaking, Mr. Gold?"

Trying to ignore Singleton's behavior, Jeff looked at Mr. Brown.

"I'm sorry for dropping the glass. I guess I was just thinking about other things. I'll pay for the -"

"You bet you'll pay. About a month's wages as much as you're worth!" Singleton said as he stood and approached Jeff.

"Just a minute, Singleton. That's enough."

"I do think it was an accident, Mr. Brown," Cindy interjected. "Jeff's always been careful about the way he's handled things."

"You oughta know, little girl. He sure has handled you with kid gloves if you know what I mean."

"Why you!" Jeff yelled, reaching for Mr. Singleton's neck.

"Hold it, hold it!" yelled Mr. Brown, throwing his arms up, trying to separate the two men.

Jeff threw a wild left hook and caught Singleton on his jaw causing him to fall on the floor. Blood dripped from his lip onto his white shirt. Patrick grabbed Jeff's arm to prevent another swing.

"Someone call the police. This guy's nuts!" Singleton yelled while he tried to get up for another round.

Bill Brown cautiously put his hand on Singleton's shoulder forcing him down.

"You just stay there for a second Jim. I think we all need to calm down," the Marine said to a more readily compliant assistant manager.

"Phone call for Jeff Carter, phone call for Jeff Carter, line one," a voice rang out over the intercom.

Jeff gently broke away from Patrick, excused himself and went to pick up the phone.

"Hello," he said gruffly at first. Then he paused and took a deep breath.

"Is this Mr. Jeffrey Carter of 201 Logan Street, Charleston, South Carolina?"

"Yes, it is. What do you want?"

"Is your phone number 843 555-2955?"

"Yes, it is. What do you need, man? I'm kind of busy."

"And is your social security number 248-00-?"

"What in the world do you want? Need my blood type too?"

"That won't be necessary, Mr. Carter. This is Ellison Graves of Lawson, Marshall, Graves, and Black located on Broad Street. Please forgive the intrusion, sir. I just had to be certain I was addressing the right party. You are the only next of kin. I don't know quite how to put this so I must be direct. I regret to inform you that your aunt and uncle were in a serious automobile accident this morning."

"What the - are they OK? Where are they now?"

"I'm sorry to inform you that they both died in the accident at 9:35, Mr. Carter."

"My Go-! No!" Jeff was stunned. He fell back in a nearby chair dropping the telephone. His head rested in his cupped hands, the tears welling up in his eyes.

Mr. Brown and the others came running up the corridor.

"What's the matter, homeboy? Lost another girlfriend?"

"Mr. Singleton, you are dismissed!" Mr. Brown commanded. "Take a long coffee break - now!" yelled a red-faced store manager pointing towards the lounge as Singleton gave a snide look and about-faced.

Bill Brown picked the phone up and asked what was going on. The shocked look on his face revealed his disbelief. Noticing that Jeff was still shaken, he talked for a few more minutes. Finally he patted Jeff on the shoulder and asked if he wanted to talk with Mr. Graves. Jeff took the phone.

"I know this is terrible news for you, Mr. Carter, but there is the matter of the estate."

"The estate?"

"Yes sir. Your aunt and uncle left you everything. The house, the land, the 1984 Buick Regal, not to mention a checking and savings account, both of minimal amounts."

Jeff dropped the telephone. He fell back but Mr. Brown caught him.

The voice on the other end searched for Jeff's response. Mr. Brown continued talking with the lawyer.

"I understand. Yes, I'll certainly tell him. Thank you," Mr. Brown hung the telephone up and placed his hand on Jeff's shoulder. It was a difficult moment.

"It's going to be OK, Jeff. We're here for you, son."

"Something happen?"

After Mr. Brown explained the situation, Patrick consoled his best friend.

"Oh, man, Jeff, I'm so sorry. If there's anything I can do... Why don't you go home and I'll cover the warehouse for you?"

Jeff stared at the floor.

"That's a good idea. Take a few days off.   Wouldn't that be OK, Mr. Brown?"

"Of course, Cindy."

Jeff sat for a few minutes as the emotional turmoil welled up within him. Finally he stood, thanked everyone, left the store and drove home.

4

Jeff awoke on a rainy Tuesday morning. He couldn't believe they were gone. No more hearing his aunt's cheery tunes at the kitchen sink. All his uncle's entertaining stories about Charleston and southern times …. Those marvelous leisurely Saturday afternoons he had spent fishing on the lake, or rocking on the front porch steeped in conversation - all swept away. He was alone.

The vigil was to be that evening at 7:00 PM. Stuhr's Funeral Home was quite helpful in this difficult task. Picking out the caskets, composing obituaries to submit to the News and Courier, buying flowers, and contacting any friends who might want to be notified of the deaths of the dearly departed took up his afternoon.

It was still drizzling when he reached the funeral home at 6:30. He ascended the stairs and was greeted by Mr. Jon Davenport who showed him to the visitation room.

"Please let me know if you need anything, Mr. Carter. I'll be right down the hallway," Davenport said as he shook Jeff's hand and gave a fatherly wink of comforting assurance.

Patrick, Cindy, and Mr. Brown made an appearance. Mr. Singleton did not.

The beautiful flowers, few as they were, provided a pleasing aroma which served to remind everyone more of life than of death. It was rather disconcerting seeing the two caskets in the same room. The lights were dimmed. Jeff had requested that candlelight be provided to create a reverent ambiance.

He and the others stood near the doorway greeting visitors. Bessie and Jim's fellow church members came to give their last respects. Mr. Graves, the lawyer, representing the estate, stayed until 8:00 when he gave his leave, reminding Jeff of their meeting to discuss the estate.

At 8:45 when it appeared that no one else was coming, a tall stranger entered the parlor. The gray-haired man with a small mustache, wore glasses and had a yellow flower on the lapel of his black, double-breasted suit. Except for his scuffed up shoes, he was well dressed.

"Hello, Mr. Carter," the man said in a distinctly southern drawl. "May I introduce myself? My name is Mr. Jimmy Morris. Your uncle's family and mine go way back." He extended his hand.

"Pleased to meet you."

"I am grieved at Bessie and Jim's passing. If there is absolutely anything that I can do, please tell me."

"You knew my aunt and uncle?"

"Well, not really. Our families crossed paths in the past. We lived right across the way from y'all's plantation."

"How did you know they had been killed?"

"I read the news. I know it might seem a bit morose, but as one involved in multi-level marketing, I have found that one of the best ways of contacting new prospects is to see who has died recently and get a whole new list of surviving relatives in the area. When I saw that my dear, dear neighbors had died and under such tragic circumstances, I might add, I was horrified. And to think that your loss afforded you much sudden gain in the form of all that land and property, I just had to come and look you up. Business, you know."

"You're right, that is morbid," said Cindy, glaring at Morris.

"Be that as it may, I didn't know if you were aware that quite a few times my family has voiced an interest in buying the house and property you have just recently acquired."

There was something foreboding about this man.

Seizing the moment Mr. Brown interrupted, "Pardon me, sir. Need I remind you that this is a wake for garsh sakes! This is neither the time nor the place to discuss the buying and selling of real estate."

"Please don't get upset, sir. I'm merely trying to -"

"I know what you're trying to do."

Patrick chimed in, "Go peddle your goods elsewhere. Let the man mourn, will ya?"

"I think you'd better leave, please," Bill Brown suggested.

"All right, all right. But I'll see you later," Morris raised his finger and pointed at Jeff. "Tah, Tah, for now."

Patrick followed him out making sure of the strange man's quick and certain departure. When he reentered the room, he asked, "Did you get a load of that guy? What century did he drop out of? Don't worry, Jeff. He's a loon. You'll never see him again."

Jeff shrugged his shoulders, turned, and walked over to his aunt's casket to take one more look.

"What a weird world we live in."

Jeff and his friends stayed at the funeral home for another half-hour and finally said goodbye.

"Want a lift?"

"No thanks, Patrick. I want to walk home. Got a lot to consider," Jeff said as he walked down the stairs to the street level.

As he roamed through the well-lit streets of the historic city, Jeff pondered the imminent changes he would face. Renting had not been as appealing as he had hoped. The apartment was roach-ridden although he had tried his best with all sorts of devices and pesticides to get rid of the filthy creatures. Now he could afford to move to a private plantation and get away from the annual raising of the rent.

When he arrived at his apartment, he was emotionally exhausted. To get his mind off things, he fixed himself a sandwich and a beer and checked out the local news on television. Still no suspects from the hit and run that had killed his aunt and uncle. The police could find little information and no apparent motive. They were offering a small reward for any helpful tips on the crime. At 11:00 Jeff fell into bed and went right to sleep.

Wednesday morning came and with it a brief respite from his job. Mr. Brown had given him plenty of time to settle details of his relatives' passing. He went to the 2:00 funeral at the Rutledge Baptist Church where his aunt and uncle had attended. His uncle had been a deacon there. His aunt had sung in the choir. There were about fifty people in attendance.

The pastor waxed eloquent about these beloved country people who had passed through life having touched so many.

"No more tears, nor anguish, nor worries over the things of this earthly existence. They are now joining the heavenly chorus, celebrating a different kind of reality with God Himself."

The graveside service was no different from any other, except for the presence of the two coffins. Fewer people had attended than were at the actual church ceremony. Cindy and Patrick accompanied Jeff for which he was very appreciative. Yet loneliness beleaguered him. He cried silently. Not only was he the sole survivor of the Carter clan, but he realized how few people he had let into his inner circle.

He missed Jim and Bessie's inner strength.

Nonetheless, Jeff would have no self-pity. He had to focus on other things. Maybe he could make a difference as his aunt and uncle had done.

The Baptist preacher offered simple words of comfort. Then the few present sang one verse of "Amazing Grace" and all were dismissed.

Though not ornate, the service was done with dignity, which typified the Carters.

Patrick and Cindy returned to work while Jeff spent the rest of the day milling around his apartment. He ate some cereal while he watched *Ghost Busters*. He had to do something to lift his spirits. Concerned with all of the next day's arrangements, he went to bed early but had difficulty sleeping. He was to be at Mr. Graves' office at 3:30 to talk about his inheritance.

Uncertainty crouched at the door of his life.

<<◇>>

It was still raining when he awoke on a drizzly Thursday. Looking at the piled up candy wrappers and small bits of chips on the floor, he mumbled, "Jeffrey Carter, you are a slob! No wonder you have roaches."

He cleaned his apartment before going to his meeting. At 3:00 he walked to the corner of King and Broad Streets and finally arrived at Lawson, Marshall, Graves, and Black. The old building had retained some of its regal charm. The three-story edifice, part of the downtown myriad of architectural structures, had weathered hurricane Hugo. The earthquake bolts installed through the walls of the building in the mid-1800's had done much to prevent extensive damage. Jeff thought of the measure of quality the architects and builders had expended to create such a stout, functional and beautiful structure. Like fine music, things that were achieved by difficult means would last through the years.

He walked up two flights of stairs to the lawyers' offices. Opening the door, he saw a prim and proper lady in her fifties sitting to the right at a desk near the far wall of the office. A golden chain around her neck suspended the glasses resting on her nose. She wore a smart black business suit, which complemented her distinguished look.

Fancy curtains adorned the windows which themselves must have contained the original glass.

The woman looked up at him and noticing his blue jeans and obvious lack of a tie asked, "Yes, may I help you?"

Her monotone voice indicated her suspicion that this young man might be a straggler from off the street.

"I've come to see Mr. Graves, please. He's expecting me."

"Oh, you must be Jeffrey Carter," she changed her tone, got up and extended her hand. "So sorry to hear about your aunt and uncle. My name is Elizabeth Warring. I'm Mr. Graves' legal secretary. Nice to make your acquaintance. Mr. Graves will be with you shortly. Please be seated," she said, motioning for Jeff to sit on a luxurious couch located across the room near a coffee table filled with current magazines. The offices themselves were practical yet ornate. To his left next to the entrance was a massive old safe.

"Nice vault..."

"Yes, it was here when Mr. Lawson bought the building. I think it dates back to the early 1840's. In fact he told me that it was one of the first ever built in Charleston."

The computer on the secretary's desk looked a little out of place in the colonial setting. History and progress were somehow blended together while displaying an air of professionalism, which so often characterized many law offices in the Holy City.

Coming down a narrow hallway beyond the secretary's desk, a tall, well-postured and finely dressed gentleman entered the room. He greeted Jeff with his condolences.

"Hello, Jeffery. Nice to see you again. I hope things have proven less difficult for you today. Let's come into my office and meet these other men."

Jeff was surprised that other people would be involved.

Graves and Jeff walked down the hallway where he introduced his client to three men all wearing attire much more dignified than Jeff's.

"We could have met in one of the two conference rooms but I thought that my office would be more conducive to a less formal atmosphere. Jeff, meet Mr. Hanover, Mr. Cunningham, and Mr. Habbersham. Gentlemen, this is the young man I was telling you about. He is primary beneficiary to the estate."

Each of the men shook Jeff's hand, and then took a seat in the nice leather-backed chairs situated around Mr. Graves' desk.

"Let me tell you why these gentlemen have come," Graves said as he retrieved a portfolio with "Estate of Mr. and Mrs. James Carter" inscribed on the front.

"All of these gentlemen were involved in business with your uncle in various capacities. There is the matter of debt against the estate –"

Noticing Jeff's worried look Graves said, "Don't worry, son. These debts are not that extensive. Mr. Hanover here is awarded by previous agreement the sum of $2,500 for the balance of services rendered concerning maintenance on the roof of the plantation house over the last five years."

Mr. Hanover looked pleased.

"Mr. Habbersham, for your maintenance of the rugs in the house, your part of the estate consists of $498.23. Mr. Cunningham, for the recent construction work done on the side of the house repairing one of the crumbling walls, your payment is $2,344.00. You were very kind to extend the monthly payment plan to the Carters. Gentlemen, if those terms seem fair then I assume that that concludes our business."

All of the businessmen agreed to the terms. Mr. Graves got up.

"Mrs. Warring has your addresses and will forward a check to you from the estate."

The three men got up, shook hands and left the room.

The lawyer called the secretary in to witness the next part of the meeting. Both of them sat down as Ellison Graves proceeded.

"Jeffrey Carter, being your aunt and uncle's only immediate living relative entitles you to the bulk of the estate which includes one of the two cars, the first," the lawyer paused, "the first was totaled but the insurance should pay the loan company in full, and the second being the 1984 Buick Regal valued at $6,500. There is a checking account with $1,235.00 and a savings account valued at $1,700.00. Also, the main house is valued at $150,000.00 and then the land itself, being 157 acres, each holding a value of $2,625.00 coming to $412,125.00. Should you plan to liquidate all, the total comes to $571,560.00."

Jeff was embarrassed. He was elated. He was saddened at the circumstances. Pressure mounting in his brain, he began to sweat. His hands gripped the arms of his chair.

"There are some features of the estate which should be discussed, however. Stipulated in your relatives' will, they, being the testators, have duly requested that I be the executor. My fee is at issue, the usual amount being 10 percent which equals $57,156.00."

"But Mr. Graves, what if I don't plan to liquidate everything? The plantation has been in our family for more than a hundred years. How can I ever pay you?"

Mrs. Warring interrupted, "Mr. Graves, have you forgotten about the double life insurance policy held by the decedents?"

"Oh, my heavens, yes. Oh my... How could I have forgotten? Pardon me..." Graves said as he hastily fumbled through the black portfolio. He finally found the policy.

"For heavens sakes. I forgot to include these two items. Your uncle had taken out a double policy, one for $2,000,000 on himself and the other for $200,000 on his spouse."

A chill shot up Jeff's spine. He froze.

"Yes, when applied," Mr. Graves ran the numbers again, "the estate totals $2,771,560. After the debts incurred and before taxes, that would leave you $2,489,061.80, a little more than you had before you came to me."

Jeff was stunned. He felt the blood rushing to his head.

Giving Jeff a few minutes to reflect upon the moment the lawyer thumbed through some papers and then continued, "Now I must remind you, property taxes are the responsibility of the new owner. And the federal and state taxes will be figured as to regular formulas. I will apprise you later of what they will consist."

"The tax man always gets his due," replied Jeff with a snicker.

"Yes, sometimes they can be rather extensive in their desire to pursue needed funds. But that's how the government is run," Graves commented.

Jeff swallowed hard.

"That concludes our meeting. Any questions Jeffery?"

"I don't want to appear too anxious but when will the estate be transferred to me, or whatever?"

"The full estate, barring any complications, should be transferred into your name in a few months time. However, there are certain privileges the new owner has. You may reside on the property immediately. The only legal obligation is that, strange as it may seem, you must pay rent to the estate to justify your temporary residence. These funds will be returned to you when the estate becomes yours."

"You mean that I'll be my own landlord?"

"Yes, in a manner of speaking. Here are the proper forms for you to sign."

Mr. Graves handed a small stack of papers to Jeff, explaining the significance of each one.

"I'll be back in a few minutes."

Jeff signed where Mr. Graves had indicated and put the papers back on his desk. Mrs. Warring notarized the documents.

Graves returned and said, "Well, I believe that's all we need to do for now. Congratulations, Jeff. You have inherited a great deal of money. Mrs. Warring will give you your copy of these legal papers. Should you have any questions, please give me a call. Here's my business card."

"I hate to be so forward, Mr. Graves, but .." Jeff paused in embarrassment, "could I keep the Cross pen... in remembrance of the occasion? Besides, it might bring me luck."

"My boy, have it with my compliments!" Graves said with a laugh.

"Gee, thanks!"

Jeff left the law offices at 5:00. He was hungry. He crossed to the other side of Broad Street and walked towards St. Michael's Church. It only took him a few minutes to reach Poogan's Porch, a restaurant he had longed to go to but never had the time.

It was a little crowded, a testimony to the fine food served there. His ten-minute wait was well worth it. Soon seated at a side table near the upstairs banister he enjoyed a delicious New York strip while listening to jazz from a piano downstairs.

Dusk came at 6:30. Jeff walked to Colonial Lake where he sat on one of the park benches. People were playing tennis while others were taking their evening jogs. The lamps surrounding the lake provided many couples with a romantic atmosphere.

"*All that money,*" he thought as he rubbed his hands together. Would he sell the land and live off the proceeds? Should he look up Mr. Morris? With all that cash, he could finally live comfortably.

Maybe he would continue at Eppy Electronics. Mr. Brown had been very good to him. But then there was Mr. Singleton. He threw his head back and gazed up at the October sky. Stars glimmered creating a soothing ambiance. Jeff closed his eyes for a minute. He would make those decisions later. For now, relaxation and daydreaming of future possibilities were the order of the day.

5

Jeff woke up Friday morning refreshed. He decided he would continue to work for Eppy Electronics until things had been fully settled with his estate.

Singleton had decided to take some (as he had stated to Mr. Brown) "well-needed vacation".

At work Jeff received a lot of ribbing from the other employees who had heard about his new residence and property.

Patrick offered to help him move his things to the grand old plantation on Saturday. He was pleased that Jeff and he were friends and determined not to let the money get in the way.

Jeff worked the rest of the day trying to ignore the admiring glances of Cindy the secretary. He could read her mind, "Now that you've got money, let me introduce you to a friend of mine, blah, blah, blah."

The store closed at 9:00. The guys and Cindy were ready to break out the beers in celebration of Jeff's good fortune. Jeff however, wanted to relax after a hectic, emotionally stirring week. He cordially excused himself. Mr. Brown understood.

After driving to a local Kmart, he got a shopping cart and put some creamer, toilet paper, and eight packing boxes he would use the next day, in his cart. Passing the sports section he spotted a glass-enclosed area with a host of different types of binoculars.

"What the hay? I can afford these now," he said under his breath as he caught the clerk's attention and was soon handed a $399.00 set of night vision binoculars.

At Block Buster he rented the movie *Gettysburg*. Jeff remembered the night when it came out at the movies. Patrick had asked him to go but a last minute call from Mr. Brown ushered him to the store for unloading an eighteen wheeler. Trucks would arrive at all hours of the night. Jeff was always on call.

After enjoying the movie, some coke and some microwaved pizza, he went to bed. Finding it difficult to fall asleep, he lay thinking of his new mansion and all that land. Interspersed with his feelings of excitement were pangs of sadness over the circumstances. But what could he do, bring his aunt and uncle back to life?

Early Saturday morning he took a shower, got dressed, and had bagels and coffee. He hadn't realized what a pack rat he had become. After doing some preliminary packing, he sat on the front porch in a rocking chair looking down Logan Street.

"I'm out of this rat hole. Goin' to higher ground."

At 9:15 Patrick arrived at Jeff's apartment. They packed both Jeff and Patrick's cars and drove 20 minutes to his new West Ashley home.

The two men turned off the highway onto the road leading to the main house. The old trees along either side of the long dirt driveway framed a picturesque scene with the elegant plantation house at its center. If those oaks could tell their stories...

Two chimneys stood on either side of the house with a white picket fence-like crown above the top center window. Painted white with those Charleston brown shutters, which were placed for decoration as well as for protection from approaching storms, the two-story house had a look of dignity.

Seven steps led up to the porch with its beveled white double columns all around. The large dwelling was surrounded by a white fence which Jeff's uncle had painted every summer. An ornate lantern hung suspended between the two main columns at the stairway. A low railing surrounded the entire porch.

When the young men emerged from their cars, Jeff just stood looking at the house.

"I can't do this."

Patrick went over, put his arm on his shoulder and nudged him.

"Come on, bro. I'm here for you. Let's go."

Through habit, Jeff halfway expected his aunt's greeting. As Patrick and he walked up the steps, he recalled sitting on the front porch smelling the roses Bessie had planted. After a long day, he would retire to bed and enjoy falling asleep in the cool of the evening. Sometimes, with the windows open, he thought he could hear the church bells of St. Phillips in the wee hours of the morning. It was a scenario that brought peace and a feeling of comfort and safety.

Reaching into his pocket Jeff got the keys that had been given him by Uncle Jim long ago.

"Anytime you want to come and we're not here, just drop in. Our house is your house..." the old man's words echoed through Jeff's mind.

He never expected this might literally be the case.

The home was officially drawn from the double house style, although it had many more quarters that had been added later. Three large rooms were located on either side of the long hallway. The stairs leading to the second floor lay some twenty feet ahead. The Oriental rug was a little worn but still held a beauty that craftsmen of old cared enough to produce.

The woodcarving on the steps and along the twelve-foot high ceiling was reminiscent of prideful work. Paintings of his ancestors lined the walls.

"Nice artwork."

Jeff took the Cross pen the lawyer had given him out of his pants pocket. "Like this? Mr. Graves, the lawyer gave it to me."

Patrick looked at the pen and nodded his approval. Jeff stuck it in his shirt pocket.

Beyond the upstairs landing was a hall leading to the screened-in porch, which stood well above the ground overlooking the backyard.

Patrick and he entered the kitchen and walked to the sink for a glass of water. This was really Jeff's home.

He remembered the times when his family would gather in the kitchen for a friendly taffy pull. It was messy. It took a lot of time cooking and stretching the molasses into strips. The taffy proved too hot for his hands at times, but the end result was delicious homemade candy.

It only took Patrick and Jeff about thirty minutes to unload. Patrick had to meet his girlfriend to move a couch in her apartment.

"I'm sorry I gotta go, bro. But maybe we'll see you tonight?"

"Thanks for your help. I only have one other load and I can get that later this afternoon. Say hi to Sandy for me."

Jeff entered the house again, walked up the stairs and out onto the back porch. A cool breeze blew across his face.

He went over to the screened-in railing and gazed out over countless acres of open land. Some of it had lain fallow for a time to give it rest in preparation for the next planting season. He wondered how he would ever do as much work around the place as his dedicated uncle had done.

He noticed a small receipt on the floor by the table.

"Huh, I wonder who left this here?"

As he bent over, he forgot about the pen he had put in his front pocket. It landed on the deck and rolled just enough to fall through a crack.

He walked to the kitchen, retrieved a flashlight and walked back to where he had dropped the pen. He carefully shined the light down into the space below. To his amazement, he saw a whole chamber he had never noticed before. A hodgepodge of implements and tools lay covered with dust and dirt. His curiosity peaked. He had to get into that room.

Retrieving a crowbar from a nearby utility closet, he placed its end between a board and the supporting underpinning of the porch. The beam wouldn't budge.

"There's got to be an entrance somewhere."

He descended the back set of stairs. Turning towards the house, he saw a small door secured with a rusted padlock. Using the crowbar, he broke the lock and carefully opened the door leading into the underground space. By the look of all the cobwebs and the amount of dust on the walls, no one had been in the room for some time.

His uncle had never mentioned the chamber. Perhaps he was unaware of its existence. Jeff had always assumed the porch covered the rear downstairs rooms of the house.

Using a small flashlight he retrieved his pen from the middle of the dirt floor and looked around.

The dark, damp room was as wide as the porch. But a makeshift inner wall constructed of clay, trash and mortar constricted its depth. A smell of tar permeated the dusty place.

Six tarred brick columns served as supports for the makeshift wall. Each of the columns had two exposed vertical four by four beams strapped to their base to provide extra strength.

Using an old broom he found leaning against one of the walls. he tried brushing the dirt floor but its bristles disintegrated. Rusted nails, a very old hammer, some metal scraps, and oddly enough, a rectangular cast iron basin three feet deep, four feet long and three feet wide littered the floor. Near the basin was a fire stoke. Tar resins were still in the iron trough.

"Mr. Carter, Mr. Carter, are you there?"

Jeff carefully exited the room and placed his hands over his eyes. The contrast between the dark crawl space and the bright sunlight temporarily blinded him. He closed the small door and saw a slender figure against the blinding sun. The smartly dressed, partially bald man carried a brown briefcase and wore black glasses that in every way intensified his stern appearance. He shook Jeff's hand as he invited him in.

Both men sat at the kitchen table.

"My name is Mr. Brody McLure and I represent the Internal Revenue Service. So what do you think of your new fortress?"

"Fortress?"

The man's disconcerting appearance and his unannounced intrusion made Jeff squeamish.

"I really like this old place. It's comfortable. I plan to fix it up over the next few months."

"Ever thought about selling it? It could bring you quite a profit I suppose."

"That's a possibility, but I really like it out here. It's so peaceful and I have my independence."

"Of course, whether you keep it or sell it, I'm sure you are aware of your obligation to the government concerning your contribution."

The man opened his briefcase.

"Contribution? Oh, you mean the taxes. But really, my lawyer told me that any federal or state taxes would be paid by funds from the estate itself. He said that I needn't worry about dealing with the federal government."

"Is this lawyer with the IRS?"

"No, but he is one of the best attorneys in Charleston and he knows his stuff. Besides, I called the IRS about the inheritance tax and someone there said the same thing."

"Well, sometimes there is a bit of confusion in our ranks concerning who gets taxed and how much. I myself am well versed in this particular area of the Federal tax code. I brought this form for you to sign. It merely acknowledges that you have been apprised of your obligation concerning the inheritance tax which is being applied to the monies or estate properties you've been awarded."

Jeff studied the paper.

"Hey, wait a minute, this looks like a transfer of title. What's going on here, pal?"

A nervous and flustered McLure cleared his throat.

"Oh, I do apologize, I handed you the wrong form. Let me look again."

Jeff got up from the table.

"I don't know who you are but I think you'd better leave."

Mr. McLure hesitated.

Jeff walked over to the phone and said, "Look, I'm calling the police!"

The man rose abruptly and gathered his papers.

"The United States Government is not one to be trifled with! I will see you later!"

The man stormed down the steps and walked briskly to his car. He sped away down the oak-lined drive in a cloud of dust.

As soon as he left, Jeff called the local office of the IRS at the Federal Building on Meeting Street but forgot that it would be closed on a Saturday. Things were getting mysteriously complicated.

6

Not wanting to go under the house again, Jeff decided to finish cleaning the kitchen. He turned the radio on and heard one of the many talk show hosts ranting and raving about the minimum wage and the need for economic relief for the common man. He always chuckled when he heard people arguing over things he thought couldn't possibly be fixed. The 11:30 weather report told of a 60 percent chance of rain later that afternoon.

At 12:30 he was finishing mopping the floor when he heard a boisterous voice announcing the daily reading of the Psalms.

"Psalm 37:3 reads, 'Trust in the Lord, and do good; so shalt thou dwell in the land, and verily thou shalt be fed'."

The man asked his radio audience if they had put their trust in God after which he gave warning of what would happen should that not have been the case.

Jeff turned the radio off when the preacher began mentioning his Share-a-thon. It wasn't that Jeff was against religion. He just had other things on his mind.

He left the kitchen and went down the hallway to his aunt and uncle's bedroom. He wanted to start using it due to its being on the cooler first floor.

He dusted the big old oak dresser. The antique had two photographs on it. One was of his great aunt and uncle Harriet and Thomas Carter standing in the front of a newer looking plantation house on a bright sunny day. The other was of his aunt and uncle's wedding. Aunt Bessie was a fine-looking woman in those days. Uncle Jim looked rather noble in his black tuxedo.

While working around the room, he realized that he wanted to pay one more visit to his aunt and uncle's gravesides. He took off his blue dungarees and flannel shirt and put on some respectable clothes. He made sure all the doors were locked and then drove to the cemetery.

The surrounding marshes were peaceful, so full of life and history. He remembered a class at the college concerning the settlers landing at Charlestowne Point, where Charlestowne Landing was. What struggles they must have endured.

With some difficulty Jeff had come to accept his aunt and uncle's passing. The headstones read, "Here lie Mr. and Mrs. James and Bessie Carter, Servants Of The Lord They Knew And Loved."

Next to the site was the burial plot of Harriet and Thomas Carter. On Harriet's headstone was inscribed,

"Born January 8, 1817, Died April 4, 1901. Beloved Wife And Dedicated Christian. She Lived As A Selfless Example To Us All". Next to her gravestone was Thomas' which gave his dates: "Born September 23, 1815, Died November 30, 1864. Thomas, A Defender Of The Faith And Of His Native South Carolina."

Below this dedication was another saying Jeff couldn't read. He went to his car and got a rag, which he used to clean the surface. He read, "Psalm 25:2, 'Gently Resting, Peaceful Sleep, Our Souls The Lord Forever Keep. A Mother Hen Doth Lay Her Young, Guarding O're Them From A Savage Realm. Life A Mystery Forever Untold, Residing Secrets In Columns Of Gold."

"*Wait a minute*," Jeff thought. "Was that how Psalms sounded in general? This sing-songy version seemed a little weird."

He went to the car, got a pen and paper, and copied the strange saying.

Jeff said his good-byes, drove to the plantation, got out of the car, ran up the stairs, unlocked the door and, and after a frustrating few minutes of searching the bedroom, went to the living room and found Aunt Bessie's Bible on the coffee table.

It was well used.

Anxiously he thumbed through the Old Testament and found Psalm 25:2.

"Oh my God, I trust in thee: let me not be ashamed, let not mine enemies triumph over me."

Sure enough, it had nothing to do with the strange saying that had been inscribed on the headstone. He looked for "Columns of Gold" in the book's concordance but found nothing.

Sunday morning came. His alarm went off at 8:30. At first he was disoriented waking up in his new surroundings.

He slept until 9:30, ate breakfast, showered and shaved. He was scheduled for work at 11:00.

Jeff arrived at 10:45 AM. He didn't particularly like working on Sundays but the employees alternated so each one could have at least one Sunday off a month. Business was slow, especially in the early afternoon. He went about the store arranging displays per the directions left him by Mr. Singleton. Removing his smock, he ate an early lunch and went out onto the sales floor to talk with the salesmen. There were great opportunities each week to catch up on the latest technologies in the audio, video and computer departments. The salesmen were never stingy about sharing information concerning their wares. Everyone was a potential customer.

A few people had gathered around the front counter. They were all engrossed in a new 2011 computer being demonstrated by a regional computer representative.

"The XP1211 model has 160 Gig chip with 256 Meg of Ram, a wireless modem, a 160 gigabyte hard drive, a DVD rewritable disk drive, a 27" screen complete with a video camera!"

"I've heard of 'D-V-T' before," said a tall brunette who had apparently been accompanied by her teenager who at that point turned his head in shame.

"Can you really get all of Sherlock Holmes stories on one single D-V-T disk?"

"D-V-D. Yep, you can even get twenty world maps, seven encyclopedias, 5 thesauruses, tons of movies and even nine versions of the Bible including quick word scan capability on this thing. That and a lot more. And with this system, this baby flies!"

Jeff thought he would see if the rep really knew his business.

"OK, say I wanted to see if a certain phrase was in a book. How fast will this thing let me do it?"

"Give me an example."

"What kind of books do you have with you that we can search?"

"I have a Bible disk we can use."

The salesman inserted the disc.

What kind of phrase ya' got in mind?"

"How about 'Dodo Brain'!" Brady Combstock blurted out, looking directly in Jeff's direction. "That ought to be in there somewhere?"

Everybody laughed.

Sneering at Brady, Jeff asked, "How about the phrase 'golden columns'?"

"Golden what?"

"Golden columns. Certainly this macho machine ought to be able to search simple words like that."

"Golden columns it is."

The salesmen initiated a search.

"PHRASE NOT FOUND. TRY ANOTHER?" the computer responded.

"Huh, not in the Bible, sorry."

"Columns of gold?"

The salesman replicated his efforts and had the same response.

"You tried every version of the Bible already?"

"Yep, this does a synchronous search, err, it searches all sources on the DVD consecutively. And neither golden columns or columns of gold is on there. What else?" he asked the crowd who was by now gaining even more appreciation for the technological advances incorporated in the small unit.

Jeff was disappointed and suspicious. He spent a few more minutes observing other tricks the computer could do. Mr. Brown walked up and Jeff and some of the others got back to work.

The rest of the day he cleaned up the back, received some computer software, and drooled over a large big screen television he'd love to have.

When the last customer left the store that Sunday, the salesmen began to chat about the day.

"So you're interested in the Bible now, Carter?" snickered Lewis Jones.

There were a few chuckles.

"Well, not really. It's just that one of my relatives had a Bible verse marked on his gravestone and Mr. 'Super-rep' couldn't find it. Sorta strange."

"Someone made a mistake, Carter. The headstone was really quoting the Book of Mormon!"

No one laughed at Grady Comstock's taunt.

The sales people took a while to talk about some interesting customers.

After a few minutes a lull in the conversation ensued. Patrick and Jeff looked at each other and simultaneously said, "Chow now, hoh!"

They gave each other a high-five and leaving the building, parted company. Jeff headed home down I-26.

It had begun to rain. He didn't like driving during the night in inclement weather. There were more cars than usual headed down the highway. He wondered what he would do that evening.

Suddenly an old red Chevrolet crossed over from another lane missing him by inches. He slowed and let the car gain distance in front of him. When he began to relax again, the same Chevrolet slowed significantly. He could see two people in the other vehicle jostling back and forth. Were they drunk?

As he passed the old automobile, he saw the driver laughing and waving one of his hands wildly out the window. The two men were yelling and cutting up while loud rock music permeated the air. The driver was definitely pointing and laughing at him while the passenger slouched out of view in his seat! Fear gripped the pit of Jeff's stomach.

These guys had certainly mistaken him for someone else. He drove faster.

He wanted to pass the cars in front to create a barrier of safety but the other traffic was breezing down the highway faster than he was. Maybe he could follow the taillights of the other cars and get out of this situation. No dice. The same car came up fast behind his and before he knew it, struck his rear bumper nearly forcing him off the road.

Jeff panicked. His car swerved back and forth on the slick highway. His palms were sweaty. To his horror his car veered off the asphalt and onto the grassy dirt median. He slowed from 55 to 45. The uneven, bumpy ground shook his automobile violently.

Everything around him disappeared as he endeavored to keep his mind on maintaining a steady speed and heading.

The stretch on which he was driving formed a dangerous V-shaped strip of wet grass. Impossible as it seemed, he was going to have to speed up, pass the other cars and get back onto the highway. Without warning his left tire hit a deep hole. His glove compartment banged open and things started jumping out onto the floor near his gas pedal and brake. He tried kicking the obstructions out of his way while maintaining his eyes on the road. The driving rain beat furiously against his window, but he couldn't take his hands off the steering wheel long enough to adjust his wipers to compensate for a better view. Then things got worse. He saw an overpass some 1000 feet ahead.

He jammed on the gas and bypassed two cars whose surprised passengers gazed at him in disbelief. In his peripheral vision he could see the other cars on the highway slowing down. Finally just 30 feet before the bridge, his right front wheel caught the road. The tires of his car gripped the asphalt so intensely that his car spun around. He actually screeched to a halt facing oncoming traffic.

In his elation he rested his head on his steering wheel, dazed by the suddenness of his escape. As he lifted his head, he looked at the license plate of one of the cars that faced him and laughed. It said, "Jesus Loves You".

Out by the highway a construction crew, taking a break from the rain, cheered and applauded. Jeff got out of the car and bowed only to be honked at by other drivers waiting for him to clear out. Reentering his Chevette, Jeff noticed the red car on the far side of the median slowly passing the other stopped vehicles. The driver looked at Jeff with more disgust and disappointment than mischievous laughter.

Jeff's comic relief turned to anger as he sped off to pursue his attackers. As soon as he drove in their direction, they got their car on the highway, nearly sideswiped a Volkswagen bus and sped off.

Jeff accelerated even more but slowed when a police cruiser behind the line of stopped cars started pursuing the red car.

As soon as he arrived at the plantation, he inspected his vehicle. He needed a new bumper. Not feeling safe out in the yard, he entered the house and called the police giving them as detailed a report as he could. Then he called Patrick.

"I can't believe it. They tried to run you off the road?"

"Yes, two of them. Didn't get a good look though. I'm just glad I'm alive. They could have killed me."

"You want me to come over?"

"Too late tonight. I'll just see you sometime tomorrow, OK?"

"Cool, Jeff. Watch your back, hear?"

As Jeff hung up the phone, he slumped on the couch, turned on the television, threw his head back, and rubbed his eyes.

"Think, man think," he said aloud. "Why would anybody be out to get you?"

He had never been into drugs nor hung out with the wrong crowd.

After relaxing for thirty minutes his curiosity was piqued by seeing a TV commercial concerning the importance of investing in gold.

"Golden columns..."

Jeff's thoughts returned to the mystery of Thomas Carter's headstone. Going to the master bedroom he noticed an old trunk with a convex-shaped top at the foot of his aunt and uncle's bed. Unfortunately he found nothing but old clothes inside.

Frustrated, he wondered where any documents or papers pertinent to Thomas' saying might be. "Many people keep old paraphernalia in books," he said and then smiled, "like a Bible with genealogies and stuff?"

He walked swiftly to the master bedroom and finally thought to open one of the two large drawers located under the rice bed. He was relieved to find a large and very dusty black Bible about five inches thick. The book had been published in 1888.

He carefully thumbed through the large volume and reached the Psalms. He found a very old, brittle brown letter from Thomas Carter dated Sunday, November 27. 1864. He plopped down on the bed and read,

"Dearest Harriet,

How I miss your tenderness in the evening. Your gentle encouragement and persuasions... I must tell you of future plans. In the past, we had agreed to limit our activity in this terrible war to that of defending our own homestead. Perhaps this was an error on my part. The fight, it seems, has come directly upon us. We have recently learned that the North in general, and Sherman in particular, plan to invade our beloved South. Grahamville and the railroad are the intended targets. Therefore, with great trepidation, the men and I have decided to help our southern forces in that town. With this, we will be leaving on the morrow, or rather Tuesday (forgive my absentmindedness in these hostile times) in hopes of becoming useful to the southern causes for freedom. Should I not return, I have but one request. So uncertain is the system of correspondence from one city to the next, that I am precluded from telling you plainly.

We have been providentially chosen to safeguard the best interest of our Native Lady, Charleston. So rare, so precious is that which the men and I have been requested to garner, that I call upon you to exercise patience.

Remember how, upon occasion, Aunt Martha had pressed the both of us into playing those obscure little games of riddles on her front porch in the cool of the evening? I used to think they proved quite a waste of time. Herein, for the utmost important reasons, I must once more ask that you have your wits about you and play, not for fun, but for the very survival of the South.

The following phrase will point you in the right direction as to what must be done,

'Gently resting, peaceful sleep, our souls the Lord forever keep. A mother hen doth lay her young, guarding over them from a savage realm. Life a mystery forever untold, residing secrets in Columns of Gold.'

This ridiculous saying should come to light if proper mental powers are brought to bear. The riddle must be preserved at all costs so that it may not be misplaced forever. Take care to reveal the saying only to those in whom you may readily place your trust.

I must leave this correspondence brief. Know that I love and adore you. I miss you all the more. May God's speed be with you and our little family as we face the unknown. Your beloved husband, Thomas."

Jeff was totally confused. What could the "best interest of our Native Lady" be? "So rare, so precious"? "A hen and her young"? Why would it belong to Charleston? He wasn't good at unraveling the mysterious so, dash the time, he called Patrick. They were soon at an IHOP evaluating the document over hot coffee.

"I don't know what this means, Jeff. The words in that Psalm and in that little saying are so strangely different; it's got to be significant. Don't you know any smart people of higher learning to help you figure this out? Maybe somebody at the library? If it concerns a whole city, maybe it has something to do with politics."

"You remember the professor at the college, don't you? You know, the one you met during one of our soccer games? Maybe he can help. I'll try to see him sometime this week. I'll let you know what happens," Jeff said as he put a tip on the table and Patrick and he walked out to their cars.

"Call me, OK?"

"Keep it real."

The two of them drove off into the night.

7

Returning from his vacation Mr. Singleton decided to adopt a better attitude concerning Jeff who also tried to make it easier on the assistant manager. Jeff didn't need any more enemies.

Monday was slow. Mr. Brown agreed to let Jeff leave work at 4:00 to tend to some personal business. He drove to the college, parked along Coming Street, walked to the Science building and bounded up the steps to the main level.

He had taken one of Professor Ernest Helm's courses in Chemistry. Everyone had told him of his interesting lectures and provocative experiments.

The educator held a keen interest not only in his subject matter, but in the students' lives. They seemed to listen and learn from this wise, although sometimes esoteric man.

Jeff walked through some double doors leading into another hallway and turned right into the Geology Center. One of the few people still in the building momentarily glanced towards the doorway and asked, "Yes, can I help you?" The girl was busily studying a geological chart, which was sprawled out on a counter. Two large stones lay near the diagram.

"Nice cleavage..." Jeff snickered as he walked over to one of the samples of shale on the table and picked it up.

"Have you seen Professor Helm?"

"Yes, I think he's in the Biophysics lab," she said as she rolled her eyes and continued on with her work.

"Thanks," he replied, as he put the rock down, bounded out the door and continued down the hallway to the other end. He took the black elevator to the ground level and walked to the laboratory.

He had always wondered about that place. The lab was reserved for the professor's use alone. The professor had certainly gained that right in his own regard. Awarded three prestigious citations by the Institute of Arts and Sciences and various societies, he had also been mentioned in countless news stories about his experiments, which always puzzled the faculty who was not given privy to the details. His popularity with the students, his impeccable character and his teaching ability more than justified his progressive and dynamic activities.

Jeff knocked on the door. A black cloth was draped over the glass. No one having come to the door, he walked to the end of the hallway, went around to the side of the Science building and peered into one of the windows. Through the black curtains Jeff could see a blurred image of the professor inside, protective goggles on his forehead. He was reading by a desk lamp. When Jeff tapped on the window, the professor looked up, squinted and waved. Jeff saw him leave the room and walk into the hallway.

"Is that you, Jeffrey Carter?" the professor asked as he met him at the entrance.

"Hello, Professor Helm. How are you?" Jeff extended his hand. The professor failed to shake it as he went abruptly over to the door of the private lab and made sure it was closed.

"Good to see you, my boy. Let's go to my office," he motioned for Jeff to accompany him to a room across the hallway, the floor of which was crowded with numerous diagrams, charts, and notebooks of documentation.

"Pardon the mess. The maid only comes on the second Tuesday of the week."

Jeff thought about the statement and laughed.

"Just seeing if you're awake."

Putting his protective goggles on his desk, the professor plopped down in a recliner near the rightmost wall and gave a peaceful sigh.

"Please take a seat, Jeff."

A thin man in his late 60's, Professor Helm had white hair extending down to his shoulders. He reached into his long lab coat, pulled out his thick black glasses, and put them on.

"How have you been?"

"Just fine."

Jeff looked around the room. Nothing much had changed since his last visit some months ago. To his left along the wall were two large bookshelves filled with scientific journals and resources. In the center of the room was a large iron stand supporting a huge rock. The professor had told Jeff he found the meteorite in Arizona. He had spent all of that summer exploring a little known canyon floor.

"Ah yes, my meteor," Professor Helm said, noticing Jeff's admiration. "It was with a lot of assistance from heretofore unmentioned helpers that I was able to have the stone transported here for display. Quite a load, heh?" he smiled with great satisfaction as he extracted a toothpick from his lab coat and swirled it in his mouth.

He leaned forward, using his toothpick as a pointer.

"This particular stone is known as a siderite. The whole thing is made of iron. It is thought to be around 4,000,000,000,000 years old."

An IBM computer sat on the desk from which Jeff had taken his chair.

"Oh yes, I just received this machine 2 months ago. It's a lot more advantageous than having to forage through voluminous works,"

Helm said as he motioned around the room at the messy stacks of papers.

The wall facing Jeff had a huge picture of Sir Isaac Newton next to the window.

"Isaac Newton, born 1642 and died 1727. He was," paused the professor with much veneration, "one of the greatest English scientists ever known. He was knighted in 1705 for his many accomplishments, namely his discovering the law of gravity and the existence of binomial theorem. He signed the book you see to your right under the glass on the credenza. It is the famous *Philosophiae Naturalis Principia Mathematica* written in 1687. That cost a pretty penny."

The old man sat back comfortably in his chair.

Jeff went to look at the book. Amazing that something so valuable wasn't in a museum. He sat back down.

"So what project are you working on this time?"

"Funny you should ask, my boy. You see, throughout my life, my favorite subject has been..." the professor seemed unsure of proceeding with this line of conversation, "time...."

"Time? Time zones? History, being punctual?"

"Time...time," the professor repeated slowly, looking up at the ceiling, contemplating the deep meaning of the subject. He smiled as he pushed his hair out of his eyes. "If you only knew, my boy." Again the professor leaned forward as if to begin an intense discussion.

"The number of books which have been written about time are endless, pardon the pun." He smiled. "The what if's of time travel, the indeterminable effects of a time-leap prospectus, the insurmountable list of boundless queries concerning the indiscernible paradigms, the catastrophic reduction of stabilizing factors..."

"Uh, Prof., can we calm down and start speaking a little English here? All I asked you about was what you were experimenting on this time."

"Yes, my boy," he said shaking his head.

"Some mundane study. You wouldn't be interested. How have you been?"

"I'm doing OK. Well, except for almost being run off the road by two crazy guys who mistook me for someone else, I think."

"Ran you off the road? Are you all right?"

"Yeah. Probably just a misunderstanding. Anyway, I have a slight problem that concerns this weird note written in 1864."

"1864, 1864? Where did you get a note from 1864?"

"My great uncle wrote it to his wife. Apparently he was headed off to some skirmish near Charleston. Could you help decipher this?"

Helm got up, walked over to his fine oak desk, sat down and read the letter to himself.

"Huh, written on November 27, 1864. That was on a Sunday."

Jeff bolted out of his chair knowing that he had come to the right place for answers.

"That's fantastic, professor! How on earth did you know that it was written on a Sunday?"

"Oh," the professor pointed to a place on the letter, "it's written right next to the date."

"Oh."

Helm smiled, "Boy, this Thomas character really loved his homestead. And it appears as though he loved his wife dearly, indeed a rare commodity in our present society..."

"Yes, but what is he talking about when he says, 'We have been providentially chosen to safeguard the best interest of our native lady'?"

A puzzled look came on the professor's face. He bit his lip, twirled the toothpick in his mouth, looked around the room, shook his head and said, "Haven't the foggiest!"

He kept on reading, "'A hen guarding her young'? Something's being protected here and I don't think it's little chickens! 'In Columns Of Gold?' What could he have meant by that? Perhaps he was projecting possible images of their heavenly life together? Strange, my boy. Haven't a clue."

The white-haired man shrugged his shoulders. "Have you found any other materials such as this?"

"No. Haven't really had time to look."

Professor Helm examined the letter further.

"Look, my boy. There's another document attached. You didn't see it?"

Jeff leaned forward in his chair.

The professor carefully separated the two.

"It's an obituary. It is hard to read."

Getting a large magnifying glass from a nearby bookcase, he read, "'Thomas Carter, Died the 30th of November, 1864, accompanied by his comrades from Charleston who withstood the northern forces led by General John P. Hatch until his final hour. Bravery described his mindset, passion for a cause his motivation, mastery of execution his strategy, and selfless service his devotion. The South shall miss him. Survived by his wife Harriet and their three children, Nellie, Orson and James'."

"Here, I found this saying at Thomas' grave sight," Jeff said as he handed the professor the piece of paper upon which he had transcribed the strange saying from the headstone.

Without thinking the professor started using the magnifying glass to read Jeff's note. He quickly realized he had no need of doing so and put the glass on the table hoping Jeff hadn't noticed.

After much thought, the professor looked around the room, gave Jeff a blank stare, carefully laid the documents on the desk, sat down and said, "I am confounded to say the least. Apparently Thomas, is it? Yes, Thomas wanted to leave a clue to a very vexing development that concerned him, his companions and even the city of Charleston. Without further documentation, I am left baffled. Time seems to have erased whatever threads of hope we might have had of solving this riddle. Boy, wouldn't it be great if you could go back in time and ask Mrs. Harriet herself?"

Helm laughed aloud as he returned the letter, Jeff's note and the obituary.

"Go back in time? With all due respect, professor, I don't think Aunt Harriet ever came up with the solution. In fact, I think that's why she had the saying put on her husband's tombstone, to preserve it for someone else who could figure it out. Besides, I really don't have much time to waste on frivolous philosophies or things that are not feasible."

"But just think about it, Jeffery. If you could go back and see your mother's wedding," the professor said as he stared at the ceiling. "The signing of the Declaration of Independence, Houdini's first trick, Erickson's final voyage..." The professor went on apparently launched into his own little dream world. "Da Vinci's painting the Mona Lisa, Edison's first successful light bulb-"

"Prof., I get the idea, time travel is intriguing, yet, unrealistic, right? I didn't think such an educated man as yourself would believe in fairy tails like that."

"Have you ever heard of Einstein's River of Time?"

Professor Helm stood and paced around the room as if he were in a lecture hall.

"We all are passing down the river in a boat without ever stopping. We enter into each day's activities, seldom thinking of the past but concentrating mainly on present or future events. What if one were to step onto the bank to pause just for a moment? And in the second of his departure, he would begin to exist in the past. Perhaps there have already been a host of people who have actually tried. No one knows of the unscrupulous experimentation going on neither in California or in New Mexico nor Massachusetts. I believe that the possibility of time travel not only exists but is more accessible to the average person than ever before," said a wild-eyed professor sitting down, his index finger pointing at his chin.

"OK, OK, maybe it's possible, God permitting."

"Why wouldn't He permit it? He certainly gave mankind the ability to reason, to fathom philosophies and logic itself, to explore the reaches of the universe. Mankind might have the ability to create such a thing as time travel."

"Man had the ability to invent cloning."

The professor pondered these excursions into the ramifications of his musings. A frown came across his face.

Jeff could see the professor was discouraged.

"All right. You're right. I mean, just think of all the good man could do, knowing all we know. If we were able to return to the past and make things right, we could improve the industrial revolution while preventing child labor abuses. We could prevent the taking of the Alamo, or World War II or even take Edison a modern day version of the light bulb."

The professor got up, leaned forward on his desk and sternly addressed Jeff's speculations, "Oh no, my young man."

He came around his desk and approached Jeff. Whispering, he said, "By no means could we interact with those of the past. Dabbling in the affairs of men would prove catastrophic for future events."

"How boring. That would mean viewing time from the bushes or a rooftop. How enjoyable would that be?"

"Not enjoyable, Jeff, educational! We could learn so much about the whys and wherefores of life. Who killed Kennedy? What really happened with the Hindenburg? Was Atlantis a real entity or mere legend as many have espoused?"

"So who would volunteer to be your first vic- I mean, passenger?"

"We would introduce the procedure with, say, a non-human subject like NASA did with their chimpanzees. Later, I, of course will - I mean, would, if such a machine existed, make the first journey. Who knows, maybe someday I would be able to show you the machine, in years to come of course."

"So you've invented a time machine. Look Prof., can I retake some of my college exams?"

"Jeffery!" Professor Helm raised both of his hands. His whole demeanor changed as excitement was replaced by suppressed disappointment. He leaned back calming himself.

"You dismiss so quickly the possibility of that which we have not yet experienced. Just because we can't see air, we all breathe it daily. Try to think outside of the box. Think logistically for a moment. What if we could take one atom, one single atom from a man's body, isolate it, and suspend that entity from the present for say... one second. If that were possible, that would be the window through which we could send the whole being into the past. That would adequately prove the feasibility of time travel, would it not?"

The professor could tell that Jeff's interest was piqued.

"Just think of it, the first real time travel episode-"

"A what?"

"A time travel episode just means that a person, animal or thing would be sent back in time and retrieved all within a well-defined space and time frame. A person could experience a presidential inauguration or the filming of a major movie like *Gone With The Wind*. The only problem would be that no interaction could take place. The subject would be like the proverbial fly on the wall."

Jeff looked at his watch and said, "I've enjoyed the talk. Maybe some day I'll take you up on that time travel thing. All I know is that Thomas Carter was killed during the Civil War. Do you think that I could borrow any books, say of quotations or who's who that might have that phrase 'Golden Columns' in it?"

"No war is civil..." the professor murmured under his breath. Clearing his throat he walked over to one of the walls of resource books and said, "Ah, yes, here we are, Martin and Dashal's *Famous Quotations*. This volume dates back to the early eighteen hundreds. Hope this helps. Let me know how you come out."

They shook hands and Jeff walked into the hallway towards the outer door. Thirsty, he thought he'd go to the student center and get a Coke. As he bounded out the door and turned the corner near the windows of the laboratory, he could hear the professor walking down the long hallway towards the off-limits lab. Without warning he saw a brilliant flash of light accompanied by a brief mechanical scream from the laboratory. He shrugged his shoulders and thought little of it.

8

The rest of the week proved uneventful. The same mini-skirmishes with Mr. Singleton were annoying but not as threatening as the major blowout. On Thursday morning, Mr. Brown reported that a computer was missing. Again the polygraph tests were administered and everyone passed. Mr. Brown was in a rotten mood until Patrick's eleven thousand-dollar sale of televisions to Roper Hospital lifted his spirits.

Jeff was relieved that his boss had scheduled him off on Saturday. His plans of playing tennis with Patrick were dashed when a local weatherman announced downpours throughout the day. He showered and shaved, got a bowl of cereal and went to the living room where he turned on his uncle's old 25" console television.

There were plenty of old movies, cartoons and documentaries available. Feeling lazy, he landed on an episode of Bert and Ernie of Sesame Street fame.   A knock at the door startled him. It was 9:00 AM.

"Hey, bro," Patrick said as he entered the hallway. Jeff and he exchanged high-fives. Patrick put his blue parka on the porch.

"Just thought I'd keep you company. Oh, watching the Muppets, huh?"

"No way... I just turned the TV on."

With renewed interest, Patrick said, "Oh yeah. This is the one where Bert and Ernie explore the attic."

Jeff looked surprised that Patrick would be familiar with the show.

"Oh, my nephew has the tape. Uh, not that I watch it or anything. I had to babysi-" Patrick could see that he was digging a bigger hole for himself.

"What's this?"

He changed the subject as he reached for the old quotation book the professor had lent Jeff.

"Oh, yeah, don't you remember that strange saying about golden columns? I looked through that book but the phrase wasn't there either. If we could only find more about Thomas and his death, maybe we could get some answers."

"Did you go to the library like I suggested?"

"No, to the college. But Professor Helm couldn't help."

"Oh, yeah. Well, didn't your folks keep any records, scrapbooks or diaries? Maybe there are some old photos that could help explain your mystery."

"That's a great idea!"

They both looked at the television, back at each other, and said "To the attic, dude!"

Jeff took his dish to the kitchen and they bounded up the stairs. On the second floor landing, they continued walking until they reached the last room on the right before the porch.

Turning into the room they saw a rice canopy bed that took up most of the floor space. On the far side of the bed were two large windows being pummeled by the rain.

The two young men ascended into the cool, dusty attic.

"What are we looking for, Sherlock?" Patrick joked using an English accent.

"Anything that will help us solve our mystery, Watson... You mentioned diaries and letters. Maybe something someone wrote will give us a clue. Just start looking."

Four large wooden trunks of various sizes lined the walls. Boxes of books and papers were stacked in the middle of the room.

In one corner hung an old army uniform and a World War I hat. Occasionally a heavy beam of sunlight revealing a break in the cloud covers shot across the room exposing the stirred-up dust particles.

"Boy, I sure am glad we didn't have to read this stuff," Patrick said as he handed Jeff an old first grade reader.

Jeff opened the front cover and read, "'If my name you wish to see, turn to page one hundred and three.'"

He turned to that page and saw Aunt Bessie's name inscribed. He chuckled and put the book down.

Jeff went over to one of the large footlockers and opened its scratched lid. He dug through some clothing.

"Jackpot!" he proclaimed. "Look at all these old diaries. They must cover the last two hundred years. We've got to be extremely careful or they might fall apart."

"You don't want a set of used hubcaps, do you?"

"Patrick. Old buddy, please quit clowning around and help me look at some of these books. Each one is a five-year diary. Here."

Jeff handed Patrick a small book dated 1866-1870.

"Can you imagine the kind of history that's recorded in these? They must be worth a lot of money. How come your aunt and uncle never did anything with them?"

"Guess they were too busy with other things. Who knows?"

Opening a diary labeled 1860-1865, Jeff read with interest how apprehensive Aunt Harriet had been about the approaching northern armies. She frequently referred to the articles in the Charleston Courier, a leading newspaper at the time.

"Boy these Southerners wanted Sherman dead in a bad way. Just reading these words makes me realize how much the South hated those Northerners."

Jeff nodded as he read on. Aunt Harriet was so concerned about the changes her South must undergo. He was surprised at how similar her words were to those of present day. He had expected to read a lot of "thee's" and "thou's".

"Let's see... when did Thomas die? Oh, what a lamebrain. I left Thomas' letter downstairs..."

"I'll go get it. Where is it?"

"Wait a while, Patrick. Dude, look what I found in this diary. It's a picture of Thomas' gravestone."

"Died: November 30, 1864."

Turning the picture over, he continued to read, "'Herein lies an honorable man who fought for his country in the skirmish of Honey Hill, South Carolina. His beloved Southerners will not soon forget him. Southern Society of Confederate Daughters of America, Chapter 14, November 30, 1904.'"

"Uncle Thomas died in a skirmish on the Wednesday after Thanksgiving, 1864! Now we can go to the library and see if any notes of the battle exist. This is cool," Jeff said. "I wonder where Aunt Harriet was before Thomas was killed."

Carefully flipping the pages, he turned to Tuesday, November 22, 1864 and read Aunt Harriet's troubling words.

"'Alas, I have had to take our children to Columbia to await the coming of my dear Thomas who has elected to guard our plantation West Of The Ashley. We have been reading recently in the Courier that Sherman has plans of taking Beaufort, South Carolina and making it into his headquarters. May our mighty God defend our faithful soldiers in their quest, for they shall affront the enemy provisioned with guns in hand and equipped with an honorable cause. God be with our men and boys.'"

"Huh. Harriet didn't know her own husband would be going into battle then? Boy, reading all this stuff is like going back into history. All those descriptions about impending invasions. Too bad we can't just take a short trip back and-"

"Patrick, don't even go there."

Jeff returned to his reading.

"Something strange was going on here. Uncle Thomas was definitely involved in some weird circumstances."

"Let me see your diary. I just wanted to see what Harriet was thinking near Christmas. I wonder if she'd had made it back to the plantation by then."

Patrick carefully turned the brittle pages until he got to December 25th, 1864 and began reading, "'How I miss my darling Thomas on this most holy Sunday morn.' Apparently she knew he had died. But it still doesn't say whether she had moved back to Charleston. The siege lasted until when?"

"I think they took Charleston sometime around January? I wonder if she even had him buried herself?"

"Jeff, bro. Wouldn't all of the men have been buried on the battlefield?"

Jeff frowned, "So you're saying that Thomas' grave is -"

"Empty. Probably! Sorry."

"Read on. Anything in the days after that?"

Patrick looked ahead and said, "Bingo! Here it is, bro. 'I am so troubled over the golden columns saying that my dearly departed left me. Lord, please help me. I am caught betwixt two positions. He swore me to secrecy only releasing me from such if I were unable to understand his little riddle. But he had told me to preserve the saying. I know I cannot even begin to make any sense of it. Thus I have decided that I shall have a new headstone placed on my beloved's grave. Perhaps someone with more faculties than I might come to some understanding. God help us discover the meaning of this haunting mystery.'"

"So I was right. Harriet left the saying in the most obvious place. And no one found it until now."

"Good work, Sherlock!" Patrick quipped. "But we still don't know what the phrase means."

"Maybe we'll find something in our research about that Holly Hill."

After searching the web for five minutes, Jeff said, "My brain must be dead, Patrick. It's not Holly Hill. It's Honey Hill. Look at all these listings. Gee, this Gary Myers has a great web page."

The two explorers soon found a plethora of old renditions of the battle written by generals, commanders and other subordinates each detailing a different perspective.

"How in the world do I tie all of these together? These reports only mention certain dignitaries and groups of men. I seriously doubt we'll ever find anything about Thomas this way."

It was getting late in the afternoon. Patrick looked at his watch and remembered that he had to leave to go with Sandy to the mall. The prospect of looking at women's dresses just didn't thrill him to death.

"It's gotta be true love..." Patrick said as he left his friend who was still working at the computer.

Jeff printed out many of the battle renditions so he could study them on breaks at work. After downloading a map of the layout of the Honey Hill site, he printed 12 copies so as to graphically draw out the troop movements described by each of the writers. Then he planned to put it all together so as to better understand what transpired during the terrible skirmish.

He returned to work Sunday morning. During breaks he would read another document concerning the battle of Honey Hill and map it out on a separate Honey Hill page. This formed a clearer understanding in his mind.

Apparently about 5,000 northern troops advanced on a small community near Grahamville trying to destroy the rail lines in order to cut off the supply line leading to Savannah. Even in the face of insurmountable odds, the small group of Southerners, 1,400 strong, held the Northerners at bay. Many more northern troops than southern forces were killed. Still, some miracles occurred. One man, a General Hatch, was shot five times but still lived to tell about it.

How the battle could have remained little known was a mystery.

After hauling stereos and televisions to the customers' cars, Jeff was ready to leave work. That evening he asked Patrick if he wanted to walk with him in downtown Charleston. He didn't feel comfortable touring the city after the two hoodlums had tried to run him over.

Always eager to look at more than old buildings, Patrick agreed. "I'm a girl watcher..." Patrick sang as the two of them headed into town.

They parked on King Street on the other side of Marion Square and strolled towards the college. As they turned from Calhoun onto Coming they walked a few blocks and noticed an abandoned parcel of land on the right side of the road.

"I hate to see vacant lots in Charleston. It always makes me wonder if some old building was torn down. Vanishing history, huh?"

"Maybe some day when you're rich and famous you could build a burger joint there?"

Jeff was not amused.

The sun was setting as they walked past some great private gardens on the lower Battery. The aroma of the seawater and cool breeze was heavenly. Bicyclists were enjoying   leisurely jaunts in the cool of the evening.

At one point, Patrick thought he saw someone staring at Jeff and him from behind one of the trees at White Point Gardens.

"Did you see that?"

"See what, one of the beautiful babes you've been gawking at all evening?"

"No, really, I thought I saw a putty cat - I mean, there was a man in a raunchy coat looking at us from one of those trees yonder."

Patrick and Jeff ran as fast as they could, dodging people having late evening picnics and a group of youth playing their guitars. They almost caught up with the man but he ducked into a waiting car and escaped.

"Who on earth was that? Was it those jerks who tried to run you off the road?"

"I don't know. Didn't get to see their faces!" Jeff said as he gasped for breath. "Different car too."

"So much for excitement. Oh well. Meanwhile, it'll be back to boring work tomorrow."

"Yes, but then there's always Mr. Singleton."

9

Jeff was a little late on Monday morning. His worries disappeared when he drove into the parking lot to see Mr. Singleton's car was missing.

"He had to go to Columbia for some sort of meeting," Cindy said. "Besides, did Mr. Brown tell you that the store will be closed for extensive remodeling from Thursday through the weekend?"

"Mr. Brown's not paying us for the days we'll miss, is he?"

Cindy just smiled, shook her head and returned to her typing.

With a short workweek, Jeff's workload increased. People were scampering to set up their layaways.

Having nothing special to do Thursday morning Jeff thought he'd visit the professor again. He wanted to apprise him of the developments in his unraveling mystery.

He drove to the college rather early and walked to the science complex. He walked up the stairs and through the double doors past the Geology Center, took the black elevator down to the ground-level hallway and approached the mysterious lab. Jeff could hear the same whirring sound that had startled him on his last visit. Curious, he entered the forbidden lab unannounced.

The professor was shocked by Jeff's intrusion. Moving his safety glasses to the top of his head, he screamed over the noise, "Jeff, whatever in the world... how are you, my boy?"

He walked to a desk in the middle of the room, quickly closed a thick notebook, and briskly strode over to a large machine. As he pulled a lever and pressed a series of knobs, the noise dissipated. After a few minutes, there was dead silence.

"Just finishing up an experiment," Professor Helm said as he motioned for Jeff to go across the hallway to his office.

"This is it, isn't it?"

Jeff didn't budge. Hands on his hips and a broad smile on his face, he stood looking at the professor.

The dumbfounded scientist meekly but ineffectively looked around the room and retorted, "Whatever do you mean?"

"Come on, Professor, this thing is your time machine!"

Helm dropped both his jaw and his notebook. He began to stutter as he fell back against a desk and put a hand to his forehead, "That's ridicu- how could you have- what I mean is, uhh?"

"Look, you're always working on secret stuff. The last time I was here, you talked about time travel. Two and two ... make four?" Jeff said as he picked up a very old newspaper dated December 17,

1903, the front page which read, "Wrights Brothers Successful At Kitty Hawk."

"Planning on going somewhere?" Jeff chuckled as he held the paper up.

The professor retrieved the notebook, walked over to a nearby chair and plopped down despondently.

"Your secret is safe with me, Professor. Just tell me a little about it, OK?"

Accepting the inevitable, Helm stood, smiled and put the notebook on the table. Closing and locking the laboratory door he said, "I've dreamed all my life of creating the perfect invention. And I think I've done it. Well, I know I have!"

He walked over to a massive object that looked similar to a large top located in the center of the room. It was cradled on its side, a six-foot shaft securing the structure to two vertical parallel steel bars.

Jeff looked with interest all around the laboratory. All of the black curtains were drawn. Across the room facing the "top" was an octagonal-shaped glass booth with its small doorway facing away from the top.

Three large computer banks lined the walls in back of the octagonal chamber. Along the right wall stood a clothes rack full of period clothing; uniforms, dresses, shirts, hats and boots. To the right of the clothes closet stood a table full of old money.

"How long have you been working on this?"

"From design to fabrication... ten years. Just completed the finishing details within the last few months. But I was having the most terrible time trying to locate a constant power source for the experiment."

"Why would you need a constant power source?"

"The energy sources, light, water, electricity, even nuclear, all have one thing in common; they fluctuate. These unstable forces would inhibit a safe and responsible period in which to prepare the time traveler for his journey. Within the few minutes it takes to initiate the time travel sequence, the traveler might lose an atom. He or she might become disfigured from the mixing up of his or her chromosomes. It could be catastrophic for his or her DNA structure."

Professor Helm paced around the room.

Then he stopped, turned to Jeff and with an excited look walked over to the control console. "But I finally came up with a system. You see, this panel controls all activity via the Time and Real Integrated Gyroscopic and Genetic Electromagnetic-Regeneration machine. I call it 'Trigger' for short."

"Good!"

"Before something is transported back into time, the item must be processed, all of its parts identified. The DNA mapping, the volume of water and chemical makeup, physical structure of height, weight, pigmentation, buoyancy, cell arrangement, physical stamina, even the mental-psychological schema wherever applicable, all must be identified in preparation for transport. In my system, in one instant, in a millisecond, in one 'impulse moment' as it were, the perspective time traveler is captured and held in a protected state of suspension. Instead of waiting for his essence to be developed into a traveling form, he is extracted from our present time instantly and thrust into a holding area - another dimension if you will, where the time travel event begins."

He proudly placed his hand on the controls.

"With the help of Einstein and others in the field, I have been able to develop a machine that can envelope a subject instantaneously and prepare it for travel!"

"Cool."

"Once that is accomplished, the spinning top projects the image and translates it into another time period. At the other end, the retrieval belt reassembles the subject to its former exact form and, voila! Time travel is born."

Jeff was amazed.

"And it works?"

"There is but one glitch. On the other side of the time wall, while coming out of the freezing process, the time traveler might experience some discomfort, a major jet lag if you will during his or her re-assembly. For a period of a few seconds, he would probably be unable to move. Breathing would be possible but all other motions suspended."

"Couldn't that be dangerous? Besides, how do you know this? Have you gone anywhere yourself?"

The top began to turn and vibrate. Jeff jerked his hand away and backed up a few feet. The noise grew to intense proportions and the professor could not hear a thing Jeff was saying. A blue light filled the octagonal chamber. A myriad of laser-like beams shot all around the laboratory. Wind produced by the colossal top was blowing papers from one end of the room to the other.

The professor grabbed onto the control booth, leaned over to Jeff and shouted, "It's happening sooner than I anticipated!"

"What's happening?"

The intense pulsating blue light from the center of the octagonal chamber changed into the form of a small body created right before their eyes. Finally, a yellowish brilliance displaced the blue light altogether and the noise and rotating motion of the top stopped as quickly as it had begun. The professor and Jeff froze in utter amazement. Standing as stiff as a board in the chamber was a chimpanzee!

"Esmeralda! You're back!"

Jeff fainted.

After a few minutes, the professor revived him.

"Jeff, are you all right? Speak to me..." he said as he patted him on the face.

"Yeah, Prof..." Jeff trailed off. "I'll take a cheese burger with extra biggie fries..."

Then he regained consciousness.

"Is that a chimpanzee?"

Jeff got up on his feet but soon sat in a chair by the desk.

"Yes, my experiment actually worked! To top it all off, I now have a credible witness; one not predisposed to disbelief. An objective eyewitness!"

"Let me get this straight, Professor Helm. Esmeralda is from the past?"

"No, my boy. She is from our time. But she has been to the past and returned in a matter of minutes!"

"This is too much!" Jeff said as he put his right hand on his forehead and moaned.

"This is impossible. I think I'm going to be sick."

"Here's further proof for you, my boy. Look what she brought back."

Helm handed Jeff a News And Courier dated December 1, 1901.

"Yes, my boy. The date in which the South Carolina and the West Indian Exposition began in Charleston. Captain F. W. Wagener initiated the idea to help the South recover from her financial troubles caused by the reconstruction of the Civil-"

"Please stop the history lesson, Professor! You just sent a monkey a hundred years back in time!"

"One hundred and nine.."

"This is a little hard to swallow. Besides, just think of what might happen if this thing got into the wrong hands!"

"I have thought about that. The ramifications are clear. Secrecy is of the utmost importance."

"And just think of the danger the chimp was placed in. I'm not a member of PETA, but any animal or time traveler might have been killed. How did you keep Esmeralda from being transported into a brick wall or underneath a moving train?"

"After years of studying physics, magnetism, gravity, barometric pressure and the tides, I was able to develop what I call a deflective automatic placement belt which you see around Esmeralda's waist. This is the retrieval device I mentioned before. The sensors on the belt act as repulsion units seeking out clearings or wide-open spaces. Upon entering the new time, the sensors actually serve as relocation devices to safeguard the health and welfare of the traveler. They push the "essence" of the person or subject away from objects to make for a safe landing. The manipulation is vertically and horizontally effectual," Helm said as he went over to the chamber, gave the chimp a hug and removed the belt. He spent a number of minutes doing some evaluatory tests to see if she was all right. With help from computer analysis, her normalcy was confirmed.

"But wouldn't the belt itself have to solidify before it could do all that?"

"Good observation, my boy. With the assistance however of my TCSU or Time Continuum Stabilizer Unit, the belt is the first thing to materialize thus giving it sufficient time to do its thing."

"That's fantastic, professor! But how did you get the monkey back? She couldn't have returned by herself."

"Esmeralda is a chimp. See, no tail. Anyway, by virtue of the belt again. With the use of my control panel, the belt records the time of departure from the present, the number of hours or days stipulated for the time travel event, the exact position of arrival, and the time of return to the present," the professor explained as he gave the chimp a banana and instructed her to sit in a chair near the clothes closet.

He motioned for Jeff to join him at the control console.

"It sounds like I've been doing this for years, doesn't it. Oh my, what a success! The time traveler has, therefore, little to do to get back. The only thing he or she must do is to be at the location where he first arrived in the past. The belt alarm lets him know how much time he's got to get there. I spent hours training Esmeralda to wander around until she heard a signal from the belt itself. She did as instructed, stole the paper and came back. Smarter than we think, these creatures. And the rest is... well, history."

Jeff was dumbfounded.

"You are the only one who knows about my time machine. I have attempted to document everything in journals located over there." He pointed to a large locked glassed-in bookshelf near the money table.

"But since you have inadvertently discovered my machine, I have also decided to entrust you with hands-on training, my boy. I deem you as a mature and serious student and also a trusted friend. I cannot relegate knowledge of this to documents which are open to misinterpretation. Someone must have experience in these matters. And that someone is you. Can I trust you, Jeff?"

"Yes, you can."

"Keep in mind, my boy, that this machine has never been used to transport human subjects. That experiment will come, but in the distant future. I myself must be the one to take the initial run. And perhaps, with your help..."

"I'd love to. But why wait?" Jeff asked eagerly, looking intently at the control console with all of its mesmerizing dials, knobs and digital displays. "We can go anywhere, anytime..."

"More tests must be performed to insure the safety of both passenger and of all history. Besides, the time traveler must be thoroughly prepared for the journey. Part of the preparation is educational. The traveler to the Rome of 44 BC must have studied the period to adapt his mindset to that time. He is then attired in proper clothing. No Nike's in 1600, my boy. Then and only then is he ready to ascend into the chamber and begin his sojourn."

Jeff was disappointed.

"Patience," the professor said, as he patted Jeff on the back.

"At least you're getting in on the ground floor so to speak."

The professor spent the rest of the evening showing Jeff how to manipulate the controls for a time travel event. While thoroughly honored by the professor's familiarizing him with the system, Jeff knew that he would never even think about using such an unsure thing on himself. He wasn't crazy.

10

Jeff's non-paid vacation ended.

"Will you just consider going out with my friend?"

"It's much too early to think about. Besides, you've begged me for the last three weeks about one particular girl. She's either homely or very boring. What's the scoop?"

"No scoop. I just think you'd like her."

"I bet she weighs four hundred pounds and has a tooth missing."

"No, look, here she is," Cindy handed Jeff a wallet-sized photograph.

"Sandra Bullock?"

"Looks like her, doesn't she?"

"Whoa.... she's a fox! OK, it's a deal. Maybe Patrick will double. Can you call her and set it up for Friday night?"

"Yes. I'll call you with the details. Her name is Hilda Macobran."

"Hilda?" Jeff rolled his eyes. "OK, OK, it's a go. Don- worry 'bout it," he said as he went to the back to begin his long day's work.

Friday night was warmer than the first of the week. Jeff called Patrick from the plantation at 5:30, drove to his house, and picked him up. The two of them went to Sandy's and continued to Hilda's. Driving down Highway 61 surrounded by those beautiful grand old oak trees was always enjoyable.

Jeff parked in his date's driveway and walked nervously to her door. The good-looking woman was even more attractive in person. She wore a sharp classy brown dress whose hemline fell below her knees. A black choker and a gold ankle bracelet completed a perfect picture. Her makeup served her well. Her dark brown hair was stylishly combed back accentuating her shapely neck.

"This is going to be a memorable evening," Jeff thought as he walked with Hilda to the car.

"Nice to finally meet you."

"Nice to meet you. Cindy mentioned you a few times. Sometimes we take an early lunch down on East Bay. She was right. You're cute."

Jeff grinned and opened the front passenger door for her.

"Oh, can I sit in the back with Sandy?"

Jeff's heart sank.

"*Red flags, red flags!*" he thought giving Patrick a puzzled look.

After everyone was seated, Jeff turned to Patrick who was sitting in the front passenger's seat and batted his eyes.

"How romantic."

Everyone laughed.

"Are these the new night vision glasses you bought?" Patrick asked taking them out of their brown leather case.

"Yeah. I thought you might enjoy looking at them. You can see over six hundred feet."

They made their way downtown and turned onto South Market. As usual, parking was difficult. Many tourists moved along the streets, weaving in and out of the market square buildings searching for good deals.

Finally a parking space opened near the corner of South Market and State. The foursome walked around for a while until they got hungry. Swenson's was busy. The ice cream factory was full of onlookers drooling over their wares.

As they approached East Bay they noticed the Customs Building, which always looked pretty during day or night, the latter of which was ensuing. They crossed over to North Market and doubled backed to where most of the bars and eating joints were. Each building they passed had its own selection of music. They went from jazz to rock-n-roll to beach.

Approaching State they saw a one-man band set up between two of the market buildings. He wore a long black coat. People threw money into his top hat as he sang Bob Dylan songs.

The foursome entered Stacey's, a large bar and grill Jeff and Patrick had frequented. Walking in, they noticed the huge circular bar with a nicely finished wood grain top. The place was crowded. "The Sandy Plains", a country band, was playing tunes from the seventies.

"Where you wanna sit, guys?" Jeff shouted over the noise.

"We could sit right at the bar if you'd like. You get faster service that way," Patrick suggested.

"Why don't we go upstairs to get something to eat? It will be quieter there. We can actually talk."

Following Hilda's advice they ascended the stairs.

On the second floor, small tables aligned each of the walls of the long narrow room. They sat by one of two windows facing the street. The air was cooler and a fresh breeze blew through the window.

Although the music boomed from the first floor, they were still able to carry on a conversation.

A waitress, who looked a little like Julia Roberts, though anorexic, brought menus. Everyone ordered beer except for Hilda who ordered a Coke.

"I don't drink," she said without apology.

"So, Hilda, where do you work?" Sandy opened the dialogue.

"Oh, I work at Roper Hospital, you know, near the old museum park. I've worked there as a nurse for three years, ever since I graduated from MUSC."

"Impressive. I hear nursing is a great profession. A lot of demand and stuff," Patrick chimed in.

"Yes, we have to work twelve hour shifts. But it's a way we can actually care for people consistently."

The waitress came again and everyone ordered the hamburger special.

"What do you do, Sandy?" Hilda reciprocated.

"Oh, I'm going to the college. Trying to get a degree in Library Science. I work at the Charleston Library on weekends."

"That's where we met," Patrick explained. "I needed help locating info in the city directory and the rest is history."

"What do you do at that electronics store, Jeff?"

"I'm in sales," Patrick broke in. "And I keep HIM out of trouble."

Jeff responded, "Seriously, I try to maintain the computer reports of merchandise and make sure the salesmen have what they need."

"Oh, you're a stock boy-" Hilda blurted out.

An awkward pause followed.

"Well, he does more than that. The store would fall apart if Jeff weren't there to keep everyone straight. Besides, the boss was saying just the other day that Jeff could move into sales any time he wanted. Right, Jeff?"

Jeff smiled.

"Is there much future in sales?"

"Sure," Jeff looked at Hilda. Her beauty mesmerized him. The charm of her complexion was enhanced by the ambiance of an early moonlit moment.

"A salesman could climb the corporate ladder. A person could sell BMW's or toasters. Just depends on what he wants to do."

"So, why not move into sales tomorrow?"

Jeff didn't like Hilda's persistence.

"Maybe when I get to know the products more," he stalled as he took another swig of beer. To his great relief the waitress arrived with everyone's order.

As they ate a delicious supper, they looked out the window at the various buildings illuminated by the street lamps. Many people were walking along the sidewalk talking about the various social events around town, the upcoming Christmas Season and life in general in the Most Holy City. The foursome could no longer hear the one-man band whose music had been drowned out by the intensifying beat of the country band on the first floor.

"Any plans for Thanksgiving, Jeff? It'll be here before you know it," Sandy said.

"None, really. I guess I might be spending it with Patrick, here."

"I heard about your aunt and uncle. I'm so sorry."

"They led a full life, I suppose. Probably in a better place."

"This is really good," Hilda said as she inadvertently slurped up the last of her Coke.

Everyone giggled.

Suddenly gunfire fractured the calm. Sparks emanated from the street level.

"What the- that's gunfire!" Jeff yelled as everyone sprang to their feet.

Patrick stood in front of the window. Another shot rang out and a piece of the brickwork flew off next to Patrick's head.

"Yeah, and someone's aiming at us!" screamed Patrick, as he moved away from the window. But he hadn't moved fast enough to avoid another shot, which ricocheted off the wall and struck him in the shoulder. He slumped over the table while the other three hit the deck.

Surprisingly Hilda reacted calmly, got to her feet and with Jeff's help moved Patrick to the floor. She took one of the red cloth napkins and tied it around Patrick's arm.

"Patrick, are you OK?" Jeff asked frantically. Jeff cautiously looked out the window. Everyone on the street had taken cover except for two men dressed in tank tops and shorts. Jeff was awestruck.

"Patrick, it's those guys!"

There was widespread panic as groups of people scurried out of the bar and into the street. The one-man band was crouching behind his bass drum.

A few seconds later Jeff could hear sirens. The two men ran down State Street towards St. Phillips Episcopal Church. A police car tore up North Market and screeched to a halt in front of Stacey's. The policemen, one short and bald, and the other tall and thin cautiously approached the restaurant with guns drawn.

The one-man band ran over to the cruiser and motioned towards St. Phillips.

"They ran down there!"

The short officer grabbed his walkie-talkie, looked excitedly at his taller partner and said, "I'll pursue. You go see what happened, OK, Clyde?"

Sighing, the taller of the two cops said, "Jim. We've been over this before. I'm in better condition than you and I've got longer legs!"

"We'll argue about this later. Meanwhile, I'm gone!" Jim carefully dodged traffic on North and South Market and ran as swiftly as his short legs could carry him towards the Episcopal church.

"Trouble again Stacey?" the tall officer asked a plump T-shirt clad man slouching in the front doorway. Raising his hands in defense and shaking his head the man said, "Not my fault, not my fault, Clyde. Don't know what's goin' down. I heard some commotion upstairs. You might wanna check it out."

"Was there any return fire?"

"This is not the OK corral!" the fat man said getting a snide look from the policeman.

The officer worked his way through the bar area, which still had a few people crouching under tables. He carefully ascended the stairs aiming his revolver in the air in guarded fashion. As he entered the upper eating area, he saw Patrick sprawled on the floor in front of the booth.

As Clyde moved over to the window and looked out, he said, "Everything looks quiet now. Everyone can calm down."

The policeman's radio came alive, "I think I saw the suspects enter a red vehicle and head up Broad Street! I'll radio headquarters for backup and will head your way. Be there in a minute."

"Ten four."

Clyde bent over Patrick and said, "Shoulder wound. Nothing serious."

"Nothing serious?" Patrick yelped, gripping his arm.

"I'm mortally wounded here. Probably got rabies from a rusty bullet."

"Let's get him to the emergency room. Listen, just apply another handkerchief to the wound to keep the pressure on it. Good work, whoever made the tourniquet."

Soon Patrick was placed on a gurney and taken downstairs. As he was put into the ambulance, Jeff gave the officer a description of the two men he had seen.

"It really happened too fast to get a good look at their faces."

The shorter officer rejoined the group. "Well, it looks like we lost them. Sorry, Clyde," Jim said as he avoided an expected look of condescension from his partner.

Clyde shrugged.

"What did they want with you all? You owe them money?"

"Officer," Jeff said, "I don't have a clue. If I knew, I would tell you. God's honest truth..."

"Can we continue this discussion a little later? I'm dying here... Can see the pearly gates... clouds all around."

"By all means," Clyde said, then turned to Jeff.

"Don't leave town."

"Can I follow you to the hospital?"

"Come on," the officer agreed as his shorter partner and he got into their squad car and led the ambulance.

11

Jeff followed the police to the hospital near the Medical University. While Patrick was transported into the facility, Jeff supplied the attendant on duty with all of the pertinent insurance information. The young, slightly wounded patient was groggy from pain medicine given him by medics in the ambulance.

"I'll take the girls home and come back in a little while. You feelin' all right?"

"Ninety-nine German-made beers on the wall, ninety-nine beers of bottl-"

"I'd like to stay for a while. Can you pick me up later?" Sandy asked.

Jeff nodded.

It took Jeff thirty minutes to take Hilda home. She was silent most of the way. He figured she would never speak to him again.

"Thanks for an exciting evening. Maybe we can do something a little less tense sometime. See ya-" she said as she closed the door.

What, no kiss?

Jeff turned out of her driveway onto Highway 61 and traveled towards Charleston. Crossing over Sam Rittenburg he noticed how busy the area was.

The drive proved pleasant. He let down both of his front windows to enjoy some of the refreshing cool night air. As soon as he passed the Eckerds store at Old Towne Road, he noticed a red streak zoom across the highway behind him. It was the hoodlums!

They must have followed him all the way from the Market area. He stomped on the gas and immediately sped to fifty miles an hour. Maybe he could attract the attention of a policeman on patrol.

Dodging in and out of traffic, Jeff gained distance between his car and that of the men following him. Seeing no cars at the corner of Wesley and 61 he ran the light and drove past the circular Holiday Inn where he carefully merged into the heavy Friday night traffic towards downtown.

There wasn't a cop in sight. Working his way into the right lane he could no longer see his pursuers. Why were they out to get him? Nothing of consequence had changed in his life, except for his inheritance.

A look of surprise came across his face as he fit the pieces together. The death of his aunt and uncle, the death of his cousin in Statesboro and the current threat to his life were linked to one common goal, ownership of the plantation. For some reason, these hoodlums wanted him out of the way to gain access to the old homestead.

The speed limit was thirty-five and he had slowed to fifty. As he reached the Marina he noticed the roughness of the road making his car jump off the pavement every few seconds. He had to concentrate hard to maintain control.

Suddenly he remembered that Lockwood ended with a sharp left-hand curve onto Broad. Fifty miles an hour? He had to reduce speed or end up in the waterway by a Coast Guard cutter!

The traffic was thinning. Every few seconds he could see the hoodlums' fast approaching car illuminated by the streetlights. He slowed to forty-five. Just when he began his turn onto Broad, another car, its lights on high beams, curved around in the opposite direction. As Jeff swerved to miss it, his right rear wheel glazed off one of the many palm trees aligning the sidewalk. His old Chevette recoiled and vibrated violently. Headed into oncoming traffic, Jeff was going to lose it.

With all his strength, he regained control of the car and sped farther down the narrow street trying to avoid vehicles parked on either side.

Just his luck, his light was red at Logan. No one was anywhere near the intersection so he slowed to twenty-five and hung a left down the quaint narrow street, smashing a newspaper stand on the corner. He nearly sideswiped one of the cars parked along the road. The sweat beaded on his forehead. His heart was racing as he slowed to pause at a four way stop near a grocery store at Logan and Queen.

He sped up to forty passing his former apartment and the public housing on the left. Approaching the next intersection, he pounded on his horn and almost went into cardiac arrest as he saw the center of his steering column fall apart due to the force he had exerted on it.

When he reached Montague a shot shattered his rear window. They were right on him! Another shot blew out one of his rear tires. The car violently careened to the right forcing him up George Street. Within seconds his right front tire hit the sidewalk directly in front of the student center. The car jumped the curve, flew five feet in the air just missing two iron lampposts and landed on its left side spewing a cascade of sparks against the brick sidewalk. The Chevette ground to a halt and struck an iron fence by a corner building.

Jeff was dazed. His ears pounding with the surge of noise caused by the crash, he thought he could hear screams from nearby. Something was burning.

He had to act quickly. With some difficulty he stood, slung his binoculars around his neck, and clinched the passenger's open window frame. Although very sore from his initial landing, he climbed out of the car and landed feet first on the sidewalk.

"Thank the good Lord for all those soccer games!"

Another shot rang out from the darkness hitting a brick wall near his head. He darted away from the vehicle which erupted into a ball of fire seconds after his departure.

After running up the street and into the nearby courtyard, Jeff worked his way over to the Science Center. Passing the circular structure in front of the Administration Building, he hid behind some of the arches where he saw the two thugs enter the gate leading into the courtyard.

One was strong and bony. Wearing a tank top, the sandy haired man holding a pistol, motioned for the other to flank to the left. To his horror, the other man was Mr. McLure who had tried to swindle him out of the plantation.

"The professor! I've got to get to the professor while there's still time."

He worked his way along the bushes aligning the left front of the Administration Building and went through a small gate leading out into the main thoroughfare. Working his way along the wall outside the courtyard, he ran silently to the Physician's Auditorium and scurried up the left arched walkway leading to a side door.

Opening the door, Jeff ran up some stairs, past the auditorium and through the double doors leading down another corridor. He continued past the Geology Center and the lecture hall to the black elevator.

Frantically pushing the elevator button, he thought he heard noises coming from the corridor through which he just passed.

The elevator finally reached his floor. Jeff's knowledge of the building would buy him a few minutes to hide.

The professor's lab was locked, the teacher no where in sight. Maybe he could enter from one of the windows on the side of the building. He heard the elevator coming down again. He finally reached the door at the end of the hallway, ran outside into the darkness, stumbled over some paint cans and landed face down on the pavement. Ignoring his skinned hands and knees and his intense headache, he ran around the corner and checked the windows of the laboratory. If he could only hide in the dark room.

YES! He was able to open a window and slip through. Gently closing and locking the window, he could hear voices. Beads of sweat formed on his face. He wiped some blood from his knee. Then panic set in. The crooks were right outside the window above his head. Pinning himself against the wall, he held his breath. His elbows ached from his fall. He couldn't let the pain of his wounds distract his thinking. He looked around the room for something he could use as a weapon. One man against two? He wouldn't stand a chance. The whole city was preoccupied with its weekend activities. No one would hear his screaming. Jeff felt like a trapped animal with nowhere to go.

"Wait a minute. If I can't leave physically, how about chronologically?"

"'*More tests must be performed to insure the safety of both the passenger and of all history....*'"

What the heck, the chimp made it. The professor was going to try it on himself anyway. But could he remember how to work the machine? He heard a rattling of the doorknob leading to the downstairs hallway.

In desperation he ran across the room to the control panel and studied its layout. As he pushed the start button, all of the machines along the wall came to life. Attached to the back of the control panel was a plastic six-foot wide four-foot tall vertical protective shield.

Jeff looked down at the large computer keyboard.

"I N I T I A T I N G   P R I M A R Y   D A T A S T R E A M   M A N I P U L A T I O N   S E Q U E N C E:" came a loud computer voice out of a small grill-enclosed speaker on the control panel.

"All right! Let's go!"

He adjusted the volume to a lower level.

"PLEASE INPUT CLEARANCE PASSWORD:"

"Oh, crud!" Jeff clasped his hand to his mouth.

"PLEASE INPUT CLEARANCE PASSWORD. YOU HAVE 30 SECONDS IN WHICH TO RESPOND. TWENTY-NINE, TWENTY EIGHT..."

No time!

He could hear talking outside one of the nearby doors.

What word or phrase would the professor use? Options were limitless.

Birthday, anniversary, license plate... Jeff glanced around the room.

"TWENTY-THREE, TWENTY-TWO..."

"The Prof.'s birthday... Let's see. "October 1, 1945."

"INITIAL PASSWORD REJECTED.   PLEASE TRY YOUR SECOND OF THREE CHOICES. TWENTY, NINETEEN..."

Jeff was frantic. He could hear the two gangsters walking outside past the window.

Feverishly looking around the room, he noticed an illuminated box-framed picture near one of the computer cabinets. He crawled as fast as he could towards the picture, which was a photograph of Albert Einstein sitting on the professor's front porch holding Helm's dog. It was signed, "Best regards to Professor Ernest Helm, a devoted colleague in the world of Science, and to Bengie as well. Your hospitality this weekend was much appreciated. Albert."

Bengie the dog! That had to be it. Would it be that easy? With this new information Jeff scurried to the control board and input "B-e-n-j-i-e".

"SECONDARY PASSWORD REJECTED. PLEASE TRY YOUR FINAL OF THREE CHOICES. TEN, NINE..."

"Oh, crud! I spelled it wrong," Jeff said as he carefully input the password for the last time, "B-e-n-g-i-e."

"PASSWORD ACCEPTED. INITIATING START-UP SEQUENCES, PROFESSOR. PLEASE ENTER DESTINATION DATE:"

The control board started to change. A long thin door rotated upward revealing a row of black dials with small screens for each. Also appearing on the shield was a small eight by ten-inch projected blue-white image of instructions.

"Did you hear something?" a voice asked.

Jeff ducked as low as he could, hoping the computer console would hide him from the hoodlums' view.

"Look, Mr. Morris said we have to take him out. That's what the contract says. I think he's in here... Can you see anything?"

"No, these curtains are shutting everything out."

Jeff again adjusted the volume of the small speaker so he alone could hear the computer's responses. He looked down at the three console windows and the black corresponding dials. The present day's date blinked at him.

"What destination date should I choose?" he tried to think under the utter stress of the situation. "Let's see. Why not kill two birds with one stone and go back and see what really happened to Thomas and the others? Got it. November 23- Gee, that's near Thanksgiving. Perfect."

He entered a destination date using the second series of black dials, "November 23, 2010".

"PRESS <ENTER> FOR CONFIRMATION:"

"No! November 23, <u>1864</u>," he said as he re-entered the date. The inputted information was simultaneously appearing line by line on the projected screen in front of him.

"TIME ARRIVAL STIPULATION:"

Jeff entered "6:30 PM".

"Should get there in the evening when no one is looking."

"DESTINATION:"

"West Ashley District, Charleston, SC".

"ENTER SPECIFIC ADDRESS:"

Jeff entered 'Southerby Royale'.

The computer searched its extensive data banks.

"'SOUTHERBY ROYALE' HAS BEEN LOCATED. ID IS POSITIVE ... COORDINATES ARE 00198-00799-01TBF AT 00198-87997-02RBF. 100% ACCURACY ACQUIRED ON TARGET DESTINATION. ENTER DATE OF CESSATION OF TIME TRAVEL EPISODE: RETURN MOTIF IS SET FOR THE DURATION OF ONE HOUR UNLESS OTHERWISE STIPULATED. PLEASE CONFIRM OR CHOOSE ALTERNATE RETURN DATEFRAME:"

"*I'll stay from November 23, 1864 until, say, December 1st. That ought to do it,*" he thought to himself as he input "December 1, 1864".

"DATE AND TIME OF ACTUAL RETURN TO THE PRESENT:"

Jeff pressed the enter key which meant a return to the Friday night from which he was making his escape.

"TIME TRAVEL EPISODE DEFINED. PLEASE REMEMBER THAT YOU CAN SAVE TIME IN PREPARATION FOR THE SOJOURN BY SELECTING YOUR PERIOD CLOTHING, MONETARY FUNDS AND SECURITY BELT WHILE THE SYSTEM MODULES ARE MOUNTING."

Across the room a row of dull green lights illuminated the costumes in the closet area.

"Fantastic!" Jeff whispered as he crawled over to the wall lined with the computer banks. He was now right under the window where the two men were trying to look in. Jeff continued to crawl over to period clothing section.

"EACH PIECE OF CLOTHING WHICH IS ILLUMINATED BY A GREEN BULB INDICATES THAT IT IS APPROPRIATE FOR THE TIME PERIOD. PLEASE MAKE YOUR CHOICES NOW:"

After choosing a shirt, breeches, vest, boots and a hat, he crawled over to the large display case of money. The case was divided into eight drawers wide enough to hold thirteen sections of coins grouped by decades. A section labeled 1860 - 1870 was illuminated. He dumped $120.00 of Confederate currency into the pocket of his old coat. He went to the octagonal booth in front of the top-shaped sphere and started putting the clothing on. Half dressed, he crouched and scurried over to the control panel to see what was happening. The projected screen said, "PLEASE PRESS CONFIRMATION BUTTON TO FINALIZE INITIATION OF ALL SYSTEMS:"

He pressed the large green button. Nothing happened. Frustration and fear filled his senses. He could hear the two men trying to pry the locked window open.

A red light flashed on the control panel.

"RETRIEVAL BELT NOT DETECTED IN THE TRANSPORT CHAMBER. PLEASE PROCURE:"

"Oh man, guess I wanna come back, huh?"

He returned to the clothes section and retrieved a thin belt three inches wide and forty inches long, lined with a series of green disks the size of silver dollars. As soon as he entered the octagonal chamber, the huge top started whirring. The thugs would be in the room any second.

"ELECTRO-MAGNETIC OSCILLATOR IS INITIATED. FINE TUNED.. CHECK. PHYSICAL FACTORS DETERMINED. WEIGHT, HEIGHT, PHYSICAL STAMINA OF TRAVELER CONFIRMED. AGE VECTORSCOPE INITIATED. D A N G E R OF C H R O N O L O G I C A L REACTION ADJUSTMENT OF TRAVELER DETECTED AND ELIMINATED. TRAVELER WILL INCUR ONLY SLIGHT DISCOMFORT UPON ENTRY.. CHECK."

Suddenly a sharp pain developed in his right arm. A shot needle had automatically extended from one of the chamber walls and was drawing a blood sample. He kept his arm steady. A few seconds passed and a green light showed on the chamber wall as the needle was extracted back into its cradle.

"DNA STRUCTURE STUDY IDENTIFIED AND COMPLETED. MOLECULAR CHROMOSOME FACTORS CONFIRMED. POSSIBLE IMBALANCE DETECTED IN MAGNETIC-CHEMICAL SCHEMA: IDENTIFIED AND ELIMINATED... CHECK."

Jeff's body tingled.

"ELECTRON VACILLATION GUNS PREPARED FOR SPARK CELL CAPTURE. SECURITY OF TRANSPORT GUARANTEED AT 99.99999% ... CHECK."

"99%?" Jeff gasped. "How about 100%! Something's wrong here!"

"Break the window. It's him!" a voice yelled from the darkness.

"TRANSFER MODE SECURE AND LOCKED:"

At the last minute Jeff screamed, "What am I doing?"

He tried to climb out of the chamber. The top was whirring and shaking the entire floor. A bright light originating from the top captured him and would not let go. The wide beam shot at one point of his body and widened encompassing his entire frame and the objects around him. He was caused to stand erect in the chamber. The light thinned to a concentrated beam, ran up his torso and pinpointed his forehead. It spanned out again. Suddenly he and everything in the chamber vanished!

"What the -" yelped one of the hoodlums as he broke the window and crawled into the room.

"Where'd he go?" asked the muscle-bound man as he ran over to the octagonal booth. "What is this thing, McLure?"

Eyeing the top-shaped form, the thin man ran over to the control console and studied it carefully. The picture within a picture projection on the safety glass read, "TIME RELAY COMPLETED SUCCESSFULLY. SUBJECT HAS BEEN SAFELY TRANSPORTED TO THE DESIGNATED COORDINATES AND WITHIN THE STIPULATED TIME FRAME. COORDINATES OF THE TIME BELT HAVE BEEN PINPOINTED AND DEFINED. AWAITING FURTHER INSTRUCTIONS:"

"Why that - he went back in time... This thing's a time machine! Crazy, huh?" McLure grinned.

"Impossible. No one has ever invented a time machine. You've been watching too many movies!"

"Is he here? Do you see him, numbskull?"

"Look, I don't know about you, but I'm not hanging around for the police. Too much risking my life for a measly five grand!"

"I've got a bit more to worry about. He's actually seen me. We've got to kill him somehow."

The muscleman started for the door.

"Where are you going, Jake? We're in this together!"

"So what do we do now? I know, let's follow him!" Jake wildly quipped.

"Oh yeah. Let's just jump right in! What, are you crazy? Just let me think, OK?"

McLure paced around the room and stopped.

"Actually, we don't really need to grab the plantation from him anymore. We don't need to harm one little hair on his head. All we have to do ... is make sure he doesn't - come – back!"

McLure pounded his fists on the control panel. Both of the hoodlums laughed.

Jake grabbed one of the wooden chairs next to the professor's desk, wielded it over his head and threw it hard against the delicate controls. A wall of sparks flashed everywhere starting a small fire. An alarm accompanied by red and green lights on top of the computer data banks went off.

"MALFUNCTION DETECTED. DANGER IS IMMINENT. PLEASE EVACUATE THE AREA. CODE 14 - CODE 14..."

McLure joined in on the destruction. He threw a chair against the top-shaped structure, which swayed off its base and crashed to the floor. A tremendous explosion nearly swept both of them off their feet. Flames began to engulf the wall adjacent to the hallway. As soon as the men gained their composure, both of them ran over to the first of three computer data banks and rocked it back and forth until it fell face forward on the wooden floor. Fire traveled to the other data banks along the wall to the period clothing on the other side of the room and engulfed the clothes. The whole room was reaching peak heat intensity.

To his surprise McLure saw Jake run over to the money table.

"Don't be crazy, man! Let's get out of here. This place is ready to blow!"

A disappointed Jake ran towards McLure, his pockets partially filled with old bills. As McLure opened the door leading into the hallway the two of them stood face to face with a frantic Professor Helm!

"What is the meaning of this outrage? What have you done to my experiment? It has taken me years to perfect -"

"This is the guy who made this thing? We can't let him live. He might reinvent the wheel. Old man, you're history!" the muscular man yelled as he drew a gun from his belt and shot the professor in the chest. Helm swooned and collapsed dead in the middle of the hallway.

The two men rushed down the corridor and escaped out of the science building into the darkness.

12

It took a few seconds for Jeff's eyes to adjust to his present surroundings. A thin dull blue cone of light enveloped his body. Sparkly crystals swirled all around, suspending him in place. The pressure on his head was intense. He thought his skull was going to explode. Nausea was setting in. It seemed that his body was being tossed about by violent winds. In a matter of seconds, he found himself within inches of a wooden wall. Abruptly his body was jerked to a new position out in the open. The cone disappeared. He couldn't move.

"Where am I? Who am I?"

His mind was blank except for thoughts of his immediate physical state. He began to fall forward. He stood in the middle of a pigsty and was headed for ground zero!

"I can't believe this! What is happening to me?" he mused over his dilemma. *"TIMBER!"* he thought as he struggled to take a deep breath.

The drop to the ground was cushioned by the thickness of the mud. To his dismay, the otherwise hilarious circumstances were quickly proving life threatening. How long could he hold his breath? Fear turned to anger. Suddenly, violently, memories of his life rushed into his head causing a severe brain freeze. Simultaneously he became cognizant that he was running out of air. He wondered what it would be like to die away from his family and friends, out of his own time and in a pigsty no less.

Without warning a pair of strong hands grasped him around his shoulders and boosted him to his feet. He gasped for air but still couldn't move his limbs.

"What's wrong with you, boy? Havin' a fit?" inquired a gruff old man.

"Houston, we have contact! No interaction, indeed. I'm dead."

Jeff looked at his rescuer. As tall as Jeff, the old man was in his late fifties. He wore a tattered gray coat some of whose threads had begun to unravel. A short flat-topped hat, the brim of which hung down to his ears, topped a slightly bald head. The bearded man wore a red scarf and checkered shirt with a dark brown leather vest. Weighing over 200 pounds, he chewed tobacco and spat into the pigsty. And oh that breath.

Jeff was glad to see the man's kind eyes gazing back at him.

"What year is this?" Jeff asked as he gasped for another breath.

"Why, this here is 1838 o'course," the man said as he smiled and gazed at the stars.

"Oh, crud!" Jeff exclaimed as he started to fall into the mud again.

The old man laughed as he steadied his newfound friend.

"Just joshin' ya', son. This be 1864, November 23rd. Day 'fore Thanksgivin'. If you-ins lookin' for a tuh-kee in the pigpen, taint too tootin' smart. Let me get you out of here," the man said as he carried Jeff to dry ground.

"You sho' is a strange one. Stranger still that ye would ask about the year and all. My, oh my, what be these things in your pockets?" the old man asked as he pulled Jeff's field glasses out of his coat.

"A double telescope? Will ya look at that? Aint seen any of them other than what the army has."

"They're new!" Jeff said as he grabbed them away from the stranger and shoved them back into his coat. Jeff was now able to move both arms and hands freely. He sat on the ground to regain calm.

Again the old man let go a big wad of chew.

"My name is Jeff Car-" he began but caught himself.

"Glad to meet ye, Mr. Carr. My name is Jed Tub. I'm a field hand for Mr. Carter who owns the plantation up the hill yonder. Time to get you cleaned up. You is strange. Wearing only your underwear and holding your britches is queer enough. You wasn't tryin' to take a bath back there, was ye?"

"No sir," Jeff said as he realized he hadn't had time to fully change in the octagonal chamber. He thought of the belt under the other clothing he clutched in his hand.

"Uh, yeh, there was a bee in my clothes. Grateful I wasn't stung," Jeff lied as he dressed.

"So where's your plantation?" he asked trying to divert the old man's attention so he could buckle the retrieval device.

"It'll only take us de few minutes to reach our livin' quarters."

Jed let Jeff lean on his arm as the two men headed up the hill. Suddenly remembering his wristwatch, Jeff removed it and shoved it into his pants pocket.

Six lanterns illuminated the long front porch of the bunkhouse. There were two large windows on either side of the door of the tin-roofed dwelling. He didn't remember seeing it in his own time.

"Must've torn it down."

"This be where all us hired hands stay," Jed said as he helped a still-feeble Jeff up the three steps leading to the front door.

"I'm OK now. Thanks," Jeff said as he withdrew his arm from the gentleman's grasp.

"Ah, pershaww," the old man said.

The bunkhouse door opened and a stout, sturdy-built man stepped out onto the porch.

"Jed, who is this stranger?"

"This is Mr. Carr. Met him in the pigpen."

The brawny man chuckled.

The old man motioned, "Jeff, meet Mr. Walter Blake, my cohort and 'bout de bes' frien' anyone could ever have."

Walter, a man of about sixty years, smiled. His boisterous friendly greeting complemented his balding head, thick white sideburns and muscular build.

"Why, hello there!" he said as he reached out to shake Jeff's hand.

Jeff extended his own but felt great pain. Walter's grip was intense. Jeff winced.

"Sorry," Jed said. "Shoulda warned ya."

He let go another wad of chew.

"So where ya from?" Walter asked.

"I think he be from a distance seeing that he be a totin' dis here green belt with all dos pretty knobs," Jed said as he raised Jeff's coat.

A shiver went up Jeff's spine.

"Got it while working in the circus. It's for high wire acts."

Both men raised their eyebrows and asked, "Circus?"

They both shrugged their shoulders.

"Well, good to have you. Plan on stayin' long?"

"Just passin' through, Walter."

Jeff started picking up the southern drawl that was more warranted than ever. The three of them stepped inside and were greeted by a roaring fire on the other side of the room. The bunkhouse was a little cramped for space.

"You can put your gear on the bed over yonder," Walter pointed to the bed by the kitchen. "You might need to clean up a bit. We have a water pump outside."

"Great idea," Jeff said. "The only thing is that these are my only clothes."

"Ye certainly does travel light, don't ye?"

Jeff nodded.

Walter gave him a towel, which may not have been the cleanest but was dry nonetheless. After sponge bathing outside, Jeff got dressed in some dry clothes Walter let him borrow which nearly swallowed him whole revealing his embarrassingly limited physique.

Another gentleman entered the room. Standing six feet two, he wore leather cowboy chaps and a large black cowboy hat. The man who looked to be forty-five had very dusty boots. His thin bony face had a small long reddish mustache. His red complexion showed years of having worked in the sun.

Walter introduced the newcomer, "Mr. O'Rork, this here is Jeff Carr. He's just passin' through, he says. Jeff, this here is our foreman. Do you suppose we can put him up for the night? Seems to be a lost lamb."

John O'Rork looked at Jeff with doubtful eyes, "So where do you hail from, laddie?"

"From the 'seer-cust'?" Jed responded.

"The seer-cust? What's a seer-cust?" O'Rork's Irish twang was as thick as his bushy red hair. The tall man approached Jeff so closely that he was now towering over his smaller frame.

"Circus. You know, Barnum and Bailey?" Jeff said sheepishly.

"You know. Workers get together and do tricks to entertain people. There are elephants and lions, people who walk across a rope suspended in mid air, beautiful ladies riding horses bareback. That kind of thing."

The cowboys looked confused.

Jeff added, "Closed down three months ago. That's why I had to quit."

By now Jeff was beginning to perspire. A lump was developing in his throat.

"Seems like a lot of wasted time to me. Anyways, I'll even hire ye if you want. I guess if this great land can accept an Irishman and his fam-ly as sech as they did me pappy and his'n, we kin accept you fer now, that is- if'n Mr. Thomas Carter approves and if'n you are a hard worker, now is ye?"

The Irishman bent down and was nose to nose with Jeff.

"Yep," Jeff gulped.

"One wee hint of laziness and you're out of it, laddie," O'Rork said as he turned on his heel and walked into the kitchen.

"Friendly guy," Jeff murmured.

"Would you be a needin' something to et, Mr. Jeff?"

"No thanks, Jed. I just ate a burger - uh a sandwich - oh fixin's at, uh, just a little while ago."

Jeff was totally unprepared to interact with this culture. Even American life in the past was foreign. It was shocking. What words would he use to describe food, current events? What slang would make him fit in?

"Coffee?" Walter asked. "We usually have some before we head out for the evening."

"Let me have yo clothes an tings. I'll take 'em up to de hill an have 'em warshed by de mornin'."

Jeff readily complied and Jed left the room.

Walter and Jeff walked through the door to the kitchen. No running water, no electricity, no fans nor Westinghouse stove. This was a true farmhouse complete with a stonework fireplace and black kettle. The warm fire gave the kitchen a homelike glow. Walter went to fetch some water from the pump while O'Rork retrieved some metal cups from a small pantry all the while glancing over in Jeff's direction.

Three other men entered the kitchen.

"Marcus, you wouldn't be satisfied if the president let you sleep in a bedroom at the White House!" a rugged suntanned man with a stiff northern accent said to the short chubby man with a boyish face.

"Tomorrow's Thanksgiving. And what do we have to be thankful for, Frederick? That we are surrounded on all sides by a blockade that's just killing our homeland?" asked Marcus whose high pitched scratchy voice was as comical as he was short.

"Be thankful that those Yankees haven't overrun us yet for starters," the tall man said.

"Will you two quit fussin'? You been at it since this afternoon. Seems that in these times you'd find somethin' more peaceable to talk about," the third man said. He wore a long white pigtail. His muscles bulged out from his short sleeve shirt and brown vest.

"Woah.. Who we got here?" Frederick asked.

"Jeff Carr, please be meetin' Frederick Hines," O'Rork pointed to the lanky gentleman.

"This be Joe English," O'Rork pointed to the pony tailed man, "and our very own Marcus Vendor," O'Rork lastly addressed the attention of all to the four and a half foot tall, chubby gentleman.

"Marcus don't have a lot of luck with the ladies, but you can trust him in a fight!"

Everyone laughed.

"Pleased to meet you."

"Where ya' from, anyways?" Marcus inquired.

"Oh, I'm from Douglas, Georgia. Just passin' through to find more work in Kentucky."

"Runnin' from Sherman, son?" Jed chimed in as he entered the room. "He's a headed this way, we hear. Burnin' every confounded thing in his way, curse de lily-livered-"

"Must we resort to this?" interrupted Walter as he put the water on the kitchen floor. "Jeff just got here, no one likes Sherman. Let's have some coffee and get goin'. Jeff, did you meet everyone?"

Jeff nodded.

"The coffee will be ready shortly."

Walter's coffee could have stood by the wall on its own. No sugar, not a spoonful of cream in the whole place. Jeff choked with his first sip. His rusty tin coffee cup which probably hadn't been washed in years, reminded him of those he had seen in many a cowboy movie.

Although he glanced a few times down in the cup to make sure no creatures had made their way in, he drank with the others. No reason to make anyone more suspicious of him.

"What do you all want to be doin' tonight?" O'Rork inquired.

"I hear dey are havin' an unofficial trot up to de Washington Racecourse. Dey don't have dem tings too often since de war done broke out but some of de rich boys makes bets, ya know."

"The track?"

"Yes. The Jockey Club has been sponsoring races for nearly, what, twenty years? Since the war started, many of the gentlemen have ceased to have official races at the track north of Charleston. Some go on Wednesdays to make simple wagers. It gives them somethin' to do and make money at the same time. Sometimes we get into makin' bets ourselves. I won a whole dollar last week when Wilkins rode in first place on Beauty Bell. Boy, that was a pretty run," Frederick explained.

"But there's a war on!"

"That only adds to the fun..." chimed Marcus, giving Jeff a curious look.

The old clothes Jeff wore afforded him warmth. He rolled up his sleeves to adjust them to his stature and put his night vision goggles in his coat pocket.

The seven men proceeded out the door into the cool night air. Saddles were located in a shed to the right of the bunkhouse. Walter tossed Jeff the saddle he was to use. It was so heavy it knocked him down. Walter grinned, shook his head and saddled up.

He helped Jeff put the saddle on Sunshine, the horse he was letting Jeff borrow. "She's a good horse, as long as you give her some of this sugar from time to time," Walter said as he gave Jeff a handful of white sugar cubes.

"Is Mr. Carter coming?" Walter called over to O'Rork.

"No, he said he had a bit a' work to be gettin' to. Too bad too. I hear some heavy racin' is on the track tonight."

O'Rork saddled up and rode over to where Jeff was standing. "You do ride?"

"Daily..."

Jeff put his left foot in the stirrup and unbeknownst to the others rolled his eyes. Getting up was easier than he thought.

"We'll have to be careful. I've been hearing gunshots and cannon all day. But we should be safe if we keep a look out, laddies."

Jeff couldn't believe they were going to venture onto the peninsula but rode along trying to adopt a cheery disposition.

He thought back to the last time he had gone with some cousins to a horse farm out on Highway 61. After riding the horse for three hours, it had to be hungry and tired, but Jeff wanted to see how fast the horse could run. Not being experienced he trotted the horse to the other end of the field, and started galloping towards the feeding barn... The horse charged the gate and stopped dead in his tracks. Jeff kept on going. A stirrup saved his life. Although vowing never to ride again, here he was riding atop old Sunshine.

The riders, led by O'Rork, made their way down a path through otherwise trackless land. Occasionally Jeff could hear cannon fire off in the distance. Charleston at this time was under siege, a condition which was to last until the end of the war. If his understanding of history was correct, the northern troops had already captured some of the barrier islands. But counter to his impressions that life had stopped with the beginning of wartime, life went on as usual for the cowboys.

The men soon reached the ferry that would take them over the Ashley River leading onto the peninsula.

A black man greeted them at the river's edge, "I hears that Sherman's a coming. Done almost reached Savannah way-"

"We don't want to hear anything 'bout him tonight, man. Just get us acrosst de river," Jed said.

O'Rork handed the man money for fare.

The horses were carefully guided onto the ferry and tied to the surrounding posts. A long rope suspended from shore to shore enabled the boatman to pull the small barge across. Some of the cowboys helped him in his efforts due to the heavy load.

The cowboys reached the peninsula and headed north. They soon arrived at Moultrie Road adjacent to the racecourse. Smoke filled the air mingled with the stench of the temporary stables nearby. It took a little getting used to but Jeff's displeasure was soon replaced by his awe of the magnificence of the Washington Racecourse. The genteel Hampton Park of his own time had been transformed into a rather large and surprisingly well attended sports arena.

"Look at this crowd!" Walter said as he tugged on his horse's reins bringing him to a halt.

"Must be the holiday spirit. Let's tie em up yonder, aye?"

Each man guided his horse over to the stables near the course and paid a nickel to a small boy who would tend to them. The group walked a short distance to the booth and paid fifteen cents to enter. They were soon standing by some of the many bleachers that aligned the racecourse.

"Yessir, this course has seen many a fine competition. It's a mile 'round of pure excitement. The gentlemen and ladies have a genuine interest in this community offerin'. Not only be it entertaining, but it surely granted Charleston an international flavor. Horse racing was very popular in England, ya know. Aye?" O'Rork asked.

Large elevated wooden seating sections located all around the course accommodated the crowd. A fence served as a protective border to keep the riff raff from the more privileged guest areas. While the most prominent of the populace enjoyed a prestigious seating arrangement, the less fortunate were able to sit on the regular bleacher-like seats farther down the track.

"What are those?" Jeff asked, as he pointed to wooden-walled structures near each of the bleachers.

"Those are refreshment stands where the ladies and gentlemen can, well, get refreshed," Walter said. "Of course, you and I aren't permitted in those areas. Neither can we go into those special bleachers where only the notable citizens can view the activities."

"Ah, yes, the privileged. Wish I was rich indeed," O'Rork said.

"At least we didn't have to pay the, what is it now to be a member of the Jockey Club, some forty to sixty dollars a year? They can have it," Walter said.

"And that?" Jeff continued, pointing to a large white two-towered edifice in the middle of the course.

"Clubhouse. Poor aristocracy. They used to be able to enjoy the racin' from those carpeted rooms, but now the current occupants are prisoners from the North. They kin view the action themselves if they can git a good vantage point from their confined cell areas, aye?"

"Wonder how they like their tea?" Frederick quipped.

Everyone laughed.

"Why are all the ladies over yonder?"

The finely dressed group with their white gloves, feathery hats and billowing colorful skirts granted elegance to the evening.

"Full of questions, aren't we? That there is the startin' post. And you know the lassies. They congregate to gab while dressed in their finest. When the winnin' jockey picks up his $1,000 purse, they're the closest to see it. 'Course, the winnins is a bit smaller these days."

Jeff noticed various groups of men dressed in work clothes standing around talking. What a contrast from the top-hatted gentlemen standing near the privileged section.

"What are they doing? Betting on the race?"

"Some of them might be, but most of them have come to conclude other business, this being a public place. They're bartering. One man might have repaired another's fence. For payment, the other has brought some greens brought from his fields. Or maybe a grocer is being paid with wheat or barley from someone's field," Walter explained.

Professor Helm had been right. This was an education.

Without warning, a young, shabbily dressed boy, brushed past Jeff, ran by the two-towered edifice, across the track and darted in between two stands on the far side of the racecourse. Jeff thought little of it until he felt for his night vision glasses which were no longer in his coat pocket.

"Oh, crud!" he muttered under his breath. Here he was supposed to be nothing more than an observer, and now he was being swept up into a more active roll.

13

The young man was quick.

As Jeff pursued the boy, crews of men still preparing the racecourse, yelled for Jeff to get off the track.

He began to sweat. If anyone discovered those night vision glasses... As he ran past the front steps of the edifice and between two of the bleachers he nearly collided with a man who had a firm grasp on the boy's arm. The man who had bushy white hair, a towering physique and a cheery smile stood over six feet tall.

"Woe, laddie. Now, where are you headed?"

Looking at Jeff and then noticing the cleric's collar on the man who held him captive, the young man said, "Reverend, this gentleman started running after me, for what reason I don't know. My mother wanted me to get some milk for the morning."

The young boy who wore dusty clothes brushed his sandy blonde hair out of his dirty face with his free hand as he caught his breath.

Looking sternly at the boy, Jeff said, "I think you have something that belongs to me. It must have fallen out of my pocket as you passed!"

The reverend chuckled as he kept hold of the boy's arm. The young boy quickly gave Jeff the glasses when he saw a policeman approaching. Jeff shoved the glasses in his own pocket.

"Sorry for any inconvenience to you, Mr....?"

"Jeff Carr. Nice to meet you. So you know this young dude- er, boy, then?"

"Gotta run-" the young man said but was pulled short by the clergyman's firm grip.

"Just you wait a while," the policeman retorted.

"Thank you officer. My name is Jon Southerland," the clergyman shook hands with the policeman whose uniform   reminded Jeff of the Keystone cops.

"Think I've seen you 'round these parts. You are the one who's been coming here to the races and gathering up boys, bringing them to your home and trying to turn them around?"

"Yes sir, this is my mission. Like most of the boys who stray from home, this young pup has probably begun to frequent the track at night in hopes a' takin' somethin' he could sell at another time. And it certainly is easy sometimes whilst some of the gentlemen discuss politics 'tween the meets. Unfortunately this makes for easy takins for lads who want to provide themselves with a wallet, pocket watch or a derby. All fer the desire to help out their poor families," the priest said in a kind tone looking at the small boy.

"And I am well aware that this young man is in need a' much counsel and guidance. Rather than arrestin' him, if'n it's agreeable to the both of you, may I take him into my care? The church elder committee has readily approved my actions. Perhaps the Lord would deal in this young boy's heart as God has in mine and we could change him into a contributin' member of society?"

Jeff could see the obvious sincerity and pain in the priest's eyes for the boy. Perhaps for the first time in a long while Jeff was actually witnessing one involved in genuine ministry.

"So what do you have to say for yourself, youngster?" the policeman inquired.

The wayward teen introduced himself as Stephen Warren. He had lost both of his parents to pneumonia the year before. It was all he could do to make ends meet. Being an only child he had been able to scrounge for food on his own.

"I have actually started my own orphanage, officer. Would you and Mr. Carr like to come and meet some of the other boys?"

"Thank you, Father, but I must maintain my station here for the night."

"And you, Mr. Carr?"

"I'm actually with a group of people. Maybe some other time, Father. Thanks."

The reverend asked the youth if he'd like a nice hot dinner and a decent bed for the night. At first, Stephen suspiciously eyed the priest, but changed his mind noticing the policeman's steady gaze as the officer tapped his hand with his nightstick.

The policeman departed. Jeff, the boy and the clergyman crossed the track and stood in better light near the clubhouse. As the reverend explained the situation into which the boy would be placed, two finely dressed ladies, headed towards the starting post area, interrupted him.

"Reverend Southerland, how are you this evening?"

"Fine, ladies. Hope you are having a fine time here at this evening's entertainment."

"You can certainly have a nice time with us up here," cackled two voices. A small crowd of men dressed in shabby prison uniforms gathered at the window on the second floor of the clubhouse.

"Don't you be mindin' them. Those are northern prisoners of war. One would think that they would enjoy the races more than indulging in seedy affairs."

"We'd love for them ladies to come up here. Reverend, why don't you mind your own business?" one of the old soldiers asked.

"Gentlemen, please try to restrain yourselves. May I bring you some water?"

"No thanks for the water, Reverend. We'd rather drink some liquor! It's darn uncomfortable in this cell. Just let us out and we'll be on our way to kill more of your useless Rebel rabble."

"I will pray for your comfort. May the graceful God lead you in the right direction. He has pulled me out from the pit I was in."

"We just pray that you'll leave us alone."

The men threw a rock that nearly hit the priest in the head.

"Sorry for this, ladies, Mr. Carr. We best be movin' on."

Jeff bid the reverend goodnight, walked towards the lower bleachers and joined his coworkers who had already gotten a seat. Large oil lanterns lighted the race track perimeter. The night was cool and brisk. Jockeys sat waiting at the starting point nearest the northeast corner of the track.

Four men in long black trench coats, some wearing cowboy hats and one wearing a black derby, stood at the entrance of the clubhouse. The one with the derby looked at his pocket watch and then motioned to another who stood at the starting gate to commence the race with his pistol.

As the shot rang out the five steeds sprang into action.

"Go Tannenbaum!" Jed yelled. "He's got 'winning' written all over him. Tree weeks ago he done come up short in de tird lap. I los' two bits. I done - come on Tannenbaum!"

The horses ran well. Tannenbaum lost.

Shirley Beau and her rider walked triumphantly to the winner's box near the starting point.

The horse's owner, Colonel Rosstrow, enjoyed receiving the small cache of money for his troubles.

O'Rork and his crew stayed for a few more races.

"Best be getting back to the farm before it gets too late," Walter suggested.

After the long ride back the men unsaddled, fed and watered their horses and went to bed. They would need rest for an abbreviated list of chores they would be doing Thanksgiving morning.

14

Sleeping under a rock would have been more pleasant. Jeff's thin mattress had afforded him no comfort and little sleep.

O'Rork, the foreman, insistent on each man's getting an early start on the morning chores, woke the others up at 5:00.

"Do you want us to fix the fence on the south forty?"

"No, Walter. Mr. Carter said we could be awaitin' next week since it's Thanksgiving and all."

Jeff was a little confused in his new surroundings. At the mention of Mr. Carter, it took his mind some time to figure out just who was being talked about.

Walter approached Jeff's bunk and said, "O that's right. You haven't met Mr. Thomas Carter. He owns the plantation. We'll have to introduce you to him later."

Jed brought Jeff his newly washed clothes from the plantation house.

After eating runny eggs and slightly burnt toast, and trying to gulp down more of Walter's military-like coffee, Jeff and the others went to do the abbreviated chores which were accomplished in the space of three and a half hours.

While cleaning one of the stables, Jeff heard someone yelling in the distance.

"Now Miss Sally, you done broke de wheel fo sho! I oughta wack you on de-"

Jeff left the stable area and looked towards the direction of the commotion. He walked to the dirt road leading out to a nearby field and saw a young black man cursing his mule. The poor animal was harnessed to a wagon whose left front wheel had become detached from its axle. As Jeff approached, the young man grabbed the reins of the animal and stood still.

"Can I help you?" Jeff asked.

The other man just stood there with a confused look on his face. He looked at Jeff's smile.

"Sorry, my name is Jeffrey Carr," Jeff extended his hand.

Very sheepishly the other reciprocated while smiling at Jeff.

"You isn't from 'round here, is you?"

"Not exactly. What's your name?"

"Jeremy."

The young man who was probably in his late teens, had short, stubby, dusty hair and wore rags and worn out shoes.

Jeff wanted to strike up a conversation but didn't know what was expected. He couldn't appear too out of character. He didn't know what to expect in relationships between the races in 1864.

He went to retrieve a large block of wood from a nearby woodpile and the two of them were able to lift the wagon, set it on the upturned chunk of wood and put the wheel back on.

Jeremy seemed very appreciative but still said nothing. He just stood there, nodded and grinned. Jeff shook his hand again and walked to the stable, which he finished cleaning.

Plans had not been set for the rest of the morning although it was assumed that the hired hands would gather around the bunkhouse table and consume turkey and vittles.

"So, Jeff, you've never seen the Holy City?" Frederick asked as the men gathered on the bunkhouse porch to take a break from their labors.

"Well, let's just say that I haven't seen it under present management, I mean, under Confederacy rule. Do you think we could go as a small group to pay a visit?"

"I'd be thinkin' that's not such a good idea," said John O'Rork as he walked up the stairs onto the porch. "It would be very dangerous there. No one knows how many looters and desperadoes be lurkin' in the ruins."

"Balderdash," chimed Jed. "Uh, what I mean wit all due respet, Mr. O'Rork is dat, dis boy hadn't been in South Carolina much long. All he is a wantin' is a little 'venture."

"Mr. O'Rork. I'm sure it'll be fine. Thanksgiving might afford a more relaxed, less active day for us all, even the looters."

"OK, Walter. Why don't you accompany these boys downtown."

"I'll be the lookout for them, sir. It might be a little dangerous in the daylight," Walter said. He went in the bunkhouse, grabbed an extra gun belt and six-shooter hanging on the wall, went out on the porch and handed them to Jeff. "Here. Strap this on for protection. You best be careful with my extras. I want these back when we return."

Never in his wildest dreams had Jeff thought he'd hold a six-shooter complete with a holster chock full of bullets. *"James Arnes, eat your heart out,"* he thought as he carefully strapped the belt around his waist. The gun was a little heavier than he had anticipated but he decided that he could get used to it.

Jed, Walter and Jeff saddled their horses and took the same route they had traveled the night before to the Ashley River crossing.

"We best be careful. Those sharpshooters will get a better chance at us, it being daylight and all. Just watch in every direction."

A stronger breeze blew across the territory.

"So is any of the city left?" Jeff asked as the three cowboys rode at each other's side.

"A lot of it has suffered from direct hits from the Yankee's cannon. But I've heard that St. Phillips Church is OK, except for the bells they had to melt down for cannon balls."

Jeff was decidedly nervous about this adventure. He wasn't on some safeguarded tour. This was "gun toatin" reality.

The line to the ferryboat was surprisingly crowded for an early Thanksgiving morning. When their time came, the three cowhands paid their fares and maneuvered their horses onto the ferry tying them up as before.

As the boat moved towards the old millpond site, an eerie fog greeted them. They could hear random rifle shots to their right in the distance.

"Probably comin' from Morris Island or Fort Moultrie," Jed said.

They reached land and mounting their horses, traveled along Spring Street. The area Jeff knew had been completely transformed. No hamburger joints. Devastation lay all around.

Either side of the street had suffered considerable damage from cannon fire across the way. They were headed through a war zone.

Several of the houses had suffered destruction because of fire. Others had been completely leveled. Dogs roamed the streets. Dirty-faced children walked around wearing tattered clothes. So much suffering.

When they crossed Ashley Avenue, things were surprisingly intact.

"Why is everything better here?"

"Well, Jeff, dem cannon balls caint reach dis far in. We be relatively safe for a while."

To their left were remnants of a fort Jeff had never seen before.

"Is that the Citadel?"

"No," laughed Walter. "I forget that you aren't from around here. The Citadel is on the square by the German Lutheran Church down in the city. That there is an old fort from, what Jed, 1812?"

Jed just shrugged and kept on riding.

The cowboys turned right onto King Street and were immediately confronted by small busy market places on either side of the road. Most of those patronizing the local shops were women, some dressed more refined than others. Jeff could hear some of the ladies talking with the vendors, "Now listen here. Mizz Blakely want two dozen eggs so I kin bake a cake. Yes, and some of dat ham fo' Thanksgivin'. Can you dress all dat up fo' me?"

A few women managed to smile at the riders while others looked curiously in their direction.

"Wonder how many of these ladies are widows?" Jeff pondered.

Several makeshift shops sold whatever wares available in spite of the northern blockade. The prices of most things were prominently displayed on large, handwritten signs carefully placed in store windows.

"Caint believe 'maters is dat high," quipped Jed. "A cup of brown sugar for ten dollars? What is de worl'- a comin' to?"

Walter answered, "People risked their lives bringing some of this to us."

In spite of it all, everyone around them seemed cordial, wanting to get along and make the best of things.

The German Lutheran Church was being used as a hospital. When Jeff took a closer look at the tragedy in the makeshift infirmary, he remembered some of the bloody scenes in the Civil War movies he had seen. But the horrors of war struck him anew. The stench and sight of blood, cries of agony, amputations and disease almost made him physically ill. Bodies were being taken out of the front of the church and being loaded into nearby wagons.

"Dey say that babies is bein' born in de streets sometimes. No doctors to 'tend to them."

"We thought that the war wouldn't last as long as it has especially with all of the war machines they've been using in the harbor. Even our Citadel Cadets got into the act by repulsing the Star of the West. I heard that they had to convert the Triboleua, that's one of those riverboats, into a ram against the enemy. The South is giving all she's got," Walter said.

Marion Square, complete with a magnificent fortification called "The Citadel", was located across King Street, a large formidable iron gate surrounding the grounds. The Old Citadel building was a three-story bastion complete with towers. In front and nearer to the road was a small remnant of rock surrounded by vertically inclined black round barrels resting on a wooden platform around the stone structure.

They progressed down King Street. It was strange how familiar things looked to Jeff from his long Sunday walks in the city. The farther they rode towards the Battery, a newfound silence surrounded them. The wind whipped up occasionally causing dust to blow in their eyes.

Every so often gunfire echoed in the distance. They slowly continued down King Street past the historic dwellings and finally reached the corner at South Battery.

Park benches aligned the White Point Gardens area.

A series of dirt dunes had been erected near the sea wall thus granting protection to the houses parallel to the street. He imagined the forts across the river were full of Northerners just waiting to take Charleston. He liked adventure but this was absurd.

Noticing his nervous look, Jed said, "Best be real careful here. Dis is de most dangerous of all places, I be a thinkin'."

"Looters?" Jeff asked swallowing hard.

"No, sharp shooters, Union Troops who kin fire crost the way yonder," Jed motioned across the Ashley towards some of the nearby islands. "It's only 'bout a half mile crost-"

Jed stopped in mid sentence. The three travelers were amazed to see a man in a gray uniform running full speed towards them. The cowboys drew their weapons.

"What are you doing here? Do you wanna get killed on Thanksgivin'?" the man yelled as he finally reached Jeff and his comrades.

"This is a restricted area! Don't you know there's a war on? This is no time to be taking a holiday ride! Get down the way. I'm not responsible for your safety. Done warned ya!" the soldier just sneered at the three stunned faces and ran back to join his comrades who were among the dunes.

"Who done he think he uz?" Jed asked in defiant pride as he ignored the soldier's warning and rode his horse down South Battery towards East Bay.

Walter and Jeff followed Jed, trying to convince him to take the nearest retreat back down King but their pleas fell on deaf ears.

The three reached the corner of South Battery and East Bay and turned towards Broad Street.

Huge potholes created likely from incoming cannon balls permeated the street. But most of the old antebellum homes had survived. The eerie and lifeless buildings were abandoned by the once proud aristocracy who used to playfully view the bombardments from their rooftops.

Suddenly, a shot rang out piercing the empty stillness. It ricocheted against a stone fence of one of the mansions they had just passed. Jed's horse bucked violently nearly causing him to fall to the ground.

"Sharpshooters! Lookout!" Walter yelled.

The men kicked their horses into action as they reversed direction and tore down South Battery towards Meeting.

The shooting behind them intensified as the southern soldiers returned fire.

After a short gallop, they slowed their pace.

"That was close! Is everyone OK?"

The cowboys made their way cautiously being very leery of people or animals hiding in the shadows.

Some distance up the street they noticed a large wall of dirt gathered in the middle of the road.

"Apparently they plan to defend the rest of the city from here," Walter said anticipating Jeff's question.

On their left the Hibernian Hall had suffered much damage. A huge gaping hole gave a very distorted look to this fine Irish establishment.

Farther up stood the Mills House barely touched by cannon ball activity.

As they reached the corner of Meeting and Queen Jeff's jaw dropped. To his left beyond the Mills House, almost every building had met its end. The whole area had been badly damaged by gunfire, cannon balls and looting. Stairways led up to nowhere. Ornate iron fences surrounded mounds of debris. Singular walls stood silent. Gas lantern posts were tilted to the side or knocked down altogether. Most of the area had been flattened. This was not a good place to be.

To his horror Jeff saw blood dripping out of Jed's horse's leg.

"O no, ol' Ranger done been hit. Best we get him home to get looked at."

"Jed, best we get a patch on that leg and get him to a doctor!" countered Walter.

Jed dismounted and taking his handkerchief from around his neck, tied it around the horse's leg to cut down on the bleeding.

Jeff was shaken. That shot had come so close to him. One never felt this kind of pain on television nor smelt the blood surrounding a dangerous moment. He became a little disoriented for a second but finally regained lucidity. The dust of the street stirred up from a cold November wind woke him from his stupor.

"I wonder if there's a hospital nearby."

"Look yonder," Jed said as he pointed to the right.

"That's the old Circular Church," Walter said. "It's been abandoned for years ever since the fire of '61."

The three men dismounted and walked slowly towards the dilapidated building. Passing a large cemetery, they finally reached the church. To their surprise, the building was still being used as a makeshift hospital. There wasn't much cover from the elements. A large tarp-like sheet had been draped over the area where only one doctor was attending some twenty patients.

When Jed asked the exhausted physician if he could tend to his horse, the man wearing a bloodstained white coat cried out, "I've no time for horses. Don't you see these suffering people? Go down Queen to the Roper Hospital. They have more room and many assistants to help you there. Besides, their building is certainly in better shape than this beloved church!"

After a short jaunt, they arrived at Roper Hospital. A tall iron fence protected a large three-story structure adorned with a number of windowed towers. Exquisite archways aligned the front walkway of each floor that faced Queen Street.

The three cowboys strapped their horses to the front gate and, entering the complex, finally found a doctor. The young man who couldn't have been more than twenty years old gladly came out to the street and helped Jed with his horse.

"Looks like some sort of sharp stone hit his leg. You'll have to let him rest a while. Perhaps find a stable in the city where he can stay the night."

Jed offered the doctor some money but he kindly refused. "We live in hard times, sir. Besides, you have a kind face. Gentlemen, please take care in these parts. The Lord be with you!" the doctor said as he shook their hands and retreated into the hospital.

Taking the doctor's advice, they walked up Logan Street, passed a large open field on the left and approached the area of the street where the college was located. Across from the school they found a small stable where Jed left his horse with the stable's owner.

Jeff looked back across the street at a younger and tinier college than he was used to. The Administration Building and courtyard were still surrounded by the retaining wall. The small building nearest them had suffered minor damage.

Jeff noted the absence of a student center, the Physicians' Auditorium and the huge science complex located on George Street where he had crashed. A few carriages aligned the dirt roads that surrounded the college. A number of gaslights stood near the road. There wasn't a whole lot of pedestrian traffic.

It was lunchtime and everyone was hungry. It looked as if the three cowboys were going to miss Thanksgiving dinner altogether. Jed walked as Jeff and Walter rode their horses towards Calhoun.

Not many eating places were still operating in that area although they were able to find a boarding house selling homemade bread and clean water at the corner of Calhoun and Coming.

Jeff remembered the time when his friends and he hid nearby where Bishop England High School would be located at the corner.

They had thrown eggs at their buses passing by one Friday night. Jeff chuckled.

Walter looked at him.

"Gas," Jeff explained as he and Walter dismounted and walked up to the boarding house.

All of a sudden someone yelled, "Get out of the way, move to the side!"

To his amazement, Jeff saw a beautiful woman in a white dress frantically trying to gain control of the stout horse dragging her carriage recklessly down Calhoun Street. Small chunks of dirt from the road were flying everywhere.

Surprisingly the shouts were not coming from the frightened lady but were warnings from the people on the side of the street.

Without thinking Jeff jumped up on his borrowed horse, prodded the animal so much so that the horse bucked a bit and then charged forward. He had never done anything like this in his life, but necessity demanded a quick response.

As he prodded his horse as fast as it could go, his cowboy hat flew off.

"What in the world am I going to do when I reach her?"

He would either have to jump from his horse to hers or try grabbing the other horse's reins. He was not overly excited about his options.

The ornate black carriage jostled from side to side spraying dirt and a cloud of dust which obstructed Jeff's vision. All of a sudden he was riding beside the other horse which, to his relief, had blinders. However, the horse sensed his presence and dodged towards the right side of Calhoun.

To his great surprise, the woman he saw was not frantically waiving her arms or screaming. She was rather calmly trying to get her horse's reins but could not remedy the situation. As she turned her head she saw Jeff and began motioning that she was powerless.

It was only a matter of minutes before he gained the courage to grab the leather reins, which were flapping wildly all around the horse's head. He almost lost his balance but managed to get closer to the other animal. Jeff gave up on grabbing the reins and decided to try for the more stationary bridle. While clutching his own horse's reins he took hold of the other horse's restraints and began slowing both his and the other horse down. With a last strong tug Jeff finally got the steed to stop in the road twenty feet from the water's edge.

Shaken, Jeff gladly and slowly dismounted, took a deep breath and approached the carriage. He tied his horse to the buggy and went to the steps where his eyes met the woman's for the first time.

What a stunning glow. Flowing brunette hair arranged ever so carefully under her white bonnet, her rosy red cheeks, high cheekbones, cute pug nose and those dark eyebrows grabbed Jeff's attention. He had never seen such a ravishing beauty.

This woman possibly in her late twenties was taken aback by this cowboy with his disheveled brown hair and slim athletic body.

With his outstretched arms Jeff gestured his assistance at helping her down. She readily complied. He couldn't believe how thin and light she was.

"*One hundred and ten pounds*?" he thought.

Then she spoke, "I have been riding horses all of my life. My father spent countless pounds on equestrian training and all for naught."

Jeff was surprised at her slightly English accent with its touch of a southern drawl. She brushed her hair back and readjusted her white-laced hat.

"Don't be too hard on yourself. Once a horse gets out of control, it's very difficult."

"Miss Crystal Montgomery is my name. I am so pleased to make your acquaintance, sir," she said as she extended her white-gloved hand.

"Whatever can I do to repay your kindness which has saved me from a terrible end?   It is another reason to be thankful on such a day as this holiday brings."

The two of them looked in front of the carriage. Had they not been able to stop the wayward horse, Crystal would have certainly landed in the water at the end of the road.

"Ah, shucks, ma'am, twernt nothin'," Jeff quipped but immediately upon seeing her confused look said, "Sorry. I'm Jeff Carr. A real pleasure to meet you."

"We best not stay here. This is a quite dangerous area of the city as you can see from looking at these damaged buildings. I do not want to appear forward or inappropriate but I would like the presence of your company this afternoon. Do you have plans for your Thanksgiving meal?"

Jeff was thrilled at her invitation. He couldn't help but notice her charming confidence and humility.

"Not really. I rode down from the plantation with two friends. One of our horses was wounded. They're probably enjoying a hearty meal back at the stables on Coming Street. We had a scary retreat from some Yankee bullets down on the Battery."

"Are you all right? No one was seriously hurt?"

Jeff shook his head.

"I would love for you and your friends to enjoy a nice Thanksgiving meal. My mother and father would be much beholden to you."

"Let me check with my friends."

He helped her into the carriage, got in himself and flicked the reins starting the horse on its way. He spotted his hat on the side of the road, got out of the carriage and retrieved it.

It took them a few minutes to reach Coming where all of the action had begun. People along the way were relieved that no one was hurt. Some waved, others clapped as the two of them passed by.

Seeing Jeff in the presence of such an exquisite lady, Walter and Jed, the latter of whom had been chewing his afternoon tobacco, adjusted their posture.

"We hadn't known you could ride like that! Is everyone all right? You took so long that I was very worried that something bad might have happened to you."

"No, I'm all right. Walter, Jed, let me introduce you to Miss Crystal Montgomery."

The cowboys shyly tipped their hats. Jed started to spit some of his chew but caught himself.

"It would certainly be my pleasure to have you all accompany me to our plantation for a warm Thanksgiving dinner."

"Well, ma'am, we'd be much obligin' to ye exceptin' dat we got a lame hoss we needs to tend to."

Walter nodded in agreement.

"Well, guys, I was thinking about going with Miss Montgomery even if it would be just for a little while. Could I meet you back here later this afternoon?"

Grabbing Jeff's coat and pulling him aside, Jed whispered, "What do ya mean going to dat fine lady's house fer Thanksgiving? Dey gots too much money and finery for the likes of peoples like us who works on a farm. Did you see dat der carriage she's a ridin' in? So jes' you uninvite yo-self right quick so's we kin git on about our business."

What would he do? Accompany his friends back to the plantation merely because of Jed's misplaced propriety, or enjoy a great southern dinner with the most beautiful creature he had ever seen?

"See ya-"

Noticing their general disapproval Jeff continued, "I'm very sorry I can't help you with the horse, but I don't want to offend Miss Montgomery. I'll meet up with you here at the livery stable later on, OK?"

Jed turned rather abruptly. Walter, concerned with John O'Rork's charge to safeguard his field hands, tried to talk Jeff into abandoning his plans but was unsuccessful.

"You just be careful, please. Will you be able to find your way back?"

"I know the way and will instruct him accordingly."

"Thank you, ma'am."

Jeff was a little concerned at Jed's anger. The old man had saved his life. Maybe all would be forgiven the next time they met.

15

Jeff was thoroughly enjoying himself as he accompanied his new friend to her house. The peaceful ride soon made him forget about his two fellow comrades. He noticed Crystal's pleasant perfume and stately form.

"That smells so good. What kind of perfume are you wearing?"

"Why, Mr. Carr... It is called Forduena. My father got it on one of his many trips out of the country last year. This came from Spain."

Being in the presence of such a good-looking lady who had apparently been brought up in style was a charmer.

The comfortable carriage ride took them to the northern portion of the Charleston peninsula where Jeff was pleasantly surprised by the sight of a very large mansion.

Beautiful flowers adorned the wide porch on both sides of the dwelling. A shiny wood-grained oak double door with crystalline glass was impressive.

Five white granite steps led up to the porch. Large columns topped with intricately carved caps supported the lower of the three level roof system. Pairs of green shutters complete with turnkey guards and flower planters augmented a most ornate scene.

"Welcome to Montebello, Mr. Carr."

To his left were five small log cabins complete with their own chimneys and windows.

"You own slaves?"

"Why, not at all. We call them indentured servants. Unlike other plantations in the area, our attendants are just like family. They have agreed to do the regular chores around the house. In return, they receive nice lodging, food and a salary commensurate with the level of their responsibility. In fact, it was mother who insisted on maintaining their well being. We have installed fireplaces, provided curtains, beds, tables, reading materials and a cooking area for each of their cabins. They can go about as they please as long as they take care of their duties. Most of them attend church near the downtown area, when the guns aren't sounding off."

This was new to Jeff. He had heard all of his life the politically correct but apparently faulty view that all Southerners not only owned slaves but mistreated them.

They reached the front of the main house. Jeff gently helped Crystal out of the carriage only to be welcomed by a middle-aged man wearing a smart, servant uniform with white gloves.

"Arthur, good afternoon. Arthur is the man of the house."

Seeing a confused look on Jeff's face, Crystal elaborated, "Our gentlemen's gentleman - our butler," she whispered. "He takes care of maintaining the household staff. He is in charge of our maids, custodians and our gardener. He actually worked for us while we lived in England. We don't know what we would do without him."

"Nice to meet you. My name's Jeff Carr," Jeff said trying to shake Arthur's hand. Arthur failed to extend his own but retorted in a very distinguished British accent, "Pleasure, Mr. Carr. Miss Crystal, need I retrieve anything from your carriage?"

Seeing Crystal's negative reply Arthur gave one last glance at Jeff and went inside.

"He's not being rude. He's very friendly but has always been respectful of maintaining his station. Now, Mammie on the other hand, is less formal."

"Mammie?"

"Our handmaid."

Jeff entered the grand hallway and embarrassed himself by gawking at the huge chandelier.

"Oh my," Arthur responded as he looked at Jeff and then the chandelier. "I just dusted it this morning."

Arthur paused.

"Might I take your hat, Mr. Carr?"

Jeff obliged. Arthur left the room.

The foyer in front of them was full of beautifully carved furniture. A bright oil lamp sat on a sturdy round wooden table on either side. There was a writing desk to the left, and a small planter to the right. Directly in front stood a grand shiny oak semicircular stairwell leading up to the second floor in both directions.

"Most of the furniture came from England. These mirrors were made especially for my father who is a businessman in the downtown area."

"Mizz Crystal, how is you a doin'?" a slightly heavyset black woman asked as she waddled through a doorway to the right of the stairs.

"Hello, Mammie. Meet Jeff Carr. He rescued me from my runaway carriage this morning!"

"Tank de Lord. Honey is you all right then?" Mammie asked as she gave Crystal a gentle hug.

"Oh, yes. A little shaken."

"Have you had a congenial afternoon or has it been somewhat obstreperous?" Crystal asked, giving Mammie a wink.

"Obstreperous..." Mammie thought for a second, her finger pointing to her chin. She then beamed, "obstreperous meaning a vexatious situation? No ma'am, obstreperous it has not been. I have had a very good morning, Mizz Crystal."

Mammie glanced at Jeff.

To his surprise, Mammie gave him a hug also and said, "Good to meet you, Mr. Jeff."

"Is Mr. Montgomery here, Mammie?"

"Yes'm. He's in the library." Turning to Crystal she whispered, "Nice cowboy you gots here, Mizz Crystal." She then left the room.

Crystal noticed the look of shock on Jeff's face.

"Oh, each afternoon at the two o'clock hour, I spend time with Mammie and her family teaching them words and phrases. It's one of the ways in which I want to help them. Today will prove the exception seeing as it is so busy on this holiday. I love to teach, though I don't do it professionally."

To the right and left of the stairway small hallways led towards the center of the house.

"Father will be so glad to meet you. He owns a jewelry store, I might have told you."

They passed various rooms along the way. Jeff couldn't help but admire Crystal's graceful walk. Again the air was filled with her perfume which intensified the moment. Crystal and Jeff arrived at two large closed oak doors, which were on the right side of the hall.

"Come!" A booming male voice answered her tender knock.

Jeff and Crystal entered a huge room filled with bookshelves lining every wall. In the center of the room, three other long shelves were well organized. Another chandelier, smaller than that which adorned the entrance, illuminated the room. The finest oak desk Jeff had ever seen was in the far left-hand corner. Emerging from between two of the center shelves was a man thumbing through a novel.

"Crystal, my darling little girl, how are you?"

"Daddy-O!"

Jeff snickered at the phrase, but disguised his reaction with a fake sneeze.

A devoted daughter hugged her father's neck. The man was in his early fifties. Gray streaks had intruded upon the rest of his black hair. A smile communicating his love for his daughter was followed by a look of curiosity.

"Who have we here, Crystal?" the man asked in a thick British accent.

"Daddy, this is Jeff Carr. He saved my life today near downtown. My horse was spooked by one of those horrible sounds of a pistol in the distance. My attentions were rather directed to the prettiest flowers in some of the shops along the way and the horse's reins were grabbed from my hands. Young Jeff here chased my buggy all the way down Calhoun. We almost landed in the river!"

"Dear boy, my heartfelt thankfulness to you for saving my precious little girl!" he said as he extended both his hands. "Charles Montgomery is my name. Whatever can we do to thank you properly?"

"Oh Father, I have invited Jeff to have Thanksgiving dinner with us. Would that be all right?"

"Certainly, he will be our very special guest. I think your mother said we will be served at the 2:00 hour."

Mr. Montgomery was a bit shaken by the idea of anything happening to his daughter.

As Crystal turned to leave the room, Charles took her arm and gave her a kiss on the forehead.

"Crystal, I am so glad you are OK. Listen, I know your birthday is coming up in a few weeks. I was going to make this a surprise but," he got a black jewelry box off a nearby desk, "please tell me if you like it."

Crystal took the black case from her father and opened it revealing a large diamond ring embedded in a black felt cushion. She was astounded. Her face flushed with tears.

"Oh, Daddy-O, this is too much for me. It must have cost a pretty penny! Are you sure we don't need to save the money especially when we are in such dire straights with the war and all..."

"I wouldn't think of it. We are doing quite well. Don't you worry your head about it. Does it look all right?"

With a kiss planted on her father's cheek and a look of great approval, Crystal hugged her father and left the room in tears. Jeff shook Mr. Montgomery's hand and followed Crystal down the hallway.

Crystal carefully placed the black box in her purse and proceeded into the kitchen.

Two cooks were tenaciously getting the Thanksgiving meal ready under the direction of a large framed woman.

"Mother, are you doing too much again? How might I be of assistance?"

"Crystal, my dear. How are you?" Crystal's mother gave her a hug and a peck on the cheek. "Would you be so kind to-oh, who on earth is this cowboy?"

"Yes, Mother. This young man's name is Jeff Carr. My horse was spooked and my carriage out of control. Jeff saved me from being dashed in the Ashley River."

"Well I declare, very pleased to meet you, Jeff. I am Haddie Montgomery. Thank you for saving my little girl!"

"Someone better save dat dere toykee," chanted one of the cooks as she saw smoke billowing from one of the ovens in the left-hand corner of the large kitchen. Crystal's mother raced over and extracted the large bird from the oven just in time.

"We'll talk in a little while. Crystal, why not sit with your young man in the parlor? Greta, Solumay, let us proceed."

Crystal blushed.

Jeff and Crystal hurried from the busy scene and sat in the parlor, which was located in the rear of the house.

Four tall windows with double louver shutters and large ornately carved crown molding adorned the comfortable setting. A beautiful, fully functional spinet harpsichord was located on the left side of the room. Solid oak chairs were located in front of each of the towering windows. A brown and blue Oriental rug lay on a superbly shiny hard wood floor.

"Do you play?"

"A little. I've been taking lessons for some time. Would you care to hear a piece?"

Jeff shook his head and Crystal was soon sitting on the brown stool in front of the harpsichord filling the house with music.

"This is Traité de l'harmonie by Rameau."

Her touch professional, her concentration admirable. Still a smile would appear every few seconds as she followed along in the sheet music.

The sun shone in the room creating a warm glow as it bounced off Crystal's beautiful hair.

When she had played a few minutes she asked if Jeff would like to bring two of the chairs together in front of the center window.

"Who's that your father is standing with?" Jeff asked pointing to a painting on the left side of the room.

Crystal giggled, "Oh, that's Robert Lee. He is a close friend of the family. That picture was painted about two years ago. My father was in Richmond during March and met Mr. Lee at a social gathering. Now, whenever he comes to Charleston, he is welcome, especially under the present circumstances, to sojourn here at Montebello. Of course these days he is honorably involved in leading our troops."

Jeff's face disclosed his astonishment.

"Poor thing, though. They say the Northerners have taken Arlington, his house, from him and Mary last January. They told him that they would be burying union soldiers all the way up to his front door because of his involvement in the war effort. Do you think that will ever come true?"

"Perhaps."

With a curious look, Crystal said, "You know, Mr. Jeffrey Carr, you are a rather mysterious individual. From whence do you come?"

"I'm from ... out of town."

"Oh, you live in South Carolina then?"

"In a matter of speaking."

"Why Mammie, how nice of you to join us."

Mammie came in, pulled up a chair and sat down between them.

"Yo mamma said I best get in here to be one dem chaperone persons. I hope, Mr. Jeff dat's all right wit you?"

"Certainly."

Looking around the large woman, they continued their conversation.

"Some say Sherman will head towards Savannah and, becoming frustrated with our boys in Georgia, give up this horrible cause to take the South. I hope that is the case."

"I believe unfortunately that he is out to bring the South back into the Union."

"I have been following the news that appears in the Courier about his exploits. He seems to be a most disagreeable man, bent on destroying everything in his path. Hard times have befallen us because of the blockade of our harbors and adjacent shorelines. Father is having a time with business dealings. Part of his negotiations comprises dealing with companies up north some of whom have quit having anything to do with him. What is to become of us, our plantation, our very lives?"

"Don't you worry 'bout tings, Miss Crystal. My belief is dat the destruction will be relegated to areas far from our habitation."

"Very good, Mammie. Thank you for your encouragement."

"Lunch is served," Crystal's mother announced.

In a few minutes, everyone was assembled in the dining room. Several oil lamps around the eating area created a comfortable Christmas-like scene as everyone surrounded the oblong table located in the center of the room. A white intricately woven tablecloth complemented the fine piece of furniture.

The table was full of plates dressed with delicious looking dishes. Warm applesauce, homemade biscuits, freshly picked green onions, cabbage, peas and corn accompanied the main course of the day. The plate on which the turkey and dressing rested was twice as large as any Jeff had ever seen. The bird itself must have weighed more than fifteen pounds.

Mammie pushed a water and tea cart into the room as Crystal, her parents and Jeff sat down.

One large lit red candle surrounded by greenery was located in the center of the table. Various paintings of dignitaries hung on the walls. This dinner seemed a rather formal affair. Jeff was careful to sit straight and watch his P's and Q's.

"We are glad to have a guest today, particularly for his act of heroism which served to safeguard our daughter's life, praise the Almighty," said a grateful Mr. Montgomery as he smiled at Jeff.

"Mightn't we pray over the meal, dear?" Mrs. Montgomery asked.

"By all means, and such a glorious meal is this, which has been prepared for us on this Thanksgiving Day," Charles Montgomery replied as they all bowed their heads.

"Gracious Heavenly Father, we thank Thee for Thy bounty with which Thou hast blessed us even in such tumultuous times as these. We have neither deserved such a grand feast nor have we truly considered the cost our Savior paid for our salvation. We thank Thee for this food, our happy friends and this glorious occasion with which You have blessed us. Food to our bodies, our hands to Thy service, In His name we pray. Amen."

Mammie and the other women served the food.

"So let us hear about your ride, Crystal. I thought we had agreed that Mammie would accompany you in the carriage, especially if you were going to the downtown area."

"Yes, Mother. I am aware what we had decided. I just needed to acquire some of that tasty bread from the market. Besides, the area north of Calhoun extending to ours lies in safe territory at least for now. But I will in the future heed your instructions. Please do forgive my indiscretion," Crystal said as she kissed her mother's hand.

Charles carved the turkey and everyone served his or her plate.

"I hate that the war has determined where we can and cannot venture. It's changed everything. I am beginning to hate this war more and more."

"Yes, Crystal. It seems to be playing havoc with everyday living. I hear many of our citizens are moving farther north to Columbia to escape that horrible man Sherman. He certainly seems to be headed our way, cutting up through Georgia. The paper said he was headed straight for Savannah."

Mrs. Montgomery squeezed her daughter's hand.

"Yes, but he won't succeed without a fight I think. Our forces of South Carolina will give him a good run for his money."

"Young man, it is proper to have confidence in our armed forces. But we do face a formidable enemy. Do you remember that just last month we suffered a defeat at Cedar Creek? Our men were doing quite well. The Northerners were even retreating when this, Sheridan, what is his name dear?"

"General Philip Sheridan, Charles," Haddie responded.

"Yes, Philip Sheridan rode his horse down the line of his retreating forces and in a moment's notice, changed an apparent defeat into undeniable victory. I am not sure as to his character nor that of Sherman, but the North does represent a sizable threat which must be considered seriously."

"I know, Father, but I think Jeff is correct. Why, do you remember when some of our Citadel boys were stationed on Morris Island in command of some cannon there? They were the first to draw an attack against the North. Remember how the Star Of The West, the boat the Northerners were using to bring supplies to the fort, was entering the harbor. These men, mostly under twenty years of age, took the crew to task and fired upon them. In response to their gallantry, the Star turned the other way. If mere cadets can do such damage to thwart the enemy, certainly our army can as well bring good results."

"And thus, they led us into this precarious position – I know, I know. Without their intervention, things could have gotten much worse. Let us talk of less heavy things. What a wonderful meal you have prepared for us, Mother," Charles said.

"With the help of our friends in the kitchen indeed," Haddie Montgomery said as she gave Mammie and the others a wink.

"Will you all be moving farther north for the duration, Mrs. Montgomery?"

"Oh, please, call me Haddie. In answer to your question, we will be staying right here, won't we Charles? We feel we can defend our land effectively. We have stored a number of firearms and our servants as well want to protect themselves and their own property against the northern aggressors."

"Your servants have property in these parts?"

"Oh yes," Charles said. "Through their hard work many of them have agreed to earn some of the property on which they are working. It is similar to the share cropper philosophy from which many others have benefited. We feel that this is only fair."

Crystal spoke up, "Daddy-O, thank you ever so much for the beautiful diamond ring you gave me for my birthday!"

"You already gave the ring to her, Charles? I wanted to be there..." a disappointed Mrs. Montgomery said and then took a sip of southern tea.

"I just could not wait. I was so excited, dear."

Seeing the funny look on Jeff's face at the mention of "Daddy-O", Haddie giggled and explained, "The reason for Crystal's calling her daddy by that name is-"

"Dear, must we go into that in the midst of present company?"

"Why, of course, Charles. Jeffrey must know... Anyway, it has to do with Charles' middle name. You see, when Charles' mother was found to be with child, Charles' father and mother thought they were to have a daughter. When it was found that a son was being born, they decided to name Charline Oline Montgomery, Charles 'O-My' Montgomery, due to the surprise of the moment. And ever since then Crystal has adopted the fond name Daddy-O for her father. Her reference is of course given with much love and kindness although Charles, darling," Haddie took Charles' hand, "you don't really like us to mention it. We do love you dearly."

With that Charles blushed and then laughed. "Do you really believe that story?" he asked Jeff and then said to his wife, "Dear, I'm just joshin with you. Let's eat this fine bird before I turn into bigger prey than he."

The rest of the meal was accompanied by discussions over the dangers of going downtown, the demise of the rice industry displaced by cotton and corn crops, and the precarious future of the way of life in the south, the latter which received not a few comments from Mammie.

When everyone had eaten their fill, coffee was served. Mammie and the others brought out three plates of desserts. Butterscotch pie, chocolate pie and flan were the choices of the day.

Everyone finished eating and got up from the table.

"Would you like to relax in the parlor or play some croquet in the backyard?" Charles asked Jeff.

Jeff and the others went in the back and enjoyed the famous lawn game, driving four colorful wooden balls through a series of hoops, called wickets.

Having never played the game, Jeff was enjoying receiving close instruction from Crystal.

Even in this zestful event Jeff could spot the serious competitive attitude adopted by Charles Montgomery.

"If you don't put forth your best effort, why try at all?"

Charles won the game.

The sunlight was beginning to wane. Jeff almost pulled his watch out of his coat pocket. Charles took his pocket watch out.

"Oh my days, it's 5:16. Where has the time gone?"

"Would you care to stay for the evening meal?" Haddie asked with Charles' approval.

"Let me take my leave of you now. I must return to my friends in Charleston so we can return to our plantation. But I would love to pay you a social call on the morrow perhaps?"

"Certainly," Crystal said. "What time would be best? Maybe we might enjoy a picnic near the house. I'm sure Mammie would be able to accompany us."

"That would be fine. I will be here at 12:00 PM."

Jeff shook Charles and Haddie's hands, went inside, retrieved his coat, got another hug from Mammie, and thanked the kitchen crew for the wonderful meal.

Mounting his horse, he gazed into Crystal's eyes, received an alluring smile, and rode in the direction of downtown Charleston.

A short ride took him to the livery stable where he waited for his friends who were nowhere to be found. The stall's owner said that Jeff's two companions had gone but would soon return to fetch Jed's horse.

"The horse should do well, even over ruff terrain, that is, if you all take it slow," the livery stable owner assured Jeff.

After twenty-five minutes Walter and a still disgruntled Jed approached.

"Have a good dinner?" Walter asked with a sincere smile.

"Eatin' with high society, humph!"

"Now, Jed, that will be enough. It's Thanksgiving, remember? Settle down. Jeff here was just blessed by providence in the saving of that girl from uncertain harm. You would have done the same thing if such a pretty lady was beholden to you with such an invitation."

Jed's anger subsided as he pretended to shrug the whole thing off.

"Friends?" Jeff extended his hand. Jed smiled a little and reciprocated.

The journey home was arduous. Stopping every ten minutes proved not only difficult for the three cowboys, but the wounded horse who, after having rested a bit, didn't want to proceed. Although the wound was well patched, the pain was quite apparent.

Nonetheless the cowboys were able to coax the poor animal along with strokes and sugar cubes. They finally reached the plantation to O'Rork's great relief.

16

On Friday morning, Jeff and the other cowboys worked on their regular chores. Jed's horse was resting in the barn. John O'Rork was getting over his anger at Jeff and the others' excursion downtown.

"Let's not be a doin' that real soon again, laddies. It be best that in these times, you be stayin' 'round here."

Jeff and Walter worked outside repairing Jeremy's wagon after which they spent a few minutes cleaning up the bunkhouse.

"Here's your gun and holster back."

"Why don't you keep them a while longer. Maybe you can pay for them out of your compensations in the coming months."

Jeff thanked Walter hoping that he would never need to use the pistol. After all, a single bullet might change history.

Jed Tub sauntered into the bunkhouse ready to take on the world.

"All of us is going for some ropin'. Wanna' come wit' us?"

"Ropin'? What kind of ropin'?"

"Occasionally we'll take some calves out in the field and practice our ropin' skills. Dey needs some exercise anyways. Come on, Jeff," Jed said as he extended his hand.

Jeff shook it and said, "Thank you very much, Jed, but I've got something I need to do."

Jed's smile disappeared.

"Oh, it's dat lady friend, huh? Mr. High and Mighty goin' a courtin'. Phesha! I kin see dat you aint one of us. Walter, you comin'?"

Jed turned on his heel and headed outside.

"Don't mind him."

"Why is he so against my courting anyone. Has he got anything against women?"

"Jed was in love with a woman living in one of the poorer districts downtown near the waterway. One night a cannon ball exploded in the parlor killing her and her mother. Although it's been two years, he never got over it. He hates those Yankees more than anything. And one would think he hates God Himself. Guess he's just envious that you found a woman and all. He'll be fine. Just give him a little time."

Walter joined the others outside.

Strapping on his borrowed six-shooter and putting on his cowboy hat made Jeff feel manly. Going back into time to find himself hadn't been the object of his quest, but such a residual benefit was not altogether unappreciated.

But this was temporary. In a few days, he would return to his present, comparatively boring time. He didn't look forward to that, especially when he had found such a lovely lady.

He walked outside to the stables where the other cowboys were saddling up.

He felt good as he retrieved his saddle from the shed and heaved it over Sunshine. His sense of satisfaction faded as he noticed a few glares coming from the other cowpokes.

Apparently Jed's reaction to Jeff's date was creating general animosity.

Nonetheless, he strapped the saddle on, mounted Sunshine and gave a halfhearted wave to them as he rode off in the direction of Montebello.

<<◇>>

He was nervous as he started up the trail leading to North Charleston. Many thoughts entered his mind.

The possibility of encountering hostile forces was ever present. Was it wise to endanger his life and future for the passion he held for a woman he would never marry? Would Crystal prove to be the woman for whom he had searched so long? How would it be to marry into aristocracy? How would he deal with her father? Would he be expected to carry on the family business-

Jeff realized the fallacy of his thoughts. He jerked the reins of his horse and dismounted.

"OK, let's just calm down. What am I thinking?"

What in the world had infatuation done to him? How could he fall in love with someone over a hundred years older than he? He had only spent one afternoon with her. Even if love at first sight did make sense, was it physically possible and morally right to remain in the past?

Jeff laughed.

"We can't live in the past, dear," his grandmother's wise words echoed through his mind.

What would he do for a living? What of his friends in 2010? This whole trip to Crystal's was a huge mistake. He had investigative work to do. He mounted his horse, rode the other way, and stopped again.

He had to know of her feelings. What were her intentions? Would he tell her where he was from?

The emotions stirring within elongated the journey.

The same ferryboat pilot greeted him, "Where you be goin' in des treacherous times, young man? Sharp shooters about, don' you know?"

"Thanks for the warning," Jeff said as he gave the man the fare.

The sounds of random gunfire made Jeff cringe. He was very careful to survey the road and surrounding terrain. He finally made it to the long dirt road leading to Montebello.

He spotted a small black girl wearing a dirty white dress with fringe on the neckline. She was working near one of the little cottages.

Turning towards Jeff she asked, "Iz you a Yankee o' iz you a Reb?"

"Good morning. You can call me a Reb if you want. I'm here to see Miss Crystal."

"Oh, she's my teacher. Ize just loves her."

Jeff smiled at the girl. In the back of his mind he thought of the professor's imperative, *"No interaction."*

What harm would giving the little girl a Snicker's have on all of history?

He dug one of the chocolate bars out of his coat pocket, unwrapped it and gave it to the child. She looked at it for a few seconds, smelled it, took one bite and excitedly ran inside the cabin.

Jeff rode on to the main house with a huge smile on his face. Perhaps he couldn't change the girl's life but he could bring her a moment of pleasure. Besides, she was now the first person in history that had tasted a twenty first century candy bar!

When he reached Montebello, all of his doubts about having taken his journey dissipated. There she was, sitting in a white rocking chair on the front porch humming as she knitted. What a marvelous creature, beauty typified by her long stately neck and regal carriage. Her genuine smile greeted his coming. He felt as if he had come home for the first time.

"Why Mr. Carr, however have you been? You are so prompt. I look forward to our time together."

"How are you? Please call me Jeff," he said as he dismounted and walked up the steps.

"Jeff," Crystal hesitated and then asked, "do you still want to go on our little picnic?"

"Certainly. Looks like a lovely day for it."

"Mammie is preparing some chicken, potato salad and other delights. She said that she would be happy to serve as chaperone for our outing. Is that all right with you, Jeff?"

"*Anything to be with you,*" he thought, nodding.

They sat on the porch until Mammie was ready. Arthur instructed the stable boy to get the carriage.

With a basket of food in her arms, Mammie stepped out onto the front porch and waited for assistance from Jeff who quickly came to her aid and retrieved the basket.

"What a gentleman you is. Uh... are."

Arthur came out on the porch and said, "It is requested that due to propriety and for discretionary issues you need to return in the space of an hour and a half." Then he whispered, "Master 'Daddy-O's' instructions."

Arthur put his hand up to his mouth, looked over his shoulder and scooted away.

Mammie, Jeff and Crystal walked down the steps towards the carriage. Jeff put the basket of goodies down and boosted Crystal up in the front seat of the vehicle. Mammie approached the carriage and genteelly extended her hand intimating that she wanted Jeff's assistance as well.

He helped her up (with all his strength), but to his chagrin, she sat right next to Crystal in the front of the carriage, necessitating his difficult entry into the back seat. Boy was he going to have a swell time adjusting to southern traditions. He placed the food in the back and entered the vehicle.

A fifteen-minute ride took them to a pleasant spot. Soon a blanket was spread out near an old oak tree on a flowing grassy hillside. A low-lying white cloud cover bordered the smooth cascading hills to their left. Crystal sat down by Jeff as Mammie took their picnic lunch from the basket.

"May I assist?"

"No thank you, Mizz Crystal. Wouldn't be proper and all. Anyways, Mammie's here to look out fo' you, Mizz Crystal. Lord knows I'd been doing dat for a long time now."

Jeff began eating a piece of chicken.

Mammie shyly said, "You know, Mr. Jeff, Thanksgiving done been over for but a day. Dat don't mean - I mean, don't we need to pray over dis?"

Jeff smiled in agreement, put down his chicken and bowed his head. After a graceful and meaningful prayer from Crystal they commenced.

In all honesty, Jeff had reflected more on the quality and humble demeanor of Crystal's voice than on the words of the prayer. He was enamored with this southern belle.

He noticed the exquisite taste of the meal. Jeff's mother had often complained about all of the chemicals being put into the food production process. Apparently this affected the flavor and, according to his mother, the toxicity of the food as well. The corn was luscious, the chicken fresh, the potato salad having been chilled on ice was delicious. Even the homemade bread was the best he'd ever had.

"This is excellent, Mammie."

"Why thank you kind sir."

"Where did you learn to cook like this?"

"Mr. Jeff, I been cooking all my life. Fried chicken is my specialty. Alls my kids likes it and Courtney my husband, God rest his soul, liked it jess fine. Poor man died of consumption, though. But not from my cookin'. He et dem eggs and dey had too much of dat brown fringe, I spec'."

"Do you like working for Mr. Montgomery? I hear some servants are mistreated, although I know you are treated well by your masters."

Without warning an upset Mammie threw her chicken down.

Honorable Intentions

"Master? Mr. Jeff, these folks is my family. De Lord, He's my master. I love working there at Montebello. I gets plenty of food, my cottage is a 'provision', and Mizz Crystal, she done- - er - she is teaching my children and myself for free almost every day. I ain't no slave for sure. I know some white folks, Caucasians - mistreat us. But I don't hears about dat much. Please, let's talk of something else, for sure, Mr. Jeff."

Jeff was beginning to like Mammie. Such a confident but gentle spirit.

"Oh my, look see yonder."

Everyone noticed a lone figure riding a horse about a quarter of a mile away.

"Who could that be all the way out here?"

"Don't know for sure, but based on the times we are living in, I'll be ready," Jeff said, patting his six-shooter.

"Oh please, no violence. We can always pray that all will be well," Crystal said.

"It hepped Dan'l in de lion's den."

"Yep, but the lions didn't have Winchesters. I'll be ready –with a prayer too, just the same."

They were all a little nervous as the man approached.

"O no," Crystal gasped, her disgust was quite apparent in her voice. "It's Mr. James Morris."

"Mr. Morris, oh, he's dat nice businessman who lives West of the Ashley, he does. Don't you like him, Mizz Crystal? He's always bringing you tings like flowers... – oh," Mammie looked at Jeff. She had said too much.

"I am very dubious about his intentions. He seems so sweet and respectful on the outside; especially when Father and Mother are about. But at other times, I think there is a certain darkness in him."

"How did you meet him?"

"One day I was tending the counter at my father's jewelry store when he ventured by. He told me that he was searching for a ring for a friend of his. To be truthful, I think he had seen me in the shop window. It's as if he has been pursuing me ever since."

Jeff stood as the man approached. He nearly dropped his jaw. Mr. Morris closely resembled the man who had bothered him at the funeral parlor in 2010! He even shared the same crooked smile.

Dressed in a tight black vest and pressed pants far too fancy for riding on the range, Morris dismounted and walked up to the group. He couldn't have weighed more than one hundred and twenty pounds.

"Afternoon. Looks like someone is having a picnic and didn't invite me?"

"Mr. Morris, what brings you out our way?" Crystal asked as Mammie and she came to their feet.

"Just headed back from Grahamville. Had a few cattle to deliver from our farm," Morris said in a thick southern drawl. "Got a good deal from the Marks brothers. No war gonna prevent them from gaining on the cattle industry. Who have we here?" Morris looked Jeff over.

"Why this is Mr. Jeffrey Carr."

"Carter? You must be related to some of my neighbors, Thomas Carter and his wife. They live right back of my plantation. They've got a nice place there."

"Carr is my name. I work for Mr. Carter."

Morris put his hands on his hips and stepped back, "Crystal, you're having a picnic with a regular farm hand? This is not a gentleman. What a shame, such a fine lady as yourself in the company of a sweaty, non-aristocratic personality."

"How can you talk like that, Mr. Morris? If there were ever a gentleman, Jeffrey is one. His manners are impeccable."

"Manners? How would you know anything about his manners? Miss Crystal, I appeal to your fine senses. I don't have any field hands of my own as yet, but at least I got my own place with a lot of land-"

"You just stop right der Mr. James Morris. Mr. Jeffrey done et wit us at Thanksgiving yesterday. And besides, Mizz Crystal wuz saved by dis here cowboy when her hoss been spooked. She wouldn't be here 'tall if'n it hadn't been for him."

Morris looked like he was going to blow a gasket.

"And who gave you the right to address the likes of me, old colored woman?"

"Mr. Morris! You render your apologies immediately to Mammie!" Crystal said as she took a step forward. Mammie was crushed and appalled.

Jeff drew closer to the thin cowboy and said, "Best you be leaving us before something happens which we'll both regret."

The tall, skinny man started to put his hand on his sidearm but thought the better of it when he saw Jeff reach for his own.

Morris quipped, "Best you be careful, son," looking sternly at Jeff. "And I'll see you later, missy," he said to Crystal as he turned, mounted his horse and whipped the animal, creating a cloud of dust at his leaving.

"Can you believe that guy?"

Crystal grasped Mammie's arm delicately, "Mammie I am so sorry for Mr. Morris' behavior. Intolerable. I'm afraid he has shown his true self this afternoon. Would you like to return to the plantation?"

"Yes'm. Best we return if dat would be all right with you."

The day had gotten a little warmer as they arrived at the main house. A teary eyed Mammie headed inside while Jeff assisted Crystal's exit from the carriage.

"Poor lady. It seems for some, things will never change. What must these beloved people endure in the future?"

Jeff could not enlighten her.

The two o'clock lesson was called off for the day due to Mammie's emotional state. Jeff and Crystal spent the rest of the afternoon in delightful discussions about anything from the terrible war to an undying hope for a better future.

As they sat out on the expansive front porch, Jeff was well surprised at Crystal's gently taking his hand in hers. Just for a second this southern belle revealed her newfound feelings for the strange out-of-place cowboy. No one was looking. Jeff was enthralled with her sensitivity. Her charm and beauty overwhelmed his good senses so much that without thinking of past, present or future, he leaned over and gave her a peck on the cheek. At this, Crystal blushed putting her hand to her mouth.

A more passionate kiss and embrace followed.

"That was the best kiss I've ever experienced," Jeff thought. What tenderness, what genuine passion, wrapped up in a single moment.

Arthur entered the room and interrupted, "Master Montgomery requires your presence in the library, Miss Crystal. Shall I tell him you are coming?"

"Oh, Arthur, you didn't see anything, did you?"

"Madam," Arthur smiled, "I was preoccupied thinking of the masterpieces of the ages, Mozart, Beethoven, Rembrandt and the like, all of whom encompass a certain unquestionable propriety not negotiable on any grounds."

Both Jeff and Crystal chimed in, "Huh?"

"No ma'am, I did not witness any indiscretion. I shall ever remain oblivious to the moment at hand."

"Arthur, you're the best," quipped Jeff.

"Undoubtedly," he said while chuckling as he went inside the house.

Crystal caressed Jeff's hand, looked into his eyes and asked, "When will I have the pleasure of your company again?"

"I don't know, Crystal. It depends on what happens in the next few days. I must tend to some business. Maybe I can see you on Saturday or Sunday. May I ask what you're thinking?"

Crystal shyly turned aside, "I can't.. quite.. think clearly. I mustn't tell you plainly, Jeffery. I must have time to ponder on .. things."

"I understand your confusion," Jeff said as Crystal turned towards him.

He looked deeply into her blue eyes and said, "We've just met. But our meeting has brought me a new understanding of how..." Jeff paused, "wonderful a person can be."

She blushed.

"I don't know when I will see you again. But I hope that it will be soon. I must leave now. Will you think of me?"

Crystal nodded, gave Jeff another kiss on the cheek and went inside.

17

It was well after dark when he arrived at the bunkhouse. His coworkers, readying for a trip, had the most serious demeanor. While Walter and Frederick held torches, O'Rork and Joe loaded some large boards in the back of the wagon driven by Jed Tub.

Two of the tallest beautiful black horses were hitched to Jed's buckboard. Each horse's chest and powerful body, awesome hindquarters and bell-shaped, hair-covered hooves made for an impressively strong, distinctive animal.

"It's a shire for sure," O'Rork was saying with pride. "Imported indeed from Ireland, no doubt. Not as strong as the Clydesdales, but they do the trick in a hurry when pushed."

"I hate to disagree, but the shire comes from England and they are about as large and powerful as the Clydesdales," Frederick said unabashedly. "Learnt it in school. Sorry."

O'Rork was not amused.

Ignoring Jeff altogether, Jed sat, reins in hand, awaiting orders.

Jed's oversized wagon looked sturdy with its reinforced axles, fortified steel wheels and ruggedly braced wooden sides.

"Hello everyone."

Frederick acknowledged Jeff's arrival with a friendly nod.

"Nice rig. Where'd you get it?"

"Never mind ye the wagon and the whereabouts of gettin' it. It's for something truly honorable we are about," O'Rork said as he mounted his horse.

Walter stepped up beside Jeff and said, "We are headed out for a small chore. You want to come?"

"He ain't invited," Jed proclaimed wiping his mouth with his dirty sleeve and letting go a wad of chew near the porch.

"Is too!" Walter countered.

A small argument arose as Walter stayed at a distance trying to convince Jed to exercise some decent kindness.

O'Rork responded, "Jeff, we haven't known you for long and we are a livin' in strange times. No offense, laddie, but we don't know whom we can trust. I would be beholden to you if you'd stay here until we got back. In fact, if you'd confine yourself to the bunkhouse for the rest of the night, that'd be just dandy. It would be safer for you. Hope you understand."

A man in clean gray work pants and shirt came walking down the hill from the house and stepped out of the shadows.

"Hello, Mr. Carter. We're 'bout ready fer ya'."

"Fine. We need to hurry a bit, Mr. O'Rork. I'll take the lead here. No time to waste," he said as he mounted his own horse.

Jeff was shocked to see his great uncle up close. He wanted to meet him but this was not an opportune time. Mr. Carter seemed very preoccupied with their current venture, enough not to have acknowledged Jeff's presence.

Feeling quite cast aside, Jeff dismounted and brushed past a compassionate Walter who offered his apologies.

He entered the bunkhouse, got some food from the kitchen and lay down on his rock-hard bed.

Two small lamps suspended from the ceiling illuminated the room. A comfortable fire warmed the bunkhouse. Shadows danced around the walls as Jeff contemplated his next move.

The cowboys were talking loudly until Mr. Carter insisted on their silence. The group, trailed by Jed's wagon, slowly headed off into the night.

While Jeff desired to comply with O'Rork's request, he had to follow that caravan. This turn of events was no doubt part of the mystery that perplexed him.

Jeff crept over to the window and seeing no one in sight, found a saddlebag at the foot of Walter's bed and filled it with bread and water. No telling how long he would be away.

He carefully edged the door open, scanned the area around the porch, ran silently down to the stables, saddled his horse and hit the trail. The night vision glasses were a godsend. That, with the slow movement of the wagon and the torches, gained him the advantage he needed.

From all he could discern the entourage was headed towards the Charleston peninsula. The trail was quite level, held few curves and was easy to navigate.

He tried to maintain a thousand feet between him and the other men. The night air was a little chilly.

He could hear a hoot owl in the distance accompanied by crickets. Occasionally Jeff would take out a piece of bread and munch.

Ten minutes into the journey he noticed movement between the cowboys and himself. Jeff nervously adjusted his binoculars to see a solitary figure following the group. He couldn't tell who this lone rider was. Even from the person's height and build and the way he sauntered back and forth in his saddle, he seemed like any other drifter. The man turned his head to see if anyone was following him.

It was Jim Morris.

Jeff bolted upright in his saddle. Helpless, he could neither warn his coworkers, nor circumvent Morris' activities. His anger over the others' rejection was now displaced by his concern for their safety. Whatever happened now was already part of a history he couldn't change.

Morris kept a low profile as he rode silently down the trail.

At one point Jeff got too close and dismounted, an action that only served to startle his horse. Morris glanced back and headed in Jeff's direction! He backtracked for a few minutes but not able to see at night, returned to his quest.

Jeff breathed easier. While he had to be aware of Morris' activity, he also had to maintain his line of vision keeping the distant torches of his companions in view.

The men finally reached the ferry. Jeff was surprised to see the boat pilot still at his station. It was 12 midnight.

The cowboys loaded their horses and wagon onto the ferry, helped the pilot pull the boat across the cold black water and reaching the other side, continued towards Charleston. Morris waited in the brush until the cowboys crossed the river and then followed suit.

Jeff reached the ferryboat ramp and dismounted. Trying not to appear anxious, he greeted the pilot with a smile. A large lamp hung from a pole mounted on the ferry illuminating the boat and the surrounding marshland. Jeff panicked. He could barely see the lights of the cowboys in the distance. He wanted to hurry but had to play this out carefully.

"See you're back again. Aren't you supposed to be with your friends over t'ere? I can call dem- Hey, cowboys! Hol' up for your -"

"That's OK," Jeff interrupted, his hand gripping the pilot's arm. He released him and said, "Sorry. I was just a little late in coming. That wagon of theirs is slow. I'll soon be able to catch up to them. Thanks, anyway."

Jeff crossed to the other side, hoping that Morris hadn't heard the ferry boatman. He also hoped the pilot wouldn't mention him to Jed and the others upon their return.

The night was clear and unfortunately, good cover was hard to find except for a few passing clouds. Still, the moonlit trail was easier to navigate.

Morris was a good tracker. He seemed a bit jittery though, jumping occasionally at the sounds of nature.

The men reached a more established road leading farther into the city. They worked their way down to King Street and finally made it to East Bay where they pulled their entourage around the backside of the Exchange Building on Broad Street.

After carefully dismounting and tying his horse up, Morris walked stealthily to the corner of a nearby building where he leaned against the edifice and strained to hear the cowboys' conversation.

Taking advantage of the shadows, Jeff tied his horse a block from Morris' position. Hardly able to see the cowboys at that distance, he came within a hundred yards of Morris.

A miner's oil lamp was hung on a pole attached to Jed's large wagon. Jeff could see another light shining from within the Exchange Building.

Marcus and Joe stood guard, rifles resting in their arms.

With his field glasses Jeff could see Joe rolling a grass weed in his mouth. He had to be deathly silent.

The time traveler thought about his time belt. He kept his finger close to the release button, which only made it difficult to concentrate on his surveillance.

O'Rork kept pushing Jed and the others.

"We need to hurry up here lads. Not too many hours till daybreak and we got to get this load over to the house. Lots of work to be done. Be kind of ya' to move a bit faster, thankyee."

No one voiced any opposition but continued with the task at hand.

What cause could spur men to such dedication?

Occasionally Jeff could hear the clanking of metal on metal followed by O'Rork's voice, "Best you be a bit more careful with that, laddie!"

In thirty minutes three of the men emerged from the Exchange Building carrying a heavy wooden crate. Seeing they were straining under the load, Joe and Marcus leaned their rifles against a nearby wall and assisted.

It took five men three hours to fully load six heavy crates into the buckboard which itself was beginning to show the strain placed upon its axles. The cowboys lastly put the thick boards in the wagon and covered the whole arrangement with a large canvas.

Abruptly a distinguished looking gentleman wearing a black top hat and tails emerged from the low doorway at the back of the building. Thomas Carter followed him into the cool night air. Jeff strained to hear their words.

"I'm sure everything is in order. General Lee will appreciate your patriotic gesture in this involvement for the cause of the South and the freedoms for which we are fighting."

"Mr. Fillmore, we will guard this with our lives. It will be well hidden and protected from enemy hands. As well, cousin, we thank you for your entrusting it to us."

"Just the same, seeing as my position affords me much responsibility, I am obligated to ask for your signature. Please indulge me in this, Thomas. I'm sure you will understand."

The gentleman handed Carter a long piece of paper and pen.

Carter signed the document. Jeff couldn't see his face.

The two cousins cordially shook hands.

"I will contact you in a few days. All will be well. Harriet and the others have traveled to Columbia. I convinced them that such a move was for their safety," Thomas Carter chuckled. "My slaves have been instructed to stay within the confines of their quarters. We shan't have any trouble."

The conversation having ended, Jed slowly directed the two powerful horses to turn towards East Bay. The cowboys formed in double file and were on their way home.

After Jim Morris retrieved his horse and started following the cowboys, Jeff retrieved his own horse and, at first, followed the whole gang on foot until it was safe to mount.

Thirty minutes into the ride, his heart almost stopped as he saw Jim Morris' horse gallop straight towards him. Jeff turned his horse violently towards a clump of trees, dismounted and barely missed Morris' view. Thank the good Lord for sugar, which Jeff liberally applied to his horse's mouth.

It was strange though. It didn't seem as if Morris was backtracking to make sure no one was following him. He was headed as fast as he could towards Charleston.

Jeff mounted his horse and cautiously proceeded. Now he had to watch both for the men he was trailing and for Morris who might try to catch up to his prey again.

The trip to Carter's plantation was precariously slow. The wheels of the overloaded wagon stuck at every turn. At one point, the men had to create a makeshift wedge to pull the wagon out of a very narrow rut.

To make matters worse, the cowboys had to stop along the way to make sure no one was following them. In addition, the poor horses, although large black brutes well chosen for the job, had to have frequent rests.

To Jeff's surprise, the cowboys bypassed the trail leading to the regular ferry boat dock and traveled farther north. After forty minutes they finally reached a much narrower section on the Ashley where they crossed with the help of the boards they pulled out of the wagon. From all indications Jeff figured the change in the route was due to the weight of the wagon. He didn't have to worry about the ferry pilot mentioning him to the other men.

With some difficulty the cowboys headed south with a slow steady pace towards the plantation.

Jeff began to sweat. There was simply no way he could get past the cowboys and make it home so as not to be discovered. He had to think of a plan.

And what of Morris' course of action? He could easily ambush Jeff's compatriots and steal whatever the men were hauling.

Reaching the plantation, the cowboys brought their load to the back of the main house.

Jeff dismounted some distance away and tied his horse to some trees. With his night visions he could see the cowboys lighting some torches for their night's work. He worked his way around in the nearby woods to gain a better perspective.

Mr. Carter dismounted. Taking a key from his pocket, he crouched at the small door and entered the chamber. A few minutes later the cowboys brought the large basin from underneath the porch.

Firewood was collected and placed twenty feet from the small door. The cowhands put the basin on top of a makeshift iron frame above a group of logs. While some of the men poured a dark substance into the basin, others unloaded the heavy boxes from the wagon and brought them underneath the house. Frederick started a fire the smoke of which filled the night sky.

Jed and the others brought some metal sheets four feet by five into the space underneath the house. There was little talk as the men quickly worked.

A steady stream of sparks danced around the iron trough. Jed and Joe took turns standing guard and churning the substance. The material, once heated, was poured in a pail and brought under the dwelling.

Occasionally one of the wooden crates and its top were brought out of the confined area and burned.

Every thirty minutes the cowboys came out into the fresh air, each of them beaded in sweat. They spent a few minutes catching their breath walking around. Whatever work they were doing was hot and burdensome.

The fire was maintained until the wee hours of the morning.

"This stuff is so hot!" a voice rang out.

"Shhh! You're wantin' de whole neighborhood ta hear?" Jed's voice shot across the clearing.

Thomas Carter, Walter, Frederick, and Marcus had been taking turns underneath the house, but where was O'Rork?

Jeff took his watch out of his pocket and gazed at its luminous blue dial. It was 5:30 AM. The men had one and a half hours until daylight. The air was nippy. Hunger was setting in so he extracted his last Snickers from his jacket and consumed it in minutes. He followed the chocolate with a few swigs of water.

Someone came running up from the bunkhouse to where the others were working. A frantic John O'Rork descended through the small door.

"I can't find that scalawag anywheres, Mr. Carter. He's not in the bunkhouse. There's no sign of his horse, nor hair of him. What shall we do, sir?"

"Calm down, Mr. O'Rork. We're almost done here."

Carter, O'Rork and Walter emerged through the door and walked to the trough. Their hard breathing could be seen against the moonlight.

"We've only one more to do. Jed, you and Walter go fetch that friend of yours. We'll be done by the time you get back. And use the better part of caution, mind you."

"Yes, Mr. Carter," Walter responded.

Jeff froze. He put his night vision glasses around his neck, quietly mounted his horse and rode parallel to the tree line towards the bunkhouse. He only had a few minutes to act while Jed drove the wagon to the barn area.

Dismounting in the front of the dwelling, he left his horse without tying her up, and ran to the back. Noticing a half-empty liquor bottle with its cap still on, he opened it and became nauseous at the putrid odor. He dare not take a swig for fear of catching some dreaded disease. Instead, he held his nose and poured the rest of the contents on his clothes.

Cautiously leaning the bottle against the building, he rounded the corner of the bunkhouse, and immediately stood face to face with Walter.

"Jeff, where have you been, son? I thought Mr. O'Rork asked you to stay inside for the rest of the night. Pheww! What's that smell? Here it is 5:40 in the morning and you're stumbling in drunk! How could you, boy?"

Jeff hated deceiving a good friend but practicality demanded it.

"Better a drunk than a spy," Jeff thought as he kept up the act, stumbled up the stairs and into his bed.

He lay still for a few seconds and turned over to see Walter standing there, a look of disappointment on his face. Jed sauntered into the room and stood beside Walter.

"Jus- went downtown to have a lil' ... drinkie..." Jeff mumbled.

"Do you know how dangerous it was to go downtown by yourself? I didn't even know you drank alcohol, son. Mr. O'Rork isn't going to like this one bit."

A smile came on Jeff's face as he rolled over and said, "Night mom." Snoring right away added an effective touch.

Jed Tub said, "Oh, bother! Well, you just sleep it off den! You've got about thirty minutes. You're sometin' else!"

Both Walter and Jed left the room to tell Mr. Carter of Jeff's activities.

Within minutes Saturday morning came and Jeff could hardly move. He was exhausted having ridden all night and staying up to see what the cowboys had been up to. He was awakened not by a tranquil alarm clock of the future but by an unpleasant nudge against his foot.

"Who are you, Jeff Carr? And where do you come from?" Jed asked. "The other boys an' me wanna know for sure."

A few of the other cowboys surrounded Jeff's bed making him a little nervous.

"Look," Jeff said as he sat up in bed and rubbed his eyes, playing like he had a hangover.

A yawn preceded a feeble defense, "Jed, I'm sorry for not hanging around with you guys-"

"Hangin'? Who said anything about a hangin'?" Walter piped up as everyone responded with either laughter or shock. "We are only asking where you come from."

"Now answer de question," Jed demanded as he drew even closer to Jeff's bed tapping his heavy foot on the floor.

Jeff raised his hands to calm Jed, "Just an expression where I come from. Like I told Marcus, my parents lived in Douglas, Georgia for a number of years but I've lived in South Carolina most of my life. I am a South Carolinian. Go Robert E. Lee!"

"You tol' me you was in a circus- dats where you-ins got dat fancy belt."

Thinking of Mr. Singleton and the rat race of Eppy Electronics, Jeff said, "Yes, I am in a circus most of the year. Look, it's just that I've been away, out of state, doing the circus act stuff."

Most of the cowboys weren't satisfied with his answer. Still, what could they do? They had no real proof that he had done anything to make himself untrustworthy.

"Gentlemen, again, I'm sorry I haven't spent a lot of time with you. What do you want to do? I'm open to suggestions."

Jed smiled.

"After chores you wanna see who's the better man at horse racin'?"

The small group of men liked the idea.

"Sure. Who are we gonna watch this time?"

"Watch nothin'. T'ween you an' me. Usually on Sat'days we go to a nice long pasture to race hosses. You gits on your hoss, dat is if Walter will let you ride Sunshine agin'. And I kin borry Frederick's, if'n you please," Jed glanced in Frederick's direction and received a nod of approval.

"Some of de boys will come and see who wins."

Jeff had no choice. He had to race or be considered an outsider.

Everyone finished what little breakfast there was and went outside to do their chores. The large black wagon was nowhere in sight.

After their work was completed, Jeff changed into some cleaner clothes and traveled with the cowboys a short distance south of the plantation to an open pasture where he and Jed made ready for their unofficial contest.

The pasture was a half-mile long.

"Plenty of space in which to be embarrassed ... or killed. Great," Jeff thought.

All of the hired hands that had come to witness the race gathered under a large set of trees at one end of the intended run. Although they weren't placing bets, one could easily surmise on the part of whom their loyalties lay.

It was a breezy day, which didn't help Jeff's nervousness. Upon their arrival Jeff and Jed dismounted and surveyed the situation. They were to run their steeds the length of the pasture, circle a clump of bushes at the end of the run and return to the set of oaks. First man to return was the winner: the prize, exemption from kitchen duty for a month.

Jed and Jeff mounted their horses and sat side by side awaiting Walter's signal.

Dusty, Frederick's horse, out sized Sunshine in height and girth. But Jeff held an advantage over a heavier Jed. Nonetheless Jeff would have to establish and maintain a good lead. No room for shyness in this venture. He took a few minutes to breathe deeply generating courage and adrenaline.

Jeff looked at the sky overhead and saw a large black bird drifting through the swaying trees.

"Look, a hawk."

"Dat der's a vulture," Jed said as he grinned.

"Great, just great."

Walter dropped the red handkerchief and high tailed it out of harm's way. The two riders spurred their animals into action and were soon running neck and neck, frantically trying to out-maneuver the other.

While Jeff was pleasantly surprised at his progress, his smile soon disappeared as Jed pulled away. He could hear Jed hollering as the old man whipped Dusty violently. Jeff responded in kind but it became evident that his opponent had the experiential advantage.

They rounded the bushes at the end of the pasture and headed back. Jeff was behind by five horse lengths when without warning a gunshot rang out startling his horse.

In the corner of his eye, he watched in horror as Frederick's steed dropped to the ground flinging Jed a good seven feet.

Jeff pulled hard on Sunshine's reins and was nearly bucked off. He finally calmed her and rode towards Jed. Another shot rang out from across the pasture. He rode over to a clump of trees where he quickly dismounted. Taking cover, he saw a billow of dissipating gray smoke near a tree across the way.

Jed had crawled beside Frederick's horse, using him as a shield. His right leg was either sprained or crushed. He cried out in pain.

Jeff retrieved his heavy gun and pointed it in the direction of the smoke. Still breathing hard from the initial ride and rough dismount, he noticed that his hands were shaking.

"Calm down, calm down, you can handle this!"

He wiped sweat from his brow.

The other cowboys, guns drawn, were in a dead run down the long field but it would take them some time to reach their companions. It was up to Jeff to do something. Another shot rang out, this time finishing off Frederick's horse.

Jeff took aim. Not being used to the large pistol's recoil, his first retaliatory shot was way to the left. He could see a rough-looking, unshaven man in a blue coat and cap flinch and take cover behind a tree as he laughed wildly over Jeff's failed attempt.

"Jed, stay put. I'll get you out of this!" Jeff yelled as he shot again, this time grazing the tree to the right of the shooter.

"You yellow bellies don't know how to ride and you sure don't know how to aim! No wonder we're winning the war," the man's words echoed against the trees across the field. He was still laughing.

"Think, stupid, think!"

Another shot rang out glazing a tree just a few feet from Jeff's shoulder.

Noticing the sun's powerful glare overhead, he took his night vision glasses, held them in his left hand while still holding his gun. He angled his binoculars so that a bright reflection shot towards the lone figure.

A cry went up from his attacker, his hands going up to shield his eyes. The gunman instinctively rose to his feet in pain and shot wildly, cursing.

"Yellow-bellied?" Jeff murmured, then stood and took aim. This time Jeff's successive shots hit dead center. The soldier in blue dropped his gun and crumpled to the ground. Blood spurted from the back of his coat.

Jeff waited a few seconds and cautiously ran across the field to the body. He kicked the revolver away from the man's hand and felt his wrist for a pulse. He breathed a deep sigh of relief, placed his gun in its holster, and ran over to Jed.

The cowboys finally arrived in a state of confusion. Seeing that the Yankee had been dealt with, the men patted Jeff on the back as they hooted and hollered.

While he was elated over his successful shooting and the receptivity of the other cowboys, Jeff felt guilty. Lying not fifty feet from him was another human being gunned down by his own hand. What irreparable damage had his bullets caused to all of history?

Jed had only received a sprained ankle but couldn't walk. He sat up with a huge grin on his face. Not only had his life been spared, but Jeff had proven his loyalty to him and the South.

"Frederick, why not find somethin' to bind that ankle of Jed's there?" John O'Rork suggested.

Frederick foraged through the woods and found some small sticks with which to make a tourniquet. After applying the restraint, he walked over to his dead horse and stroked her.

"I've had old Dusty for so long. I know I still have Marcelle, but-"

Then he glanced over at the dead man in blue and said, "May you rot."

"Listen, it'll be OK. At least we're all alive," Walter replied.

Marcus, the shorter cowboy with the boyish face, secured the Yankee's wallet and papers.

"You won't be needin' these anymore, I 'spect."

Joe English and Walter dug a shallow grave for the soldier. Walter insisted that they say a small prayer for him although he had proven to be quite a scoundrel. They used two of the other horses to drag Frederick's steed into the woods.

"You can ride Grady to the plantation, Jed. I'll walk. But we better high tail-it back to the farm. No telling if there's more Yankees where he came from."

"You're very kind, Walter."

"Walter, here you have two horses and you're not riding either of them, my friend," Frederick said.

Honorable Intentions

O'Rork and the cowboys laughed as Walter smiled back.

"I need to walk off all the good vittles Marcus has been cooking us lately."

Marcus smiled as the cowboys walked to their horses, mounted and were soon on their way in double file.

"Where was the Yankee from anyway?" Joe asked.

Marcus looked through the papers.

"Look, he wrote a letter to his mother just a few days ago. Walter, you read a bit better than I do."

Marcus handed the letter to Walter who began to read,

"'Dear Mother,

Things have become progressively worse since my last communiqué. We have been incurring some loss in our efforts to secure the rest of our lost nation. Going through the southern poor farmlands of Georgia has been rather easy except of course for the Atlanta campaign. Resistance has not been formidable. Yet I can see a pride in these backward people that has diminished within our ranks. Some of our men see us as aggressors, prodding where we have no place. The majority, however, know of the importance of preserving the union. I will send further correspondence to you in the days to come. General Halleck of Kingston, Georgia received word from General Sherman that we plan to cut off the southern rail line at Grahamville. This action hopefully will transpire on or before the twenty-ninth of November. May our actions have their full effect in weakening the resistance. My best to you and Grandmother.

Lovingly,

Jim

November 21, 1864'."

Walter stopped dead in his tracks. The other cowboys looked at each other in disbelief.

"So the northern forces are headed right into our own territory?" Frederick asked.

"Not only that but past us and farther north. What will they do, end the blockade and invade Charleston itself?"

"Walter, there are plenty of waterways that lead within miles of the Grahamville area."

The men looked at Jeff and curiously pondered the scenario.

"We've got to get word to Colonel Colcock. I heard that he's the commander of the district up in that area."

"Frederick, we can't just be ridin' up to Colcock's camp and announce this. We would be losin' all manner a' credibility. His forces don't know us at all. Mr. Carter didn't want us intervenin' in the affairs of either side, which is something I never agreed with.

Colcock's men might be thinkin' we were trying to divert their attention from another area the Yankees really plan to attack," John O'Rork said.

"We have the letter in hand. Certainly we can just show it to them," Frederick responded.

"How do we a'know dat dis Yankee isn't jus tryin' to trick uz?"

"The letter's written to his mother. No one lies to his mother," Frederick said and then became embarrassed over his statement.

"Is this an official dispatch?" Walter asked.

"Nothing official about it. Maybe it can be trusted even more, it being a personal correspondence and all."

Everyone nodded at Frederick's point.

"We need to show this to Mr. Carter."

The group moved slowly towards the plantation cautiously watching the surrounding areas.

On the way Jed made his gratitude quite plain to Jeff. He even volunteered to clean the kitchen and bunkhouse for him in the next few weeks as soon as his sprained ankle healed.

Thankful that the dark times between Jed and himself were over, Jeff offered to go into town and buy some liquor to help Jed's pain while some of the others consulted Mr. Carter about future actions.

As usual Mr. O'Rork didn't want his field hands gallivanting into the city but at Walter's request, Jeff and Walter saddled up.

"You two best be careful. Tis a'bot 3:00 on a Saturday afternoon. I'm sure the bars will be filled with the hopeless. Watch for sharpshooters. We don't want a repeat of the last adventure."

Jeff bought two bottles of hard liquor and a copy of the daily newspaper.

On their way back, he let Walter lead the way while he read the news.

Most of the reports had to do with the approach of northern forces. Wiping out farms and pillaging small towns was a way of Sherman's demoralizing the South. Sitting safely in a library at a microfiche machine in the year 2010 while reading reports of Sherman's advance was quite different from reading articles reflective of his now present times. News of imminent invasion haunted him.

To his horror, he read that a distinguished citizen of Charleston, a Mr. Fillmore, had been found dead in an alley off Tradd Street. He had been clubbed to death and robbed.

The story concluded, "Mr. Fillmore had served as First Lender's Vice President for more than twenty years. The Charleston Police Department has the situation under full investigation."

Honorable Intentions

Thomas Carter's cousin dead? Morris had doubled back that Friday night to grab the document Carter signed!

Jeff wanted to warn the others.

"Do not interact, do not interact," the professor's instructions echoed forever in Jeff's mind. Did it really matter what his next move might be?

Mr. Carter and the others must find out about Fillmore's death on their own as if Jeff had never entered the past and bought the paper. By supplying information to Thomas and the others, Jeff might cause the men to do something they wouldn't have normally done. He let the paper fall to the ground.

When the two men arrived at the bunkhouse at 7 PM, Jed took immediate advantage of the benefits of alcohol consumption and was soon laughing his head off.

"Mr. Carter sent Mr. O'Rork and Joe English with the letter from that Yankee attached with his own letter of concern. This whole thing may be a hoax, but nonetheless, we have no other choice," Walter said as Frederick, he and Jeff sat on the porch in the cool of the evening. They could hear a few gun shots in the distance interspersed with the sounds of a hoot owl chanting away.

"Frederick, where do you come from? Did you attend school somewhere?"

"I'm actually from Virginia, Jeff. My family represents one of the steel industries up north. Enough for my brother to attend West Point, at least."

"Pardon me for asking, but how did you get down here from there?"

"Unfortunately my father wanted all four of us, my three brothers and me, to join the Union forces. I told him that the South had just as much cause to enjoy the freedoms of states rights as any other. I left assuring him that I would return upon the end of this whole affair. The divisions in the families both in the north and south have done much to cripple relationships. I'm trying not to let that happen. Who knows? Maybe Father will have respect for my having stood up for my convictions."

Frederick stretched back in his chair and gazed up at the stars, "Still miss them, though. I hope they're doing all right. Anyway, I had heard a lot about Charleston and the rich cotton and rice industries. I guess I thought I could get into the business somehow."

"I've wondered all along why you and the others hadn't joined the Confederate forces."

"I've wondered that some," Walter said. "We are first loyal to Mr. Carter and his interests. Most of us are from different places, but none of us has any children. I guess you could say that we cowboys have become like a family."

"Many people have been killed over this tearing of the Union. Some of the Northerners think it's all about slavery. But how about any decisions made by the states? I know we've got to struggle together so that all will be prosperous and safe, but if they do away with the right of a state to decide issues more particular to that area, what next? Will the president and Congress tell us how many horses we can own, or what kind of buggies we can purchase? Where will it all end?"

"So Frederick, why didn't you jump right into the battle?"

"You're right to ask these questions. A call to arms is a call to arms," he said as he sat up in his chair and looked at the floor in retrospect.

Walter responded, "Defending our freedoms is important. I guess that I felt that defending this place in particular, though, was more practical that prancing all over the country looking for a fight."

Walter shooed away some mosquitoes and continued, "Everything has changed due to the war anyhow. I mean, like the fact that Mr. Carter and his family have usually stayed in town during the nighttime hours to avoid these mosquitoes. Of course, that's from late April to, well, about now. The war has made it unsafe to stay in town, anyways. It's face the bugs or the bullets."

"Walter, I gather that you're a religious man," Jeff said.

"Religious?" Walter asked.

"Yes. I mean, I haven't heard you cuss. You don't smoke or drink, except for that strong drink of coffee I've tasted," Jeff chuckled.

"Religious, no. I just have a relationship with the Savior. It's quite rewarding to know that, because I know Him, come long-living or instant death, my soul will be found in His care. I didn't do anything to deserve Him, just placed myself in His hands."

"Have you ever been married?"

"I had a wife of some twenty-seven years until she died of malaria, God rest her soul. My Beatrice was a pioneer woman, strong of character and muscle. She could even whip me at arm wrestling! She was a plain looking lady for sure. But she was beautiful in the heart where it counted. Always the last to sit at the table and the first to serve, the most selfless person I've ever known."

Walter grinned, closed his eyes for a while and let his words settle on any listening ears.

"We best be getting to bed. Church comes very early and the chores must be done before that," Walter reminded them.

Honorable Intentions

Jeff thought, *"Church? Gag, I haven't been to church in, well forever."*

He picked his chair up as did the others and brought it inside.

"Some of us go to Jerusalem Church near Calhoun Street. It's a bit safer than the churches nearer the water. There is still a formidable gathering on Sunday mornings. Would you care to join us?"

"Sure, Walter," Jeff said, uneasy.

Jed was dead to the world by the time they ended their discussion. The fire's warm glow filled the room. The other cowboys had already hit the hay.

Jeff was psychologically and physically drained. He wondered what the next day might bring. Moreover he lay in his hard bunk pondering on how he might keep from interacting more with those of the past. He began to wonder if it would even make a difference.

He grinned as he heard Jed's heavy snoring on the other side of the room. Nonetheless, he was fast asleep in no more than a few minutes.

18

Roosters made for an effective alarm clock, especially at 5:30 on a Sunday morning. Jeff wanted to throw his boots at the unlikely chorus.

"Wake up, there, Jeff Carr. Good morning to ya. We best be getting on to the chores, then we'll be going into the Lord's house if you'll be wanting to join us," Walter greeted Jeff.

The cowboys ate a quick breakfast before lighting out. It was a black and chilly morning. The sun was rising above the level of the trees.

Moving the cowherd from one range to the other, milking the cows which was normally done by Thomas Carter's daughter Nellie, and gathering the eggs from the chicken coup were some of the chores of the morning.

Jeff volunteered to feed the chickens and gather the eggs. "Just you wait," he said to two of the roosters in the pen. "Thanksgiving may be over but Christmas is-a-coming. I might volunteer one of you for the main course!"

The rooster nearest him paused, seemingly contemplated his tone and slowly walked to the other end of the compound.

Jeff gathered a dozen brown eggs, put them in a basket and brought them up to the main house.

"So you are Jeff Carr," asked a tall handsome man when Jeff entered the plantation kitchen.

"Mr. Carter, nice to finally meet you, sir."

Mr. Carter's eyes and smile resembled those of Jeff's uncle.

"Are you going to church with us this morning? I don't require that any of my field hands attend, but whoever wants to should be getting ready."

"I am sorry about the drunk thing Friday night. It won't happen again. You'll find that I am a good worker."

"Mr. O'Rork had mentioned your behavior. I don't tolerate drunkenness, Mr. Carr. It's not good for the individual or for the constitution of the other men. Nonetheless you will have plenty of opportunities to prove yourself."

Carter looked out the window and commented, "Looks like a pretty day. Bit chilly, though. When last have you heard from your family during this dangerous occupation of the South?"

"My family's all gone. How about yourself, sir?"

Thomas nodded, "I sent my family to Columbia for safe keeping. Until we regain our strength and political posture, I must communicate with them by letter. I can't bear thinking about what might happen to the Carolina's over these escapades. I've not had the opportunity to be around you much, Mr. Carr. Come from good stock, do you?"

"I think so," Jeff smiled. He stood in the same room with his grand uncle, yet separated by years and position. What could a usually tennis shoe clad, soccer-loving guy from 2010 say to a rather well to do farmer from the 1860's. All he was to Carter was an insignificant field hand, and one perhaps not to be trusted at that.

"Think it might rain?"

"We certainly need much precipitation for our crops."

The landowner was a good, level headed man, humble in his station yet aloof in his demeanor.

"Where do the women cook?"

"We have a smoke house on the far corner of the main structure. I miss those rutabagas, cabbage, fresh corn and such. How I long.." Carter stopped himself short, scratched his head and said, "I will join you and the others in a few minutes at the stable area. Thank you for getting the eggs."

Walter, Frederick, Marcus, and Jeff accompanied Mr. Carter on the trip downtown.

The cowboys rode in double file and soon reached Jerusalem Church where a group had already gathered.

"This is the only Methodist church open during these horrible times," Walter told Jeff as the men dismounted. "There was a church split about thirty years back."

"Over what, Walter?" Jeff asked anticipating some infighting over some spiritual issue.

"Well, from what I heard, the congregation used to be made up of both races until one of the colored men wanted to sit on the ground floor where the Caucasians were due to the heat. Some of the members insisted that the coloreds sit in the rafters. It was a shame that both groups were worshipping Christians but they were split by their different cultures."

Jeff shook his head. Church splits were not foreign to congregations even of the past.

Some of the congregation sat in the balconies on either side of the church and to the rear, conversing as they fanned themselves.

A distinguished gentleman in a white robe came to the pulpit and announced the first hymn, "Rock of Ages". The congregation stood as a unanimous outcry of praise filled the air.

Jeff was surprised to see men standing on each side of the sanctuary looking out of the windows.

"Guards," Walter said as he redirected his attention to the preacher's apt words.

The hour and a half service included an encouraging sermon among other things usually present in worship.

"'Bout time for it to be over, I think," Mr. Carter whispered to Jeff. "Quite a powerful preacher, don't you think?"

"Shhh!" Marcus gestured and then shrunk back in his seat when he saw that it was his boss speaking. Marcus looked like a little boy from where Jeff was sitting.

After the benediction, everyone filed out and went into the warm sunshine to visit.

Refined gentlemen and ladies were conversing with some of the cowboys. Perhaps not only due to their corporate worship but also because of their having been thrown together behind the lines of an unforgiving blockade, lines of station had been overlooked.

The cowboys gave their leave of many friends and mounted their horses. They rode up Calhoun and turned left onto Coming Street. Riding in double file, they discussed the gist of the sermon.

Suddenly a boisterous thick Irish voice rang out from the street.

"Jeff Carr, how are you on this bright and cheery day?"

On the right side of the road a group of boys was standing in front of St. Paul's Church. A sign out front listed a number of priests, Jon Southerland among them, who was now approaching the group.

"Someone you know?" asked Thomas Carter glaring at Jeff.

"Yes sir, I met him at the racetrack."

Noticing the white collar around Southerland's neck, Carter stretched back in his saddle and responded, "Racetrack?"

"Yes sir, he picks up boys."

Another strange look.

Jeff could hear Marcus snickering, "Guess he's collectin' them for some sort of museum."

"Mr. Carter, the reverend runs an orphanage near the Washington Racecourse. He rounds up homeless boys and tries to set them straight," Jeff retorted.

The clergyman walked up and shook Thomas Carter's hand and smiled.

"Nice to meet you. I've only had a short conversation with young Jeff here. He seems to be an upstandin' individual. A young man stole something of value from him," the white-haired clergyman said as he looked in the general direction of the boys who were themselves in conversation in front of the church.

"Jeff handled it very well."

Jeff appreciated the endorsement.

"I'm sure the boys wouldn't be mindin' some extra company if any of you would like to eat with us this afternoon."

"Very kind of you, Reverend. The boys and I will be quite busy attending the affairs of our farm."

"Even on the Lord's day?"

"I think the scriptures say something about getting the ox out of the ditch," Carter countered. "I do respect you for the work you do, Mr. Southerland. Certainly you can respect my rights as well."

Mr. Carter saw that the reverend was a little surprised at his stern reply.

"Pardon my demeanor, Mr. Southerland. I am a businessman in troubled times. I am also a believer. Perhaps one or two of my men would like to see how things are done at your orphanage?"

No doubt most of the cowboys were weighing the decision, escaping extra work at the farm by visiting a religious establishment or working and avoiding having to talk with someone who might try talking them into getting saved.

Walter volunteered to go. Jeff felt obligated since he had met the clergyman previously.

"I will see you two about supper time. Nice to have met you, Reverend," Carter said as he and his field hands departed.

Walter dismounted and walked towards the reverend. Before Jeff was able to warn the clergyman of the cowboy's hand-crushing greeting, Walter shook Mr. Southerland's hand. The greeting only lasted for a few seconds but Walter was the one who was left wincing in pain.

"Nice grip," Walter said with a smile.

"OK, boys, let's be getting into the wagon. Got a ways to go," the clergyman said as he got up into the buckboard.

It took them forty-five minutes to reach Moultrie Street where the reverend's house was located.

Accompanied by two boys, Reverend Southerland fixed vegetable soup and corn bread steaming hot. A beautiful small oak-grained icebox in the kitchen stored a bottle of milk and block of cheese. The house was in a quiet neighborhood within a few minutes' walk of a market place around the corner.

When all was ready, everyone was summoned to the two tables. The clergyman and Stephen Warren, the new boy Jeff had met at the racetrack, served the main meal.

After a prayer, the boys began politely serving themselves and then passed the food off to their left. The reverend went around the table and introduced them who cordially nodded at the visitors and dug into their food.

Reverend Southerland began, "Summerton Inn is a place for a new beginnin' for our youth. It's a place to restart our thinkin', to steer our young ones in the right direction. With the war we have seen an increase of opportunities of service wherein we can help our new arrivals."

"May I say something, Father Jon?"

"Certainly, Warren, but mind that ya don't spill your water there laddie."

"I am glad we have a new friend to play with."

"Play with?" responded Stephen. "I don't 'play' nothin'. I do whatever I please and the least I'd want to do is spend time with the likes of you!" Stephen laughed.

Some of the other boys put their sleeves up to their mouths and snickered softly. Warren burst into tears.

"Stephen, please don't be rude. Brother Warren is only paying you a complement. We try to encourage each other in our home."

Stephen abruptly rose from the table and headed for the door.

"Don't mean to be disrespectful Reverend. I mean, my thanks for rescuin' me from the policeman and all, but Warren here aint no brother of mine. I aint got no brothers."

"Excuse me gentlemen. Stephen, may I be seein' ya in the kitchen for a minute?"

Stephen hesitantly complied. Walter, Jeff and the boys could hear a heated discussion from the small kitchen but the words were not discernible.

Stephen reentered the room with the concerned priest trailing.

"Son, I am asking you to stay here with us. Returning to your world especially in these times is dangerous. Please reconsider," the clergyman asked as he followed the young rough-looking boy to the front door.

"Again Reverend, thanks for trying. Boys, it was nice making your acquaintance," the young boy said as he opened the door and left the gathering. The reverend called after him but reentered the room and quietly shut the door. He looked at the other boys and shook his head.

Jeff would have made an effort to go after the wayward teen if it hadn't have been for the reverend's signaling him to relax.

"It's all right. He knows of our open invitation."

Walter and Jeff spent thirty more minutes visiting the boys, looking at pictures they had drawn and viewing some of their woodworking projects.

"Thank you very much for the fellowship, food and that lemon pie!"

Honorable Intentions

"Please be comin' back whenever ya can, Walter, Jeff. Lord be with you on your journey."

It took an hour to get back to the bunkhouse. When they arrived, there were still a few small chores to be done before dinner. Jeff and Walter took some time to groom and feed their horses at the stables.

"Supper's ready. Come and get it or we'll throw it out!" a voice came thundering from the plantation house.

The cowboys were being allowed to come up to the big house to eat that night since the women were away in Columbia.

Thomas thanked some of his cooks for a wonderful meal and instructed them to eat their own supper, clean up the kitchen and retire to their quarters for the night.

Plenty of red rocking chairs out on the porch made for a comfortable setting.

"So, Mr. Carter, what are you a-plannin' to do 'bout the troops headed our way? Joe and I talked with Colonel Colcock. He's readyin' his position up at Grahamville," a curious John O'Rork said.

"We're a gonna go tuh Grahamville and teach a few Yankees a lesson 'bout invadin' our land, dats what!" Jed defiantly broke into the conversation as he briskly rocked back and forth.

Thomas calmly sat in a vacant rocker and directed his remarks to the entire group.

"The news is bad, men. Sherman aims to take the railroad. We must, at all costs, prevent this from happening. The lines of communication and supplies must be kept open. Our current way of life is at stake. It wouldn't be proper for me to insist on your involvement in this Grahamville affair. Accompanying me would be voluntary, you know. So, if you desire not to participate in this venture, please feel free to say so ... now."

Without hesitation, one cowboy after another affirmed his decision to join the viable quest. Jeff hesitated. What was he to do? Through reading the documents concerning the battle of Honey Hill he knew that a few southern soldiers and participants would die in the confrontation. He also knew that Thomas himself would definitely meet his end. The desire to warn his relative burned in his heart. But what would that do to all of history? And how could he explain his knowledge of future events? Peer pressure in the 1800's. He agreed to go.

Jeff was quite relieved when Mr. Carter broke the silence.

"I have already sent correspondence to Mrs. Carter and the others in Columbia concerning our intentions. They will undoubtedly be in much prayer for us in this endeavor."

Thomas gave a reassuring smile to his field hands.

Honorable Intentions

"Who is gonna take care of dis her' farm, though, Mr. Carter?"

"Why, Jed? Do you need to stay? How is your leg?"

"Well, sir, I might ought to stay around here for a day or two, though I'd love to whip up on some dem Yankees indeed!"

"We won't be leaving until Tuesday morning. There are some chores that need attention. Maybe your leg will be healed in time."

"I sho' do wanna kill me some Yankees. They done shot a hoss right from under me and give me dis her' limp. Yessir, the only good Yankee is a dead Yankee!"

Most of the cowboys shook their heads in agreement.

"Now boys. I know how we must feel concerning our land and other interests. Certainly this seems a war of aggression on the part of Mr. Lincoln and the others. But keep in mind that some of those Yankees worship the same God as do we ourselves. If we move against them, it will be for principle and not for blood vengeance."

"Just the same, with all due respect, Mr. Carter," said O'Rork, "I've heard tell of many abuses against the wonderful families of Georgia and the other regions. They are tryin' to break our backs with the horrific treatment given to our own kind."

"I'm sure that each of you will take the appropriate course of action on the field of battle whenever called upon to act," Thomas said as he got out of his chair, stretched and yawned. He walked over to the door leading into the hallway and paused, "Defend yourselves, defend the South. But may the history books record that we did so with honor. Gentlemen, I will see you all on the morrow. Get some good sleep."

The men went to bed earlier than usual in order to get a good start on the next day's activities.

19

A dense fog covered the plantation and surrounding areas that Monday morning. Jed's ankle felt much better due to the full day of rest he had had.

The cowboys dressed in the warm bunkhouse.

"There are many things to do this morning. Mr. Carter wants us to do the regular jobs as well as complete that new fence in the southern section. I don't think it will do any good. I think he assumes a new fence will deter the advance of the enemy, even albeit for a little while."

"I love how you talk, Frederick," Joe said.

"Yes, and we caints be too mean to dem der Yankees cause some of dem goes to chu-ch and sings as bad as Marcus Vendor!"

Marcus threw a pillow across the room at the old man.

Everyone laughed except for O'Rork who gave Jed a hard look.

The men rode a short distance to the work area and put their tools by the fence.

Jeff was beginning to feel more comfortable. They trusted him.

The men worked hard for a few hours, sometimes humming old southern tunes.

They took a water break at 12:00.

"Where did you learn to sing like that, Frederick?" Jeff asked.

"His mother done sent him off to dance school!" Jed quipped. The others chuckled.

"I have been in a few plays here and there. Along with a proper education, Mother and Father wanted me to be well versed in the arts. Doesn't hurt to polish a rough stone," Frederick said as he took a sip of water and winked at Jed.

"About de only ting I ever polished off was a few bottles of dat hard liquor!"

"And look how well-rounded you are!" Walter said as he jiggled his own belly.

Leaning against one of the newly installed posts, John O'Rork reflected, "Will ya just look at all this land? A hard-working man, that Mr. Carter. I'll never be that rich, indeed. Talkin' 'bout a well-rounded gentleman."

Jeff realized that having traveled back in time had benefited him with a meaningful group of friends. Then his sadness deepened. In the years to which he would return, he wouldn't have anyone with whom to share his life or great wealth.

Pangs of longing surged through his heart for the one who had become the woman of his dreams. He missed her smile, her touch, her gaze into his eyes. Why did things turn out the way they had? Impossible situations so frequent and unannounced.

He had to see her once more even if it were merely to say goodbye.

As they returned to the task, the others noticed a renewed energy in Jeff.

"Why the hurry, young laddie? We'll surely get it all done by the afternoon."

"Got something I gotta do later. That is, if it's OK with you."

"Somethin' goin' on in town? Circus comin'?" O'Rork asked with a wink.

"Might it have something to do with a sweet young lady?" Walter asked, nudging Jeff.

Snickers abounded as the men returned to their work, putting their hearts into their labors.

John O'Rork complemented the others on the straightness of the enclosure.

"Wait till Mr. Carter sees this!"

The men gathered their tools, gave their horses some water from a stream nearby, mounted up and rode to the plantation.

Upon their arrival, Jeff went to the bunkhouse, grabbed some grub, filled his canteen, and bid the other cowboys farewell assuring them of his return before nightfall.

The trip to Crystal's plantation gave him a lot of time to think. The improbable solution for his life would be to stay, never returning to his own time. How crazy was that?

The stark practicality of the moment was inescapable. What impact would he have in the current epoch? Even if this reality were removed from his pensive deliberations, he was uncertain as to the built-in capabilities of the time belt system. Couldn't it automatically metamorphose his body and then transport him first to the pickup area and then back to his own time? All of these uncertainties upset him. His passion for her grew by the minute.

By the time he reached the plantation it was late afternoon. As he passed by the servants' quarters, the little black girl he had seen greeted him with a big smile. Still the same tattered dress and hole-ridden shoes. Feeling a great deal of pity, he leaned down and handed her some of the Confederate money he had, which she promptly took. Her mother who had been watching from her window emerged from the servants' quarters with a distraught look on her face.

"Thank you, Mr., but we don't needs no chair-ty," she said as she smacked her daughter's leg and had her return the money.

The woman's gentle pride and peaceful spirit were quite surprising. She pulled her daughter towards their living quarters.

"Iz you a goin' to visit Mizz Crystal?" her daughter asked.

"Sheila, what a question to ask. Now you git on inside, ya here, and finish tendin' them dishes!"

The little girl hastily complied.

"What is your name?"

"Emily Cantlin. I been livin' here with my family fo' 'bout thirteen years."

"My name is Jeff Carr," he said as he extended his hand.

Emily timidly shook it and continued, "We tend the grounds for Mr. Montgomery. I am sorry if Sheila done been bothering you, sir."

"No bother at all. She's a delightful little girl."

Emily grinned, her face turning shyly towards the ground. She looked alarmed and said, "I am terrible sorry, Mr. Jeff. I taught my chil-rens better dan dat. Dey knows if dey don' work for money, best not ask for it. Just isn't right to do so. The good book done say if'n ya don't work for bread, ya shouldn't eat. Anyways, thank you fo' your kindness. I best be goin' inside now."

The polite black lady turned to go.

Jeff tipped his hat and said, "Mrs. Cantlin, have a nice afternoon."

Emily turned, looked at Jeff with a smile and entered her quarters.

He rode up to the main house and dismounted. He was greatly relieved that the long ride had ended safely and ecstatic over the prospect of seeing Crystal again. He walked up the front steps and knocked on the Montgomery's door.

Arthur the butler answered and said, "Mr. Carr, what a pleasant surprise."

"Nice to see you, Arthur."

"Have you come to visit Mr. Montgomery?"

"No, Arthur."

Arthur ushered Jeff into the vestibule. Looking over his shoulder and grinning Arthur said, "I have dusted the chandelier for your inspection. May I take your coat?"

"Thank you, no."

"You have come to see Mrs. Montgomery then?"

"Is Miss Crystal here?"

"No, actually she moved to Boston this morning..."

"What?"

"My apologies," Arthur chuckled under his breath. "Yes, she is inside. I will advise her of your arrival."

Jeff entered the house and sat on one of the two chairs in the main entrance. The sound of exquisite music from a harpsichord floated throughout the house.

After waiting for five minutes he grew impatient, got up and followed the sound to the music room. There she sat, beautiful, back up straight, intensely playing one of the classics with which he was not familiar.

Surprised to see Jeff enter the room Crystal jumped up from the bench.

"Oh, Jeffery! So good of you to come."

His heart was swimming with infatuation for the young lady. He wanted to throw caution to the wind and reveal who he was and from where he had come. He wanted to wrap his arms around her and show her his affection. But this was 1864 and such behavior was out of the question.

Abruptly Crystal walked over and threw her arms around him. Sparks flew as she gave him a kiss on the lips! At the height of passion, Mammie barged into the room.

"Mizz Crystal! Please control yourselves. Dear girl!"

Jeff and Crystal backed away from each other, a broad smile on both of their faces.

Jeff took the bull by the horns.

"Now, Mammie. You know that I like you. I think you are one of the finest ladies I've ever met-"

"But Mr. Carr- Ize married!" Mammie exclaimed as she backed up near the doorway.

"That's not what I meant. I just wanted to compliment you before asking you to leave me alone with Crystal for a few minutes."

Mammie stepped back farther and put her hands on her hips, "Do you think for one moment that I, Mizz's Crystal's Mammie, could leave you in a room with her by yourselves? I jes cain' do that, Mr. Jeff. It would prove to be inconceivable on the better part of me!"

"Mammie, you can trust me. I just need to talk with Crystal for a minute. I promise I will behave. Scout's honor-" Jeff said, forgetting that the Boy Scouts weren't even in existence.

"I gotta go git Mizz Montgomery. I be back in jez a minute, Mr. Carr. Leave dis here door open," Mammie turned to go and then turned back, saying, "WIDE OPEN!"

Jeff led Crystal to a small couch near the harpsichord, had them both sit down and clutched her hands in his.

"Have you been thinking of me?"

"I must admit, Mr. Carr- Jeff. Every morning when I awake, every evening before I enter a deep sleep, you fill my thoughts with pleasantness. I don't know what it is. I have never met anyone like you before. Have you thought of me as well?"

"Yes, I have. I can't get you out of my mind," Jeff said as he squeezed her hands.

"Listen. I am on a mission. I must find out the solution to a mystery that has been bugging me, er, taunting me for some time. Do I seem strange to you in any way?"

"Why, a little ... different. You seem to be quite forward yet in a gentle way as if it were such a proper thing for you to do."

"Anything else?"

"Well," she answered as she looked at him. "The clothes you wear seem a little out of place. That green belt which I have seen showing from time to time, where does that come from? I've never seen anything like it."

Jeff sat straight up, preparing himself for whatever response Crystal might have and then began, "Crystal, I'm going to take a chance. I'm going to tell you something that might be very hard for you to believe. You might not understand a word of it but it's true. Are you willing to hear it?"

Crystal nodded.

"Crystal, I'm not from around here."

A look of concern crossed the young girl's face.

"Are you a Yankee, Jeff Carr?"

Jeff laughed but quickly grew serious, "No, not at all. I am from the south but I'm from... well... a different ... time. I'm from ... the future," Jeff said as he raised his eyebrows.

Crystal withdrew her hands from his and looked at him with intense scrutiny.

"You're from what?"

"The future. Look," Jeff said as he looked towards the door through which Mammie had exited, "I don't have a lot of time to explain so just hear me out. I came to your year 1864 through the use of a machine that transported me here. I do live in Charleston, South Carolina but in the year .... 2010. Have you ever heard of time travel? Ever read Charles Dickens and his ghosts in the Christmas Carol?"

Crystal was dazed. She lifted her right hand to her forehead as if she were going to faint. She took a deep breath and said, "I believe I have read something about a new French author who is very popular. A new book has come out, Journey to the Center of the Earth. But it hasn't been translated yet. I wish to read of these things-"

She grabbed Jeff's hands with both of hers and gave him a serious look, "Jeffery, please don't dash my hopes of a bright future with ... well. You are not talking ... rationally. It is too difficult to believe what you are saying, my dearest."

Crystal started crying. Jeff carefully caressed her. Then he pushed her away.

"Do you see this belt? It is a retrieval belt. I had to come back to your time to escape some men who were trying to harm me and I think it has something to do with the house I inherited."

Jeff cleared his throat in frustration.

"It's a long story. Suffice it to say that I can't stay here forever. I am supposed to return to the future so as not to mess up the past. I wasn't even supposed to interact with anyone. Boy, I sure messed that up!"

Crystal could see Jeff's concerned look and cautiously gave him a peck on the cheek. "This is all too bizarre Jeffery. But you see, you have won my heart. My hero has become my beloved. I know it's all too soon, but I am taken aback by you." She shook her head, "I can't believe my forwardness. Please forgive me. What is to become of us?" she asked, hanging her head, perplexed.

Jeff smiled and continued, "Crystal, if I could change things, I would. But the way the time machine is configured demands my return. I must be at the place where I first arrived in 1864 this coming Thursday morning at 7:30."

Her dreams were evaporating before her eyes.

"Jeffery, can't you just ignore this ... this time machine? Throw the belt away. Stay with me here at Montebello. We shall enjoy a wonderful life together."

"I don't know what would happen if I didn't make it to the rendezvous point. I might be evaporated for all I know. But my mission here isn't complete yet. I have to do some things first." Jeff paused, took a deep breath and continued, "Crystal, my real name is ... Jeffrey Carter. Some people in the year 2010 want to take my plantation house from me and I've come back to 1864 to find out why. I thought things would be simple but then I met you. I fell in love, yes, in love with you. You're the most wonderful thing that's ever happened to me. And I don't want to leave."

"Carter? You aren't Jeffrey Carr? This is all too confusing."

With a new resolve she rose to her feet, went over to a nearby window, turned and said, "If you can't stay with me, I shall accompany you to your own time!" She walked over to him and grasped his arms.

"The belt will only transport the person who went through time. My body and everything was ... prepared. It has everything to do with molecules and physics and all."

"You really are from the future," Crystal finally realized as a look of austere contemplation crossed her face.

She began asking questions, "And what of my family? What will happen to the South? Will Sherman succeed in his quest?"

"Crystal," Jeff paused, grasped her hand and kissed it, "I can't tell you anything that you don't already know. You might decide to do something you might not have done otherwise thus jeopardizing your own safety and that of your family. It could change your entire life and the history that's already transpired."

A wounded expression appeared on her face, "Why can't you-don't you want to help us? We won't know what to do," she said tearfully.

Jeff replied, "If I hadn't come, you wouldn't have known the future anyway. No one knows the future."

"And what of us? Is there any way you might return to me, Jeffrey Carr- Carter?" she cried again but then stiffened her lip.

With great uncertainty Jeff could only say, "With all of my heart I want to be able to caress you forever. I want to talk with you, spend time in your arms, and gaze at the stars in your presence. I want to plan our lives together. But it's just not up to me. I'm not the one in control of this infernal machine!"

Grasping both of her hands tightly, Jeff could see that Crystal was understandably upset.

"Crystal, if it is within my power, I will return to you. I don't know how. But I will return. Please trust me."

"Jeffrey Carter, I will trust in my God to bring it about. I will wait for you and shan't give up on our lives together!"

The two of them embraced and kissed as tears rolled down their cheeks.

Mrs. Montgomery accompanied by a defiant Mammie burst into the room.

"Young man, what is the meaning of this? Crystal, distance yourself from him at once!"

"I sorry, Mr. Jeff, but it aint proper to -"

"Mammie, I will handle this," interrupted Crystal's mother.

"I'm leaving now, Mrs. Montgomery. Please don't blame Crystal for her actions or me for my feelings for your lovely daughter. I assure you that I have only her best in mind."

"If you care for her, you best leave. Proper courting is done differently where we come from. Would you jeopardize her very reputation for these momentary displays of affection? I think not!"

"I understand, ma'am. I do apologize," Jeff said, as he gave Crystal an endearing look. He walked out of the room, and exited the dwelling.

A heated discussion between mother and daughter ensued. Jeff mounted his horse but quickly dismounted. He wanted to explain his intentions, to come to the defense of his lady. Then he decided that he would only make things worse if he interfered further. He mounted his horse and rode down the trail.

How in the world had he gotten into such a mess? No one else had ever spanned worlds of time. Difficult decisions beleaguered him. Surging emotions concerning how to establish meaningful relationships, different customs even in the United States, various expectations as to behavior; he had not been aware of such things.

"Good ole boy," Jeff said as he patted his horse's neck. "All you have to do is eat, walk around, sleep and enjoy life..."

The horse shook his head and whinnied as if in disagreement.

The night had grown chillier as he finally reached the bunkhouse. The other cowboys whistled as he entered the room.

"There he is, Mr. Debonair," Frederick chided with a big grin.

"I know, just call me John Wayne," Jeff said imitating the not-as-yet existent actor.

"John who?"

"Never mind," Jeff said as he prepared to eat a cold supper. The others were just finishing their food.

"We'd best get in bed early, boys. We'll be riding a'bot five hours up ta Grahamville in the mornin' and that will be after all the chores is done."

The men were soon asleep except for Jeff who was consumed by the agony of many questions. He was worried about how things were going to play out the next day. How would he escape the battle of Honey Hill? Would he ever see Crystal again? What was the answer to the mystery concerning Thomas' strange letter?

Midnight sounds bathed the outside air creating a tranquil setting. His nerves calmed a bit as he lay in his bunk. The uncertainties haunting him were displaced with a profound curiosity about what was under the main house.

What other time would he have to explore the situation? He wondered what the cowboys had done that Friday night that had cost Mr. Fillmore his life.

When he was sure that everyone was asleep, he carefully sneaked out and ascended the hill in the moonlight.

He finally reached the small door leading underneath the house. A large padlock had been placed in the hasp. He had never been adept at picking locks but remembered when Patrick and he had ordered a lock picking kit from one of those novelty magazines and spent a lazy afternoon around Jeff's apartment trying their hand. He extracted his Swiss army knife, got a pair of small tweezers from it, bent one of the ends back, took out a paper clip he carried in his wallet and started working the lock. Surprisingly within a couple of minutes, he had the lock off.

"WARNING! WARNING! THE TIME-TRANSFER RETRIEVAL DATE FOR THE CURRENT TIME TRAVEL EPISODE WILL OCCUR IN LESS THAN SIXTY HOURS. YOU MUST BE WITHIN TEN FEET OF THE ARRIVAL POSITION. IF FULL COMPLIANCE IS NOT MET, ANY FURTHER AUTOMATIC RETRIEVAL ATTEMPTS WILL BE JEAPORDISED. WARNING-"

Jeff fiddled around in the dark and shut the time belt off. In horror he heard voices from above on the porch. He quickly secured the lock and darted around the house nearly kicking some potted plants over.

Having run around the other side of the house, skirting down the hill and finally making it to the bunkhouse undetected, he quietly scooted into bed. He could hear footsteps ascending the stairs. Pretending to be asleep, he cautiously opened one eye to see Mr. Carter peering around the door scanning the room for activity.

"Hump!" Carter mumbled to himself as he closed the door.

With great relief, Jeff finally dropped off to sleep in a cold sweat.

An early hastily prepared Tuesday morning breakfast followed by regular chores made for a hectic morning. The cowboys were to leave for Grahamville at 11 AM.

Jeff would not be deterred from seeing what was underneath the house. While the other field hands were gathering their grub and gear for the trip, Jeff, throwing off all caution, ran up to the main house and jimmy-rigged the padlock.

Closing the small door behind him, he could hear Thomas and John O'Rork talking overhead. Jeff must have been insane to take such a risk. He always carried a miniature flashlight in his pocket, which he used to examine the room.

Everything was as he had seen in his own time, the wall separating the small section from the rest of the area underneath the house, the trough and implements, and some buckets of tar. After closer inspection of the trough he found remains of newly formed tar the stench of which nearly made him gag.

He went to the small entryway, silently took a deep breath and retreated back into the inner chamber. His eye caught a faint glimmer towards one of the brick columnar supports. He nearly tripped over one of the two vertical four by four beams at either side of the column but caught himself.

With his Swiss Army Knife he carefully picked away at the shiny spot. A chunk of tar the size of a coffee lid thumped on the floor. Training his flashlight towards the newly revealed material, he saw a sheet of metal strapped to the column itself. Using the blunt blade of his pocketknife, he silently chipped away. After a few minutes he finally made a hole about the size of a silver dollar and saw a yellowish metal plate with three letters imprinted on the material, "CSA".

"Confederate States of America!" he whispered to himself. Suddenly a big smile came across his face. "GOLD!"

He looked briefly at the six columns of tar lined up in a row supporting the inner wall. "Columns of gold!" he whispered excitedly.

That was it! The cowboys had received the gold from Fillmore. They had carefully stacked it around each of the six regular brick supports of the house, formed some sheets of metal and strapped them to the columns and to the vertical beams, and used tar to hide the whole arrangement! The four by four beams on either side of the columns were used to compensate for the weight of the gold so the house wouldn't show signs of settling.

"A hen guarding over her young," the phrase rang in Jeff's mind. Carter was the hen and the gold was the young. "The best interest of our native lady!" Gold that would strengthen the South's position.

The voices above him sounded as if they were getting nearer. As he turned towards the doorway he tripped over a shovel he hadn't seen and landed hard against some empty metal buckets causing a loud collection of clanging noises. Beginning to sweat profusely, he scrambled to his feet and was immediately confronted by Thomas Carter standing in the small doorway.

"Well, well, what do we have here?" Carter asked, his gun drawn and pointed towards Jeff's head.

"Gotta shoot you now!"

20

Walter and O'Rork joined Carter. The Irishman lit a lantern hanging from one of the underpinning supports.

Thomas looked around the room and noticed the column with the patch of tar missing.

"You found our little secret. That's rather unfortunate. I thought you were a young man of good character... But you must be a spy for the North ... or worse yet, wanting something for yourself. How long have you suspected?"

Jeff was speechless at first, then defended himself, "I assure you, Mr. Carter, that I have no plans of telling anyone or taking any of this from you."

"Why are you here, then, Carr?"

"I just had to see what was going on. Mr. O'Rork wouldn't let me go with you all the other night. I figured that something worth while was being kept from me. Just had to know, that's all."

"Nonetheless, you must be dealt with. There's no way to trust you now. My apologies... O'Rork, see to it that Mr. Carr here doesn't tell anyone."

"Sir?"

Mr. Carter shot back an enraged, panicked glance. O'Rork drew his pistol and pointed it at Jeff.

"No!" Jeff screamed.

"Wait," Walter stepped forward and pushed the gun aside.

"Mr. Carter, I know that our secret is very important to the South. But to kill an unarmed man? Is that what the South's cause is all about? Surely there's some other course of action."

"I won't reveal anything to anyone. I am for the South. You've got to believe me."

"Gag him!" Thomas told Walter.

Pointing his finger at Walter, Thomas said sternly, "And tie him up tightly. He can stay in the bunkhouse while we go up to Grahamville to help the troops there. We will deal with him when we get back!"

Carter placed his gun in his holster, looked up in the air and then at Jeff.

"Mr. Carr, why did you have to go and do this?"

"Sorry laddie. Tis fer your own good, I guess," O'Rork said as Walter tied Jeff's hands securely and O'Rork stuffed a cloth in his mouth.

After locking the small door, O'Rork and Walter took Jeff to the bunkhouse. They sat him down on his bed and made sure he was firmly tied up.

"Who's going to guard him while we're away?"

"One of the slaves, me thinks. Mr. Carter went to get him. Don't ya be a-worrying 'bout nothing, Walter."

Jeff leaned his head against the wall, downtrodden. His eyes glazed over, what could he do?

The door swung open and in walked Jeremy, the black man whom Jeff had helped. He held a pitchfork in his hand. While Walter went to get the horses for the ride to Grahamville, O'Rork whispered to the timid slave, "This laddie stole something from Mr. Carter. Don't harm him but don't let him go either. We will be back in a day or two. You are officially in charge of the place until our return. Remember, guard him well," O'Rork said as he slammed the door behind him.

Jeff needed to escape as quickly as possible. He wanted to follow the men to Grahamville but he didn't want to alarm his new captor with any sudden movements. What could he say to convince the man of his innocence?

Unexpectedly the black man held the pitchfork high in the air and charged towards Jeff. Jeff recoiled in horror, yelling with the rag in his mouth.

Suddenly the black man slammed the pitchfork down into the floor's wooden slats right beside Jeff's bed and laughed. Jeff felt sick. Held prisoner by a masochist?

"Here, let me take your mouth cloth off so's we kin talk."

"What the- Jeremy, thank the Almighty that it's you!"

"Hello, Mr. Jeff," the young man said as he dragged a chair nearer Jeff's bed.

"I appreciated you heppin me wit dat der wagon de other day. I knew you was friendly. 'Sides, my cousin Sheila, she lives over der to the plantation owned by dat man what wit' all dem rings and t'ings."

"Your cousin Sheila works for Mr. Montgomery?"

"Yessir. My older brother, Abram, and my sister goes over to de plantation and sells molasses that we makes. Mr. Carter likes us producin' money fo' him. He also say dat dat makes us feel good about ourselves. Anyhow, Abram tol' me dat my cousin Sheila done say dat you been kind to Mizz Mammie. He even say dat you give Sheila money 'til her mamma done protested. I can't think dat you done nothin' bad 'gainst Mr. Thomas, Mr. Jeff."

"Oh, that was Sheila. She seems like a nice person."

"Yessir. She and her sissers and her mamma Emily is kind peoples."

A curious look came across Jeremy's face.

"But why is Mr. Thomas a keepin' you here? It caint be for dat you done stole nothin'."

"Why did you lunge at me with that pitchfork? You nearly scared me to death!"

"I wuz jes practicin' for dem Yankees when dey come. Sorry 'bout dat, Mr. Jeff."

"I don't understand. Aren't they coming to free you and your family?"

"We likes it here. Mr. Carter is kinds to us. He let us get food from de fiels, he gives us clothes and we even have our own homes. Dem Northerners is goin' to take all dat away."

"So you're actually in favor of Mr. Carter and the others fighting the Yankees at Honey Hill?"

"Honey Hill? You mean, Grahamville?"

"Uh, yeah. Then, you have to let me go help them in the fight. They may need an extra hand."

"No sirs, I caint let you go. Mr. Thomas, he wup me fo' sho'," the black man said as he scooted his chair a few feet away.

"Jeremy, just think. Has Mr. Carter ever whipped you?"

After pondering seriously over the past, he shook his head and said, "Naw sir."

"Look, Jeremy. I don't know what I can say to convince you that it's all right to let me go. Just let me think a second."

Could he give him money? Maybe he would be offended. Maybe something more substantial would convince him of his honesty. Credit card? Boy, would that blow his mind! Keys... Jeff's upraised eyebrows revealed the existence of a solution.

"Jeremy, if I give you the keys to everything I own, would that help you decide? I need these keys back to get into my car- carriage. I mean my house. Yeah. I can't get into my house if I don't come back and get my keys. Will that do it?"

"Where does you live, Mr. Jeffery?"

"Relatively nearby..." he glanced towards the plantation house.

Jeremy scratched his head and said, "All right, Mr. Jeff. I will let you go."

Jeremy collected his keys, untied his hands and stepped back.

"Do you need me to knock you out?"

Jeremy looked very surprised and distanced himself from the time traveler.

"I mean, if Mr. O'Rork thinks I bonked you on the head..."

"Dat's all right, Mr. Jeff. Miss Sally done figured that out for de bot- o' us."

"Miss Sally?"

"Yessir. Remember dat hoss dat wuz pulling dat broke wagon you-ins helped me fix ta other day? I was 'round her stall when I dropped a hammer 'hind her. When I went to pick it up, she done whopped me in the heyd! I got a big bump right heye on my noggin'. I didn't tell Mr. Carter cause I was ashamed an' all."

"Thank the good Lord for small blessings – er - that he worked all this out for us."

"I'll keep these keys fo' you, Mr. Jeff. But make sures you comes back, now, ya hear?"

Jeff smiled and gathered an extra blanket, two canteens of water and some bread he had spied wrapped up near the stove. The two men emerged from the bunkhouse and carefully surveyed the area. There being no movement around, he turned and shook Jeremy's hand.

"I really appreciate this, Jeremy. You have shown how great a person you are today. You will not regret this."

Jeremy grinned from ear to ear and walked towards the main house.

Jeff walked to the stables, saddled and mounted his horse and lighted out towards Grahamville.

21

It took six hours to reach the area just south of Honey Hill. Jeff didn't meet anyone on the trail the entire trip.

Darkness had made it difficult to identify the region. But with the use of binoculars, he distinguished the hillsides and landscape resembling some of the pictures and drawings he had seen on various web sites.

Clouds gave some cover from the moon as he carefully made his way through the woods assisted by his compass. Once he found Grahamville Road, he dismounted and, leading his horse, stayed to the right of the main thoroughfare to avoid any troops.

At 7:30 Jeff positioned himself two hundred yards in front and to the northeast of Honey Hill, taking cover behind a line of trees parallel to the elongated mound. The twenty-five foot high knoll in front of him ran from his northeast position, crossed the Grahamville Road and passed to the southwest.

A small creek and swamp covered with sparse trees and underbrush ran parallel to the southern position. A dam lay up stream between a bridge whose planks had been removed.

Three cannon were positioned in the fort. He knew that others would be placed higher on the ridge. The fort was strengthened with cut timber along the bottom half of the inside perimeter. Flat rocks and bricks were stacked on the timbers to keep the dirt in place.

Along the wall were openings for various types of cannon. Rifle pits were stationed around the cannon holes for support.

Fifty men were sitting behind the works keeping watch.

Five thousand northern troops would come marching up the road from the southeast pushing the Confederate troops back to their guarded position.

Some of the southern troops had already trained their muskets on the road. The cannon were loaded and ready to fire. Many muskets, which had been loaded for the ensuing clash, had been stacked together in teepee fashion. Although the men were keeping their campfires to a minimum, Jeff could smell some late night vittles. He satisfied his hunger with two pieces of bread and some water from his nineteenth century canteen.

He didn't look forward to viewing the battle, which would turn this peaceful place into a quagmire of death. Watching his great uncle die in the field was incomprehensible, especially when he could not intervene.

Jeff decided that he would get his mind off dreadful things and compose a parting letter to Crystal. He might not have the opportunity to fully reveal his inner thoughts at a later date.

He poured his heart out. If he could only be granted one more opportunity to show his enduring love... But would time permit? After concluding the epistle, he folded it up and put it into his coat pocket.

At ten o'clock he set his watch for 6:00 AM. That should give him time to move to another location if needed. Putting his blanket on the ground, he curled up for the night with his gun by his side and fell asleep dreaming of her.

He awoke at 3:00. A few more soldiers who seemed very alert to the task at hand had gathered on the Honey Hill mound. A sparse fog had formed over the land, which had partially blocked his view. He covered himself against the early morning frost and went to sleep again.

In the middle of the night Jeff froze. Just ten feet from his head, a tall man silhouetted against the moonlit sky towered over him with a Remington rifle pointed straight at his skull.

"How are you doing, stranger?" the man whispered. "Are you a yellow-bellied good for nothing Reb?"

The man's breath hauntingly hung on the midnight air. His glassy eyes were barely viewable under his large black cowboy hat. He held a cigar in the corner of his mouth. Sturdily built, he could have easily overpowered Jeff who was nervously, defenselessly lying on the ground.

Jeff's hand moved ever so slowly under his blanket towards his gun. What would he do now? Not get involved? He should never have come.

"Let's see what your scrawny little self looks like," the man in the dark coat and pants said as he motioned with his rifle for Jeff to get to his feet.

Jeff reached for his gun but it wasn't there.

"Looking for this," the dark man asked as he dangled Jeff's weapon in his left hand and snickered under his breath.

The chill of the night air and the danger of his situation gripped Jeff. He couldn't move. He couldn't die in such a lonely place as this.

The black-bearded man grew impatient.

"I said get up, boy!" The man walked aggressively towards Jeff and pointed the muzzle of the cold steel barrel against Jeff's forehead. Jeff braced for the worst and –

Jeff's watch alarm went off waking him from a horrible dream. Cold sweat beaded on his forehead. He felt for his six-shooter. He was so happy to be alive and so angry at the stupid nightmare.

22

Hiding behind the tree on that chilly Wednesday morning, he carefully stretched and yawned. His blanket and surrounding campsite were drenched with the morning dew. His breath floated across the air. Using his binoculars he spotted some birds atop one of the trees nearby. Some crickets sounded out in chorus oblivious to the death and destruction that lay ahead.

Stale bread and day old water made for a skimpy breakfast.

After relieving himself he withdrew a few feet into the woods. If scouts from either of the warring parties discovered him, he would be sent to one of the prisoner of war camps where he might die of malnutrition or unbearable living conditions.

There was much more activity on Honey Hill. A few fires were burning along the dirt structure sending up clouds of smoke into a now clear morning sky. Perhaps the Southerners had already been informed of the impending conflict and were less worried about being discovered.

Nearly seventy-five men had amassed along the upper level of Honey Hill. Cannon were stationed behind their respective openings in the dirt wall. Muskets were manned behind the rifle pits on both sides of either gun. Two of the large ten-pound howitzers, "Parrots" they were called, were like some Jeff had seen at Fort Sumter. Their black wrought-iron barrels were mounted on an iron frame with wheels that ran perpendicularly on another iron track that made for easier swiveling from side to side.

Another smaller cannon was being brought into position. It's shiny brass-colored barrel was mounted on wheels, had a wooden stock, and was attached to an ammo chest.

The weapon was unhooked from its caisson and swiveled into place. Men wearing red caps and beige-colored jackets surrounded the gun and began preparing it for use. One man swabbed the bore of the gun. A second brought a load of packed gunpowder and placed it into the barrel after which another man rammed it down the barrel's throat. Subsequently a cannon ball was loaded into the weapon and pushed to its inner back. A steel bar with a perpendicular wire-looped device was shoved down a fuse hole. Lastly a man stood at the rear of the cannon and with the help of the other soldiers, aligned the weapon towards its intended target, in this case, straight down Grahamville Road. The actions of the men were being duplicated at the other cannon positions.

The camaraderie was high as soldiers from different geographic enemy activity. Others were finishing an early breakfast while a few leaned against the wall awaiting orders.

Jeff spotted a man whom he thought to be a chaplain, Bible in hand, wearing a side arm, making his rounds encouraging the men before the awesome battle. In the distance a series of white tents had been set up to shelter the troops. Many colorful banners and flags were mounted to designate the companies they represented.

While most soldiers wore gray uniforms, others wore anything from long plaid breeches and bulky hats, to double-breasted coats and derbies.

The officers were easily discerned by the red and blue insignia on the shoulders of their uniforms as well as from the many salutes they received.

Jeff noticed three men riding through the makeshift gate at the front of the fort. The small group trotted down Grahamville Road, first through the swamp, around the plank-less bridge, up a slight incline and back onto the road towards the woods. Two details of men trailed behind the group. Their horses pulled two caisson-like brass cannon mounted on wheels. It was 6:30 AM.

"Scouts?"

He grew uneasy as he assumed that more patrols would be filtering through the woods on either side of the road.

After a few minutes some of the men returned at a gallop and talked with an officer who had emerged from the fort.

Mounting his white horse the man in black motioned and twenty other men followed him briskly down the road.

At 7:30 Jeff heard a strange sound coming from behind the Honey Hill wall. To his amazement a small group of musicians was playing tunes on their drums and fifes.

At 8:00 Jeff arose from his crouched position. His legs had cramped. He had to hold back a yelp of pain. He could hear various noises from beyond the woods which covered Grahamville Road. Occasionally cannon and musket fire erupted.

At 8:30 he noticed another officer riding through the Honey Hill gates down the road accompanied by four other men.

Just by the way he carried himself he was of formidable rank. The thin, tall officer, who was dressed in a light gray uniform adorned with yellow insignia and gold chevrons on his sleeves, had a thick black beard. His horse had a blue blanket complete with a series of golden stars and double striped borders. He and his group were soon out of sight.

A loud thunderous blast came from one of the front cannon. Jeff nearly fell back in surprise. The cannon ball soared down the road followed by a trail of fire. It was 9:15 AM and war had begun.

Officers called down some of the younger Confederates who cheered and shot their muskets in the air.

At 10:00 a new round of shouts came from Honey Hill when a rather stout man without any facial hair, high cheekbones and a high hairline rode past the gate. This pristine figure must have been more important than the one Jeff had seen. His presence garnered salutes and admiration. He circled his horse and waved at the row of young men manning the fort. As he turned back around to face the road only Jeff could see the pain he was experiencing. Maybe an old war wound. He rode a little way and stopped, examining the situation with his field glasses. Then he continued beyond Jeff's view into the wooded area.

Jeff noticed some smoke coming from the forest down the road. It was not the kind one would see from cannon activity but rather from a brush fire. He thought he smelled burnt corn. Maybe some of the southern scouts had started a cornfield on fire to impede the advance of the Yankees.

In a few minutes another cheer came from the southern mound. A group of Southerners led by the two officers was returning from the wooded area. Every twenty yards they and their men would face down Grahamville Road and fire their cannon and muskets.

When he looked again at Honey Hill, Jeff's mouth dropped open. Standing within the confines of the fort were over a thousand men readying their muskets to fire.

The small force still retreating to the fort was now receiving sporadic musket fire from the enemy. Jeff was surprised that the northern army wasn't utilizing more of its cannon.

Part of the retreating forces lay with rifles in hand outside the Honey Hill structure. The rest of the entourage entered the fort. It was 11:00 AM. A new feeling of impending confrontation permeated the air.

Yells throughout the camp energized the scene. A smile of southern pride came on Jeff's face. Somewhere in that feisty crowd, Thomas Carter and his workers were readying themselves for battle. But Jeff's smile disappeared as he looked down Grahamville Road. In the distance he could hear a steady pattern of cadence drumbeats ricocheting off the forest walls. Within minutes the first wave of blue coats arrived 600 yards in front of the Honey Hill structure. A battery of four cannon was stationed in front of the southern position.

A team of eight Rebel cannoneers fired their guns and the whole area was filled with smoke. Loud booms rocked the scene. Jeff could hardly hear.

A small group of Northerners left the main road towards the swamp on the southwest of the mound. Their advance to the front fortress wall was subverted by the low-lying swampland.

Muskets and cannon blazed from both sides of the arena. In the midst of the violence, a regiment of black soldiers rushed down the road towards the causeway. Perhaps they wanted to take advantage of an early advance and surprise the southern army with an aggressive frontal assault. Nonetheless, most of the southern muskets responded in kind bringing the first casualties upon the field.

Many were slaughtered by the sheer power of the guns on the hill. Others of their number fell back in confusion in all directions. Anguish, pain and anger dominated the moment until another regiment pushed its way through to approach the swamp area.

Jeff thought it strange that this new wave of men wore blue sailor's uniforms and caps with long white strings of cloth attached. The muscular troops, eager for vengeance, formed part of some naval brigade accompanying the northern offensive.

The artillery to the right of Grahamville Road shelled the Confederates thus lending support to the newcomers entering the battle. Enduring all of the bullets, the two groups at the front could hold the line no more but swerved to take cover on the right. What a sad sight to see the remaining forces stripping their dead of weapons and ammunition.

What a scene! Death and Hades were weaving their way through the northern forces. Many men were cut in half by cannon balls launched from the Honey Hill wall. Severed legs and arms strewn the bloody battleground.

The smell became unbearable. Even as he had distanced himself from the war zone, Jeff had to tie a handkerchief over his face to help with the stench. Innumerable cries of endless pain were intermingled with those of victory from the southern side.

Just as the groups of the first advance filed to the left, another larger body of men marched up the road accompanied by a defiant drum cadence and thus a new effort in the fight. The new entourage formed a line on the small hill leading down to the swamp. They were six hundred yards from the Confederates. It was 12:00 PM.

When this new group arrived, they started firing their muskets over the swamp grass into the woods. But soon a northern officer came running from the thicket and ordered them to stop. Jeff could barely hear the man yell, "You're killing our men of the 54th!"

Friendly fire in 1864? Jeff was well surprised by the confusion.

The South was having its own problems. One of the cannon on the ridge had jammed. Seven men were working feverishly, trying to get it to function but to no avail. They dragged the heavy piece from its position on the dune and another was put in its place.

Some of the cannoneers along the Confederate line had to wait between shots in order for their instruments of death to cool before loading another round.

Jeff couldn't believe the devastation brought by war. How many would have to die before the North gave up their quest? As the medics tended the wounded, they dodged musket balls and shotgun-type grapeshot used by the South.

Northern desperation turned into panic as if some thought the war effort were already lost. Then pure hatred gave them new vigor.

Jeff's attention was drawn to a lonely figure located one hundred yards to his left. An exhausted Northerner sat resting at the feet of a large pine tree. His face blackened by dirt, his shirt soaked in blood, he coughed profusely, trying to catch his breath from the turmoil. His filthy, weary, bloodstained face revealed the horror of his consternation.

Jeff looked in amazement as he saw a southern cannon ball careen through the air and slice the pine tree in half not twenty feet above the man's head! The man dove out of the way as large limbs came crashing down where he had been sitting. Jeff was relieved that the man was not hurt, but snickered at how quickly the man had exited the jaws of death.

A rush of movement grabbed Jeff's eye as the larger group to the right of the road approached to within two hundred yards of the Honey Hill wall. A small group of Confederates who had been stationed in front of the large Honey Hill dune now took sanctuary within its gates. The body of northern troops extended from the far right of the road to where Jeff was hiding.

As time drew on there was more firing from the northern troops in the swamp. It seemed the North was preparing for a major onslaught to finally overrun the "Rebels".

A man of some importance, slightly balding with a large wide mustache and no beard, rushed to the front of the group and to the left. He had great command of his horse and his troops. Some of the men in front were ordered to lie down and not to fire unless they saw the whites of the enemy's eyes. Preserving ammunition became the order of the day.

Jeff noticed a newfound desire of the South to take more careful aim. The muskets were ordered to fire in waves. Every fourth volley, the men on the hill trained their guns on the North's farthest side nearest Jeff's position. Perhaps this was due to the fact that that side of the road didn't have as many natural obstacles such as the swamp and thick trees to dissuade the North's advance.

As well, the Southerners on the hill would switch positions. One company would move to the left replaced by another, perhaps to keep a fresh effort of stopping any flanking by the opposing troops.

Damage to the South was minimal. The northern troops were getting nowhere. With all of their massive numbers and fire power Jeff thought they could have easily overrun the southern side and captured the railroad they so earnestly desired. But the concentration of so much southern firepower at an elevated position preempted their efforts thus creating an impassable situation.

Another group of black soldiers passed right in front of the main body of northern troops stationed in front of the swamp. Unfortunately for them, the southern muskets were ready for their coming. What followed could be described as nothing less than a severe loss of life. The Southerners were now alternating the amount of powder and shot being put into their weapons. With every other shot they were using double the amount of powder which proved very effective against the advancing forces.

The fiery-hot gunpowder illuminating the field was scalding human flesh. Scores of soldiers fell in waves as both cannon and musket balls filled the scene. Jeff had to turn his head at the ghastly sight. He almost threw up. He forced himself to take a deep breath and then looked back at the slaughter.

The rest of the advancing forces retreated to the right next to the dam for sanctuary.

Suddenly there was deadly silence as both sides contemplated the gravity of the moment.

In the midst of the silence Jeff heard a voluminous yell.

"Follow your colors!" an older man with a thick beard, thin eyes and heavyset body rallied troops ready to take the day.

A mixture of black and white men on horses and on foot followed the mounted leader and charged up the road in two columns.

As they rounded the bend in the road a yell of victory, however brief, rose from their ranks. Yet their short-lived enthusiasm turned to denial and death. The Southerners gave it all they had with double cannon shot and more than a thousand muskets mowing down the northern forces. There were too many of them grouped together to miss.

Nearly fifty men fell dead or wounded all around the older soldier who had been leading the charge.

One of the northern flags fell to the ground when its barer doubled over in agony. Just seconds afterwards, a black soldier gave a yell of defiance, turned towards the incoming cannon balls, raised his hands and shook them at the enemy. He hurried to retrieve the flag, grabbed it with a newfound determination and disappeared into a cloud of swirling smoke. Others followed him into the hellacious advance. Jeff was impressed by the black man's heroic effort.

Jeff's attention was drawn to the elder gentleman still atop his horse barking out orders. He was mesmerized by this man's courage. The gentleman was hit with a musket ball in the hand. He nearly fell from his steed when it reared up on its hind legs. The man clutched his horse's reins with his one good hand, garnered control and fired his pistol across the swamp. All around him men were picked off by a wall of musket balls. The lone rider again, though in pain, led yet another charge down the road.

Another fifty men were wounded by horrendous cannon fire from the fortress. Not willing to give up the fight, the older gentleman led his men in a third advance. This time, however, this valiant leader was broadsided by a nearby exploding shell that instantly killed his horse and knocked them to the ground. The man cried out in pain as he lay pinned under the weighty animal.

"It's General Hatch!" Jeff whispered recognizing the man from his research.

Again a musket ball hit the man, this time in the ankle while simultaneously powder-shot struck his chest. Another brave officer, seeing his comrade's precarious position, rushed to the scene dodging musket balls and explosions that were churning the earthworks around him. As he rescued his fellow soldier from certain death, a musket ball hit the older officer in the square of his back.

"*Dead meat,*" Jeff thought. But sure enough there was still life in the old soldier. In a newfound respect for this warrior Jeff was happy and relieved as he was safely extracted from the gruesome battle.

<<◇>>

Encouraged by the northern retreat from the swamp area, a small group of Southerners advanced with a yell from Honey Hill.

In the midst of them were Thomas Carter and his friends.

The small group of southern soldiers who advanced towards the enemy was violently driven back by the Yankees. They commenced fighting hand to hand. Jed Tub was yelling at the top of his lungs, swinging an empty musket over his head. A Yankee stabbed him in the shoulder with his bayonet with such force that it broke his collarbone. Jed fell to the ground screaming in pain, doused by his own blood. With all of his strength he rose to his feet, hit and killed the soldier with his fists, jerked the bayonet out of its gaping wound and yelled defiantly before collapsing.

With his field glasses, Jeff saw Walter Blake crawling on his belly in the swamp rushes, his musket readied for action and a knife between his teeth. For some reason he was headed towards the plank-less bridge. Jeff noticed a young man who couldn't have been more than fourteen crouching near one of the vertical bridge posts. Occasionally Jeff saw the youth stand up in full view of the northern soldiers and shoot his rifle. He winced as he hoped beyond hope that the young boy would come to his senses and take cover. Apparently Walter had seen the boy as well as he continued towards him. Musket fire from the northern forces erupted just over Walter's position.

A musket ball hit the youth in the leg followed by a second piercing his stomach. The brawny farmer finally reached him, put him over his shoulder and began a treacherous retreat towards the fort gates. A musket ball hit the selfless hero in the square of the back and he went down. Jeff could hear Walter crying out to his God. Two more shots rang out finishing both Walter and the poor youth. Jeff grimaced in deep remorse.

Nearby, a stout John O'Rork fought as bravely as he could. It took two Northerners to overpower the spirited character with both of their bayonets. O'Rork collapsed, grew silent, and slumped against two other soldiers' bodies.

Twenty-five feet to the right, Joe English and Marcus Vendor were fighting valiantly back to back when a cannon ball exploded snuffing out their lives.

To his sorrow, Jeff saw Frederick charge the northern line only to lose his life in a scuffle with a grizzly brute of a man. Frederick's foe towered over him and thrust a knife into his neck. His body grew limp as his enemy raised his rifle and plunged its blade into Frederick's chest.

Jed Tub was dragging Walter to safety, not realizing his friend was dead.

Thomas Carter fired two handguns killing three enemy soldiers. A musket ball coming from the Confederate side struck the back of Thomas' skull. Jeff's heart sank as his great uncle lay dead upon the field.

With his binoculars he looked behind where Thomas once stood. To his alarm he spotted a smiling Jim Morris holding a smoking gun pointed in Thomas' direction!

Not thinking, Jeff extracted his gun from its holster, yelled at the top of his lungs and was about to shoot when Morris jerked his head to the left. A northern musket ball missed Morris by inches. The villain disappeared from view.

Jeff finally knew the truth of Thomas' demise. He had lost his life not for the purpose of valor or for God and country but due to greed. Morris was going to take care of all who knew about the gold so he could keep it for himself.

"WARNING, WARNING! YOU HAVE LESS THAN NINETEEN HOURS UNTIL THE DESIGNATED TIME OF DEPARTURE RENDEZVOUS. SYNCHRONIZATION IS INITIATED. LATITUD-"

Jeff pushed a stop button and the belt silenced.

The battlefield metamorphosed into a sea of confusion. Smoke and screams obliterated the shouts of victory, as both sides grew increasingly aware of the horror that lay before them.

Wagon hospitals crowded the neck of Grahamville Road as medics tended the northern wounded as best they could.

Men's bodies were strewn over the ground as wayward horses fled incoming cannon balls. Bullets split the air like invisible arrows, having their way with unsuspecting victims. Both sides of the conflict were agonized with fear as they strove for victory. All the while, the commanders and officers tried to maintain an orderly and effective presence.

Jeff had been so intensely focused on all that was going on that he forgot to watch his own back. He felt a sharp pain in his side.

He looked in its direction and saw a rusty bayonet aimed at his ribs. The man behind him swiftly twirled his rifle around so that it struck Jeff's right leg and landed him on his back. Slowly getting on all fours, he doubled over in pain and dropped his night vision glasses.

His toothless adversary had a dirty wrinkled face. His black, unkempt beard disclosed his backwoods nature. To his dismay, the Yankee was wearing a hat he had stolen from a Rebel.

"So I 'spect you are just as useless as them cowards on that field over yonder!" The man spat some chew in Jeff's direction.

Out of the corner of his eye Jeff could see Jed crying out in agony still dragging Walter back to the fort.

The Yankee just laughed, "Get a load of that lazy old school boy. Everybody knows that nothin' good ever come from South Carolina!" The man in blue just about doubled over with laughter.

Jeff's anger grew. Not only could he do nothing to save Jed and the others, but a countless nobody was jeering at his helpless friends.

In seconds another cannon ball exploded right on top of Jed and Walter closing the door to any hope of Jed's survival.

The Yankee laughed at the destruction. Jeff's body tensed.

"Well lookie here," he said as he spotted Jeff's binoculars. Overconfident, the man bent over to retrieve them. Just at that moment, Jeff drew his six-shooter and hit the man in the groin. The old codger dropped his rifle and fell to the ground in pain. He hit him harder, this time crushing his skull.

Jeff had seen what he had come to see. He finally understood what had happened to his relative and the others, which pointed to the clues Thomas Carter had left behind. Those who could tell the story had died. Thus the secret would be buried for a century. He turned towards his horse to make a hasty departure.

It had been such a horrific battle. He wanted to get away from that morbid place. He had a rendezvous to keep.

23

He hurriedly put the bedding and other things on his horse and took one last look at the torrid field of death and his helpless friends.

It was 1:30 PM when he carefully mounted his horse. He felt relieved that he was going to another world, grateful that he was being forced back to a less harsh reality.

All of a sudden a hail of musket balls flew past him and struck several trees sending pieces of wood everywhere. He led his horse behind a tree and carefully looked towards the direction of the shooting. The shots were coming from the Southerners who no doubt thought him to be another rag tag northern soldier separated from his regiment. His horse bucked in terror as additional projectiles struck even closer. He calmed Sunshine and steered her deeper into the woods. The Southerners wouldn't track a lone person when they had to deal with so many others of their enemy.

Time was of the essence. A lot had to be done before the 7:30 pickup time at the pigpen.

With five thousand troops around he couldn't be too careful in his wanderings through the woods. Luckily most of the Northerners would be concentrating their activities elsewhere. Jeff finally found a dirt road that led due south.

A long ride lay ahead of him. He had less than five hours to see Crystal, get his keys from Jeremy and get to the pickup point.

He was not surprised at the battle's outcome, yet his sorrow remained. Was he now responsible to tell Thomas Carter's wife how his life had ended? Was he to reveal to southern officials the presence of the precious metal which could help their cause? To whom did the gold belong?

The precariousness of his situation prolonged his sojourn. His caution was enhanced by his nervousness. He would not want to fall into Yankee's hands especially after they had suffered such a formidable defeat.

He almost ran right into a northern brigade but was able to duck behind some tall bushes forty feet from the road.

The long journey afforded him time to think about his final words to Crystal. What could he do without this wonderfully confident, levelheaded girl? Cindy, the secretary would have been proud of his gentle advances.

It was 10:30 PM when Jeff arrived at Montebello. He was saddle sore. His horse was spent. Moonlight shadows danced in and among the servant's quarters as he cautiously rode towards the main house. A dog barked in the distance.

Only one light shone in the right front window of the mansion. His uneasiness at the eerie silence subsided as he thought of the surprised look on Crystal's face at his unannounced coming.

A cool damp breeze greeted him as he approached the front porch. It was much too late to be calling on a southern belle but he was driven to reassure her of his love. Her window faced the left front of the house on the second floor. Luckily her parents' bedroom was located in the rear of the dwelling.

His heart pounded with conflicting emotions. Disgust of war, passion of a real but elusive love, anticipation of his return to his present, and uncertainty as to whatever moves he might make upon his return. His mind was swimming.

Jeff dismounted and tied his horse to a bush under Crystal's window. If he could only spend a few brief moments with her, perhaps lasting memories could be formulated which would satisfy both of their longing hearts.

He found some smooth stones and lobbed them to awaken his beauty. The first landed too softly unnoticed, against the corner of the window. The second ricocheted off the left wooden corner of the building missing the target altogether. The third bounced perfectly off the pane. Candlelight illuminated the room and a petite figure appeared. Her hair somewhat disheveled, Crystal put a candle on a nearby night stand and quietly opened the window. She lifted the candle to eye level and put her other hand up to her forehead to focus.

A big smile came on her face as her gaze fell upon Jeff who motioned putting his finger to his lips, "Shhhh! Don't wake your parents. I just had to see you again."

Crystal quickly donned a robe and hurried downstairs and onto the front porch. She rushed down the outside stairs into his waiting arms. They embraced and kissed immediately.

"How I've missed you, Jeffrey Carter. I didn't know when I should see you again."

Her perfume made Jeff's head spin.

"I had to see you, Crystal, even if it might be our last time together."

Crystal let out a little gasp of disappointment but Jeff delicately covered her mouth.

"Where can we talk?"

They ran hand in hand in the cool weather to the barn located at the distant side of the main house. Entering through one of two large doors, they climbed up a ladder into the loft.

She lit a lantern and adjusted its flame to a lower level.

"I love you Jeffrey Carr, Carter!" Crystal exclaimed as she plopped down in the hay beside him.

"I knew it when I saw you trying to rescue me from my runaway carriage!"

"And I you," Jeff said as he grasped her dainty hand.

"I knew it when I saw you defending Mammie from that Mr. Morris!"

"Don't even put a 'Mr.' by his name. He is much less a gentleman than you are," Crystal's hand stroked Jeff's face.

"Can there be such a thing as an instant love?"

"You mean, love at first sight?" Jeff said as he took both of her cold hands in his.

"What a sweet way of putting it. How clever you are," Crystal said as she delicately leaned her head against his strong shoulder.

"I love how you look at me. I love how your dark hair glistens in the sun. I love your laugh and your dignity. I love your soft lips, and your dark blue eyes."

Crystal blushed.

Sitting up Jeff looked directly at her and said, "You are everything I ever wanted in a woman." He stroked her hair and kissed her forehead.

"I'm so happy," Crystal responded. A long embrace commenced. Then Jeff lightly pushed her back.

"But I'm so confused. What can I do? What should I do about us? Here I am with the most wonderful woman I've ever met, and I've got to whisk myself away to return to the future. That's crazy!" Jeff said as he gazed around the room.

"I'm so different from anyone here. The things I know, the technological advances which I've become used to. It'd be hard to revert back to, well, times like these. Look," Jeff took her arm and asked, "Have you ever seen a time piece like this one?" Jeff removed his Casio calculator watch from his pants.

She looked stunned at Jeff and then back at the watch.

"What on earth is that?"

"It's a watch that can add, subtract, multiply and do most arithmetical equations. That's just one of the advantages of my time. The medical improvements alone would stagger the mind. Of course there are the medical horrors as well. You wouldn't want to hear about them."

"Jeffery, you may be different in many ways, but you are still human. You have your alluring charm. You are sweet to me and many others with whom you have come into contact. You eat and sleep and do many more things that will never change, no matter what age in which you live," Crystal's sweet English accent and intellect charmed him.

She looked rather pensive for a few minutes. Jeff let her contemplate their situation as he gently rubbed her arm to warm her.

"But you are right, my love. We have no recourse as to the future. God has set things in motion. He has allowed you to temporarily visit this place in this time. And even if it has given us a brief moment together, I shall cherish this night in my heart," she said as she kissed Jeff passionately.

Jeff knew that any indiscretion on his part at that moment would ruin things. He wasn't going to let his immediate desires cloud his judgment. Even if she were to offer herself to him, he would dissuade her loving gesture.

She didn't offer and he was relieved. Instead the couple spent the next few hours discussing the future, anything from electric toothbrushes to horse-less carriages, from the invention of the Internet to the production of Titan submarines, the latter which greatly alarmed her.

"Uncertain times will face all of mankind in the future. Who knows what's going to happen? But I can tell you, I must tell you of what is to become of the South, Crystal."

"No my darling. You mustn't. As you said yourself, no one knows what will come to pass."

They spent more time discussing their likes and pet peeves, favorite foods and deserts, and best-liked pastimes. Who would want to talk into a piece of plastic? If one didn't have real money, why not barter instead of depending upon the government or some credit system? Crystal couldn't understand why men were allowed to actually carry the ball in a football game instead of just kicking it like everyone else.

It was late. He wrapped his bulky coat around her to keep her warm. She snuggled up against him and they fell asleep in each other's arms.

A mild morning accompanied by cheery sounds of some birds nearby greeted the both of them. At 6:00 AM, Jeff's loud watch alarm startled Crystal. She awoke first not knowing what the incessant beeping was. She found the watch, held it closer to her face and chuckled, "Mr. Rooster, you've simply been outdone!"

"WARNING! WARNING!" the green belt suddenly came to life nearly scaring poor Crystal to death.

"THE TIME NOW IS 6:00 AM. RENDEZVOUS DEPARTURE TARGET IS SET FOR 7:30 AM. PLEASE BE ADVISED. WARNING! WAR-" Jeff reached down, nonchalantly clicked off the belt, and smiled at Crystal. He stretched. The cramps in his side and arm were well worth having spent their evening hours together.

Faint beams of morning sunlight shone into the barn.

Crystal said, "I'd best be getting back to the house or Daddy-O will think something is amiss."

She took something out of her robe and quickly put it into Jeff's coat pocket, "I don't know when or if we shall see each other, my kind gentleman. You are my hero, my love... but this is for you."

Jeff looked at her charming face. Even in the morning she looked like an angel.

"Please don't open it for another ... one hundred and forty-six years," she said as she briskly kissed him with tears in her eyes and descended the ladder.

"Crystal, Crystal!" Jeff called after her as he tried to descend the ladder but she all too quickly rushed out of the barn into the morning light and entered her house.

He had no time. Getting to the rendezvous point was of the utmost importance.

It would be very dangerous now to travel to West Ashley. The Northerners would probably be more cumbersome in the outlying areas. He decided to ride past the Washington Racecourse, then to the ferry he had crossed the previous night and finally make his way to Carter's farm.

Mounting his horse Jeff looked up at Crystal's window. He was glad that her absence during the night had not been discovered. She blew a kiss to him and turned.

Traveling past the servants' quarters onto the lonely main road, he glanced back at the mansion, gave a sigh and rode on.

24

What was he going to say to the young slave who held his keys, "You're free to go? Your masters have all died in battle while I watched from a safe, convenient distance?"

He finally reached the dock from where the ferry usually launched. To his dismay, the boat was floating, unsecured, ten feet from its moorings. A note that had been tacked to a post read, "Gone home. Ferry service spended. Grover."

Jeff cursed at the inconvenience but abated his anger. He understood Grover's desires and respected him for them. Still, thinking about having to get into that cold, dirty water, his anger flared up again. Jumping down from his horse startled Sunshine. He gave her some sugar and tied her to the post. Although time was running out, a few minutes were needed to calm himself in the midst of his dilemma.

Taking a deep breath, he closed his eyes and slowly exhaled. Warming his hands, he felt in his right coat pocket and pulled out the letter he had composed to Crystal near the battlefield. He hated himself for not remembering to give it to her.

Focusing his attention on immediate concerns, Jeff stretched hard against the dark sky and wished all of this were over. With his night vision glasses he saw lanterns dotting the marsh's shoreline.

"Just gotta do it," he murmured as he walked over to his horse, strapped the binoculars on the saddle, removed his coat, shoes and socks and neared the water's edge.

Taking a deep breath he jumped feet first.

"I hope they're not any snakes around," he thought to himself as he plunged into the frigid river.

He swam over to the ferryboat and took one of the ropes attached to it. Luckily the line was long enough for him to return with it to the shore where he would have more pulling power. Just as he climbed up on the bank a cold breeze hit him square in the face sending chills up and down his body. He dragged the rope over to Sunshine, tied it securely to her saddle and led her away from the shore. The barge was soon bumping up against the dock.

"Good girl."

Jeff was freezing. A headache was coming on. So much trouble! In his anger he violently brushed some of the grass weed from his water-soaked pants. The horse's eyes grew wilder with his sudden movements. Finally when Jeff jerked her reins to lead her onto the ferry, Sunshine bolted upright. When she came down, one of her hooves struck an uneven metal piece on the boat breaking her shoe.

"Crud! That's all I need. No time, no time-" His nervousness increased.

He stroked the horse's face and strapped her to a vertical pole on the ferry. To his relief, the heavy rope suspended from shore to shore was still in place. He started pulling his load across the river. It was hard to believe that the ferryman had to do this on a daily basis. His hands growing tired and chapped, he stopped pulling for a few minutes, found two dirty, worn rags, wrapped them around his hands and continued across the water.

Finally reaching the other side, Jeff secured the ferry to the dock, and guided his horse over to the river's edge to take a drink.

"We're going to make it, girl. Just a little while longer. All we have to do is stay alert."

Walking alongside the animal, Jeff proceeded down the dirt trail towards the plantation. In spite of all of the difficulties incurred, he reached Carter's place at 6:45 am. The sun was beginning to peak over the horizon.

He surveyed the scene for any activity. An eerie loneliness crept over the homestead. The usual early morning cackling of the chickens and roosters was mysteriously missing. Something was wrong.

His first step onto the porch of the bunkhouse let out a loud creek as the step flexed. To his horror, the front door was halfway off its hinges. Some of the windows had been smashed. His muscles tensed as he drew and quietly cocked his weapon.

Dead silence unnerved him.

His throbbing head and his breath against the early morning air dulled his senses.   Jeff suddenly froze. A dark shadow through the doorway was moving around the room. He raised his gun, carefully put his other hand up to the broken door and gave it a nudge.

"Ruff! Ruff!" a scared dog rushed past him, out the door and down the stairs.

"Idiot! Idiot mutt!"

Gritting his teeth, he noticed a note on his bed.

"Massa Jeffery. I intended to meets up wit' you and give you dese keys but, massa, dem Yankees done got everybody. Dey sayin to de others (I kin hear through the window) that we will serve in the Union army and be free. Don't know if I be free but I gots to git so's I can hep de others. Taint right for me to stay here. It was nice to be meetin' with you. Take care of yourself.   Sincerely, Jeremy."

Wet from his dive into the murky waters, haggard from his long trip and emotionally drained from his observation of the Honey Hill battle, Jeff was baffled. His keys were nowhere to be found.

He quickly got dressed in some of Walter's dry clothes, all the while keeping a watchful eye on any activity outside the window. Apparently the Yankees had finally made at least a piecemeal incursion into the West Ashley area but had decided not to set up headquarters at Carter's place.

Jeff wrapped the green belt around him along with his gun belt and walked towards the main house. He had a little more than thirty minutes before having to head to the pigpen for retrieval. Just one more look to see if the cowboys had covered the patch of gold around the column he had disturbed.

A cool breeze made for a crisp morning. The darkness of the night had all but dissipated. With each step up the hill towards the plantation he grew more self-assured that the area had been abandoned. He secured his weapon in its holster.

"WARNING! WARNING! THE TIME-TRANSFER RETRIEVAL DATE FOR THE CURRENT TIME TRAVEL SESSION WILL OCCUR IN EXACTLY THIRTY MINUTES!"

Jeff punched the button on the obstreperous belt.

The little door leading underneath the house was locked.

"Great! No one's been here to disturb anything. Safe and secure, baby!"

Starting to pick the lock as before, Jeff decided against it.

"No time," he moaned as he took his six-shooter, removed the bullets, and smashed the large lock and hasp. Three blows and the lock fell to the ground. Unlatching the door, he firmly pushed it and entered the small chamber.

Lighting the lamp dangling overhead, he marveled that all that gold lay within his grasp. What would he ever do with it? He didn't have to lift a finger to transport it to his own time. Time itself would accomplish that task.

Why had Morris' family waited until Jeff's present day to get at the precious metal? Everyone on the plantation had been killed.

He walked over to the spot where he had done his investigative digging and noticed that O'Rork and Walter hadn't re-patched the column.

"Lookin' for somethin'?" someone asked.

In shock Jeff spun around towards the small door leading to the outside. A man silhouetted against the incoming sunlight held a six-shooter in his hand.

"Morris!" Jeff grabbed for his gun forgetting it was empty.

"Don't move. Got ya' covered cowboy! Just don't know when to quit, do ya?"

The villain stepped into the dark room with a condescending smile.

"Throw the gun down or else!"

Jeff slowly threw the weapon down.

"Get on your hands and knees."

Jeff did so, but without thinking looked at his wristwatch. Jeff's heart was on fire with panic. Time was running out.

"My, my, where did you get that pretty bracelet? What is that anyways? Throw it here!"

Jeff tossed it over in Morris' direction.

"Well, looky there. Huh. It's some sort of ... timepiece. Look at all them numbers. Where'd you git this, anyways?" Morris asked with a glimmer in his eyes.

"Can't tell you."

"You'd best tell me, boy. Or else!" Morris flexed his arm extending the gun.

"You wouldn't believe me even if I did!"

"WARNING! WARNING! TIME RETRIEVAL PROCESS IS DUE TO ENTER INITIAL PHASE. TWENTY MINUTES UNTIL RENDEZVOUS POINT. CROSSVECTOR ESTABLISHED. 2010 IS STIPULATED TARGET YEAR. WARNING!"

Morris cocked his gun and pointed it directly at Jeff.

"Oh, great, thanks," Jeff said as he clicked the belt's alarm and looked up at a startled Morris.

"Time retrieval, huh? What's goin' on here?"

Jeff maintained his kneeling position and didn't say a word. He very gradually gathered some dirt in his right hand. He eyed a small brick just inches from where he crouched on the floor.

Morris' eyes opened wide as he realized what was happening, "My God, you came from the year, what was is, 2010? That's impossible!"

Morris was beginning to feel quite uneasy. How was he to deal with the unexpected, the unbelievable? What unknown powers did his enemy have? He was on his guard.

Jeff began to get up.

"You just stay right where you are," Morris warned him. "That explains your strange behavior, why you wouldn't join the others when they went downtown. They didn't trust you," Morris sneered.

Seeing Jeff's reaction Morris replied, "Oh, yes. I seen you a couple of times. A baby could have tracked you easily. Surprised the others didn't know you were there. And then the way you were riding your horse. Strange all around. And it makes sense how the others done tied you up 'fore they left for Grahamville."

"How did you know?"

"Yeah, I been watching this place. Been concentratin' on it for a few hours now, ever since I got back from the skirmish. Surprised the cowpokes left it unguarded, well, except for them there coloreds. I even had a plan to get rid of Mr. Thomas and his friends but the war took care of that. Then I just had to wait until the slaves abandoned it. But they wouldn't go. Queer behavior," Morris mused. Then he chuckled, "The funny thing is that the Yankees came to my farm first. They agreed to leave me alone if'n I knew where any slaves was."

"You turned in Jeremy and the others? You cad!"

"Yeah, but I got you to thank fer that. Remember on the battlefield when I gunned down Carter? Just seconds after you yelled at me, I ducked. A musket ball nearly blew my head off. Thanks for savin' my life."

Jeff almost rose to his feet but Morris flexed his muscles.

"Just try it, boy."

Morris grinned from ear to ear and began to snicker, "I got the gun, I got the gold, I got the girl!"

Jeff's body flexed.

"Yessir, with you out of the way, I'm sure that lady friend of yours will become awfully lonely," Morris laughed.

Threatened with his life, angry at Morris' murdering Thomas Carter, shocked at his handing over slaves to suit his own interests, afraid of losing his only love to a scoundrel, and quickly running out of time, Jeff threw the dirt in one of his hands and the brick in the other. As he lunged at the unsuspecting cowboy, Morris flinched backwards before taking his shot. His gun went off, its bullet missed his intended target, struck the iron trough, ricocheted and hit the middle of Morris' skull. He fell dead on the floor.

Jeff yelled out in relief, pressing his hands against his temples trying to rub his headache away. Pressure was mounting. His difficulties had increased. Now he had to get rid of the cowboy's body.

Jeff led Morris' horse to the little door, went inside and dragged Morris's body out into the open air.

He mumbled, "Morris was supposed to die on the battlefield. That's why he hadn't taken the opportunity to grab the gold back in 1864 when Thomas and the others were out of the way. There had to be a link, some sort of note that Morris' family would have found in my own time. That explains why my cousin, aunt and uncle had been recently killed."

Twelve minutes to find out. He had to risk it. Jeff wasn't about to take a chance on leaving something behind that would point Morris' family to the treasure.

Honorable Intentions

Finding nothing in Morris' pockets he tied him securely to his horse. "He-yah!" he yelled, as he slapped the animal who would undoubtedly travel to the familiar surroundings of Morris' farm.

Jeff ran past the bunkhouse, through a field and carefully approached the corral on the right side of a building centrally located on Morris' property. To his dismay, smoke was coming out of the chimney. A brother or sister, or any other family members living with him? He felt ill not knowing anything about the surly villain.

As silently as he could Jeff approached the porch. No saddled horses or threatening dogs around. An empty clothesline next to the house, no tools lying on the ground where people might have been working... The coast seemed clear.

He ascended the steps leading up to the porch and quickly but carefully looked in the windows. The house only had two bedrooms and a main living room. He took a deep breath and went in through the front door into the main living area. The house was empty.

A fireplace on the middle left wall had a warm glow. Over the mantle he noticed an old photograph of Morris standing near a woman and a small boy. A vase with some dead flowers was on the other side of the mantle.

A large scuffed-up wooden table and three chairs were in the middle of the room. He walked over to the table and, noticing some papers, read a letter from Morris' wife dated November 3, 1864,

"Jim,

I have arrived safely with Harmon at Mother's in Richmond. We will continue to stay here until such time as you will start acting responsibly. Your son has asked whether I love you. I have assured him that I do. But my heart knows that all is but lost. Your evil dealings with those cattlemen in Grahamville over the last two months struck a last blow. I married an honest man, but you have turned out to be someone else. Let us know of your true intentions. We will be waiting for your coming or some correspondence.

Marie"

"What a poor sap. Lost his honor, the respect of his woman, and lost his family."

Lying beside Morris' wife's letter was one Morris had started. Dated the morning of Saturday, November 26, it read,

"My darling Marie,

How I have missed the both of you. I am glad that your travel has seen you safe to Virginia. Better that you were there than in this war torn land. Oh what I've had to endure. Our Charleston has become all the more desolate. Marie, I am a changed man, my love. I myself just found out about the corrupt nature of those cattlemen and have done broke ties with them hence. I also have wonderful news that will joy your heart. Mr. Thomas Carter has agreed to sell me all of his land for real cheap seein' as he had decided to up and move northward with his family. And Marie, I think there might be gold on that there land! We can make a new life if you would consider -"

At least Morris' wife would know nothing about the treasure of the golden columns.

Nonetheless, Jeff had to discover how Morris' distant relatives of the future would find out about the gold.

Lying beside the two letters was a framed picture of Morris and Marie.

"Why would it be lying on the table? Shouldn't it be hanging up somewhere?"

Jeff looked at his watch and panicked.

"Get a hold of yourself," he murmured as he began to scan the walls. He saw a recently patched place. Knocking out the fresh surface, Jeff reached in and felt something on a horizontal two-by-four. To his delight, he extracted a small bundle of papers and brought them to the table.

The documents were tied together with a string. Among the papers was the agreement between Thomas Carter and his cousin Fillmore. Hauntingly some drops of dried blood had stained the bottom of the document. Also wrapped in the package were Jeff's set of keys!

A folded letter enclosed read,

"November 29, 1864

To whoever this concerns,

I have discovered a little secret that the Rebs would rather not let out. A group of them have stolen a wagonload of gold from a local bank in Charleston. They transported it to Thomas Carter's farm across the way and have off-loaded it underneath the main house. Rumors have it that a battle will soon occur at Grahamville. I think these Rebs are headed that way. I will track them to see what would become of them. I don't wish to have a confrontation with them because they outnumber me. Don't want to lose my life for the likes of them.

The South is done for anyways. It is my intention to recover the gold from these scavengers. So what if I keep some of the find for my family and me. Who knows? Maybe I could do some good for us all.

If I should not make it back from the battle and you discover this note, perhaps the gold has been meant for you all along. Do with it what you may. Good fortune be with you!

Sincerely,

Mr. James Morris"

Jeff grimaced at all of the lies in the correspondence. Morris' frivolous accusations concerning Thomas and the others who died on the field of battle and his painting himself as some sort of hero heightened Jeff's indignation.

He grabbed Fillmore's document, Morris' letters and his own keys, stuffed them into his coat pocket and started out the front door.

Doubt haunted him. Had he secured all of the clues that might hint towards the existence of the gold?

"WARNING! WARNING! THE TIME IS 7:25 AM. FIVE MINUTES UNTIL RETRIEVAL SEQUENCE INITIATED -"

Jeff stopped the alarm. He held back his hysteria.

The uncertainty of the situation nagged at him.

"Details, details. Think about the details!"

He remembered the crack he had left in the tar, which had exposed the gold in one of the columns and the broken lock he had forgotten to put back in its place.

He ran to the house and through the small door leading under the porch. His muscles were writhing with pain.

The lamp was still lit. Jeff walked over to the column. He got a dirty rag off the floor and carefully put some of the tar from the trough in the crack. That would have to do. As he was exiting the chamber he noticed a small pool of blood where Morris had fallen.

"WARNING! WARNING! CROSS VECTOR LOCATIONAL SCHEME PROCEEDING. TARGET SUBJECT NOT FOUND. PLEASE PROCEED TO THE LAUNCH SIGHT IMMEDIATELY."

Jeff silenced the belt again. He kicked some dirt over the blood and smoothed it out with his foot, ran over to the lamp and blew it out and then emerged from the chamber. He closed the small door, closed the hasp and put the broken lock in its place.

Looking down the hill towards the pigpen he noticed a very strong thin field of pulsating yellow, like a vertical open-ended glass. He dashed towards the pigsty. Forty feet, thirty feet - he could hear a constant low electrical hum from the yellow circular cone.

Twenty feet-

Abruptly the cone disappeared! Jeff tripped and fell to the ground in frustration. Late again! Anger, fear, disillusionment, uncertainty.

He missed it! Caught back in time, without any hope of regaining reality as he knew it. He would remain distanced from familiar things. The safety of his world thrust beyond his grasp. What kind of a life must he endure in a world where he could easily fall prey to some disease that could be treated with only outdated medical techniques?

He contemplated his next move and defiantly rose to his feet. He would not be conquered! He was going to Crystal's!

As soon as he had walked a few yards, a strange glow and electric sound once again filled the space behind him. The sphere emanating up into the sky glowed invitingly.

"SUBJECT LOCATED BUT DOES NOT RESIDE WITHIN THE PERIMETER OF THE ELECTRICAL TIME PORTAL. PLEASE ADVANCE IMMEDIATELY. THERE WILL BE NO OTHER OPPORTUNITY!" the belt screamed, this time in the professor's recorded voice.

Jeff was elated, relieved. He readily complied and stepped into the center of the sphere where his body was immediately held stationary. A whirlwind of activity surrounded him. Five beams of light shot from the outer edges of the sphere at different pinpoints on the green belt and a wall of greenish light enveloped the contour of his body. Fully submitting himself to the will and control of the machine, he purposefully relaxed. He closed his eyes. He felt light-headed, as his body floated in mid-air.

Mental images began entering his brain. The final retreat of the Yankees at Honey Hill, Lee's surrendering to Grant, Lincoln's getting shot at Ford's theater, the fire destroying part of the old city, the Charleston Earthquake of 1886, and many more scenic images that briefly passed through his conscious state all served both to educate him and to distract him from any panic. Scenes more modern in nature began to appear. Images of technological advances interspersed with wars, which permeated the ages, passed through his consciousness.

"WARNING! WARNING! CAPTURE ENVELOPE ESTABLISHED. SUBJECT PREPARED FOR REENTRY METAMORPHOSIS AND REASSEMBLY. SEQUENCE COMMENCING IN FIVE - FOUR - THREE - TWO - ONE. TIME TRAVEL MODULE EPISODE REACHING CONCLUSIVE STAGING MODULE."

He felt that he weighed a thousand pounds. The professor had never mentioned anything about the effects involved in reentry. Again, he felt so ill prepared.

"WARNING! WARNING! FOREIGN OBJECTS DETECTED AND IDENTIFIED. IMMMEDIATE MOLECULAR ADJUSTMENTS REQUIRED! MODULE INITIATED."

Jeff had forgotten about the papers he had stuffed in his coat pocket, the gift Crystal had given him, the different clothes he wore. He wondered what effect they might have on the reestablishment of his own molecules. Would he ever be normal again?

"DNA MAPPING STRUCTURE STUDY IDENTIFIED AND COMPLETED. MOLECULAR CHROMOSOME FACTORS CONFIRMED.. CHECK."

"MENTAL IMAGES AND MEMORY STATUS RETAINED AND RECORDED.. CHECK."

"SKELETAL AND MUSCULAR SYSTEMS STABLE.. CHECK."

"DERMIS AND EPIDERMIS LAYERS CONFIRMED AND INTERLINKED TO SKELETAL SYSTEM.. CHECK."

"CRANIAL AND SPINAL NERVES RECONSTRUCTED.. CHECK."

"PERCEPTORY SENSE ORGANS REESTABLISHED: AUDITORY, OLFACTORY, GUSTATORY, PALPITATORY, AND TACTILITORY SYSTEMS IN PLACE.. CHECK."

"WEIGHT, HEIGHT, PHYSICAL STAMINA OF TRAVELER REESTABLISHED.. CHECK."

"THERMAL EQUILIBRIUM AND RESPIRATORY VARIATIONS IDENTIFIED. SUBJECT MAY INCUR SOME INITIAL DISCOMFORT IN RESPIRATORY FUNCTIONALITY. TEMPORARY NON-LIFE-THREATENING CONDITIONS APPLY.. CHECK."

"REESTABLISHMENT OF SUBJECT IS FULLY SECURE AT 100%. PLEASE PREPARE FOR DEPARTURE FROM THE CHAMBER," the computer console abruptly and methodically completed the scope of the time travel event.

25

Something was very wrong. Jeff couldn't open his eyes. Like before, his body was frozen from free activity. A bright reddish glow was blazing right in front of him. A loud roar was all around. He stood frozen, unable to take any evasive action.

His body tingled as if a thousand sharp objects were pricking his skin and increasing the temperature of his body a hundred fold. He coughed violently, trying to clear his lungs.

Finally the loud roar subsided, leaving him motionless and temporarily blinded. Over his coughing, he could hear the time top spinning. A burning smell alarmed him. The top decelerated until it ground to a halt. After a few worrisome moments, he opened his eyes.

The reddish glow proved to be three coats, the kind of which had been worn by English soldiers during the Revolutionary War. The garments had been placed in a display case under a bright fluorescent light straight ahead of him.

A clock on an adjacent wall revealed that it was 7:30 PM.

No fire, no hoodlums, no destruction. He stood still in the chamber for a few seconds until he was able to regain full motion of his limbs.

Suddenly there was a loud banging on the window. The hoodlums! With all of the effort he could muster, Jeff crouched on the floor of the chamber, rolled out of the booth and crawled across the floor behind the control center.

In a sweat he started setting up for another run. He looked again at the window. A white garment flashed past and he could hear some loud swearing. The man stuck his head right up to the window. It was the professor!

"Who's in there. Hey, I locked myself out again. Who's in my lab? Hey, can you let me in please?"

Jeff clumsily got to his feet. Cramps developed in his newly formed muscles which made it difficult to walk. Nevertheless, in exhilaration over seeing the professor he walked as briskly as he could down the hallway and let him in.

The professor laughed embarrassed at his absent-mindedness. But then his countenance changed into confused anger, "What are you doing in my laboratory without my supervision? Why are you wearing those old clothes? What's going on here?"

Jeff raised his hands in surrender and turned his head towards the ceiling, "Prof, you have every right to be upset with me, I know. I took a risk. Could've messed up everything, but, I had to, well, sort of use your time machine."

"What! I can't believe my ears. I've worked all of my life and finally came up with a functional project and –" the professor stopped short. "It worked? It really worked? Wait just a second, Jeff! How did you know about my time machine?"

"I'll explain, Professor. But look at the good news! Not only did it work but you have me as a witness! I am able to speak about it. I can tell you what I went though which is a whole lot better than depending on a chimp! Yes, it worked!"

The professor's pensive look turned into an understanding grin. He was so happy that he gave Jeff a high-five.

"Besides, I had to use it to escape from some guys who wanted me dead ..."

The professor looked befuddled, "Dead? What have you gotten yourself into, my boy?"

"Remember how I told you that I had inherited that plantation from my aunt and uncle who got killed in that traffic accident? Remember my telling you that some guys ran me off the road? They chased me to the lab and –" Jeff stopped, seeing that the professor had a look of utter confusion on his face.

"What do you mean you're living on some plantation now? I just called you yesterday morning at your house on Logan Street. I needed some extra parts for my newest experiment and you said you'd be right over with them this afternoon.

Then he backed up and plopped down in a chair near the console with a horrid look on his face. "Did you interact with anyone in the past so that the future would be changed?"

"I might have, just a little."

"My heavens, what have I done? You could have changed the structure of world events, my boy. We need to discuss your adventure in further detail. Let's go to my office across the hall."

The two of them entered the room and took their seats. The professor was curious as Jeff beamed with joy.

"Wait a minute. If I'm still living on Logan Street, that means my aunt and uncle are still ... alive!"

Jeff realized that his plan to discover the secret of Thomas Carter's note resulted in assuring a safe future for his extended family.

He removed the green belt and handed it to the scientist. "Professor, I'm sorry I used your machine on its human maiden voyage. But look at it this way, it worked just great. I'll explain everything later. I promise. Right now I've gotta run."

At first the professor objected to Jeff's leaving before a proper debriefing but he would not be dissuaded. The professor took the belt, held it up to the light and grinned from ear to ear. He bade Jeff goodbye, turned and started dancing in his office singing, "It worked, it worked..."

Jeff extracted Crystal's wrapped gift and the important documents he had brought back with him from the jacket, discarded the western clothes and money putting them on the coin table and left.

Not finding his wrecked vehicle at the Student Center, he ran all the way to his Logan Street apartment. It was difficult discerning what had and had not actually taken place.

He excitedly drove to his aunt and uncle's house, knocked on the door and yelled to his Aunt Bessie.

"Why hello, Jeffery," she said opening the screen door. "What are you doing here? I didn't know you were going to come this weekend, dear."

He gave her a hug and kissed her on the cheek. "I love you a lot, Aunt Bessie! I'm just glad to see you again!"

"Your uncle is in the kitchen getting ready for supper. Go say hi to him too. Jeff, are you OK, honey?"

He squeezed her hand, winked and then went to the kitchen. Thoughts of inheriting a small fortune dissipated, replaced by something more important, those whom he dearly loved.

"Hello Uncle Jim!" he greeted the older man who was drying his hands at the sink.

"Hello Jeff. What you doin' here? What's the hug for? You act as if you'd been away for a whole month."

"You wouldn't believe me if I told you."

The uncle gave Jeff a strange look and asked, "Love it that you came, even unannounced."

"Just thought I'd come and spend some time with you all. Mind if I go upstairs and take a little nap? It's been a hard week for me."

His uncle motioned his approval, "I'll be sitting in the living room."

Jeff ran up the stairs, went into the guest bedroom, and sat down on the bed. He paused for a minute to settle down from his impossible adventure. He lay down on his firm mattress and shut his eyes. "*Everything had changed for the better*," he thought. He would return to a normal, non-threatening life and get on with things.

Melancholy overtook him as the ramifications of his actions set in. He calmly felt in his pocket for Crystal's gift and, without taking it out of his pocket, held it for the longest time. Something so special from so long ago. He didn't know if he could handle whatever message she might have conveyed. Finally per her wishes, he took the gift out, unwrapped the colorful paper and read a note that had been attached to a small black box.

Honorable Intentions

"Dearest love,

How might I ever scribe the words of affection I feel for you on this lonely Friday night? The picnic was ever so enjoyable. Even though we have met only yesterday, I thank you greatly for rescuing me. Certainly you saved my life from certain peril when you delivered me from that precarious situation. But as well, you have saved it in another sense. How I had grown weary of waiting for someone special to come into my life. And here you are, Jeffrey Carr. I am unsure as to when I shall impart this special letter to you. I know that this is so forward on my behalf but I am unable to keep from expressing my true feelings for my newfound hero. For this, I ask that you would forgive me. Hopefully we will be able to spend time together soon. Please stay well my friend."

Scratched at the bottom of the note were other words, "A parting word, my dearest. I know not if or when, Jeffrey Carter, I shall see you again. I now know who you are and to the time you must return. I will tell no one of your adventure but shall keep these things in my heart. I am giving you this special gift in hopes that some day, through some miracle of God, of Science or both, you might be enabled to place it on my finger. Yours for all time, Crystal."

His heart fell. A lump developed in his throat. How he missed her. Such an excursion into an otherwise delightful world had ended so abruptly.

He carefully opened the black box. There was the diamond-studded ring her father had given her for her birthday. It still looked brand new. Apparently time travel had preserved it. He lay on the bed and wept, letting the sounds of his sobs be absorbed by his pillow. He put the ring with its box back into his jacket, took his jacket off and hung it on the bedpost. In a few minutes exhaustion overtook him and he fell fast asleep.

He awoke with a start. Aunt Bessie stood at the door.

"Jeff, did you want to eat supper with us? I made some pork chops and mashed potatoes. And there's lemon pie to boot? Come on, honey. You're probably hungry. You've been sleeping for nearly two hours."

Jeff sat up in the bed and looked at his watch. 9:45 PM. Splashing water on his face, he sorted his feelings of accomplishment with those of lost romance and friends. He must concentrate on the task at hand.

The biggest "problem" he faced was the gold. Did it belong to the government? Whose government? The Confederacy? The IRS? The State?

What would all that gold do for their plantation, their health and livelihood? He had to tell his aunt and uncle, but how could he convey the truth without their becoming suspicious of his activities? He had to make the gold so obvious that it could be easily discovered by his uncle.

He would drop his Cross pen down through the cracks like he'd done before to direct his uncle's attention to the lower chamber. But when he felt for the pen, it wasn't in his pocket.

"Dummy!" he scolded himself. "There is no pen because there was no lawyer because, thank God, Uncle Jim and Aunt Bessie are still alive! Okay, Plan B."

He walked down to the first floor, told his aunt he'd be back in a minute, and arrived at the small door leading underneath the house. Removing the old lock he had broken more than a hundred years before, he entered the dusty chamber. Using his flashlight he went to the place where he had patched the brick column. As he picked up an old broken sickle and softly tapped away at the dust-covered black tar, a bright shiny patch of gold was revealed.

After dropping his keys on the ground, Jeff went out into the nighttime air, quietly ascended the stairs and, standing near a large crack in the floor, yelled, "Oh, gosh!"

His uncle came running out onto the porch, "What's the matter? Are you all right?"

"I'm sorry, Uncle Jim. I dropped my keys and they fell through that crack there."

"It's all right, son. We can get them with no problem. I've been meaning to clean that area for years. It gives me an opportunity to get at it once and for all. Let's go."

"Supper's on the table. Can't you get it later, Papa?" Bessie called after the two men.

"Just a second, Mamma. We'll be right back," Jim said as he went to the kitchen counter and retrieved a large yellow flashlight.

It took a little more effort for the old farmer to enter such a small doorway.

"Here they are," Jeff said shining his light on the floor.

"Good. Glad you found them," Jim said as he looked around with his flashlight.

"Never been down under the house. No need to, really. Some old farmer must have used this space hundreds of years ago. Hum, something on the tip of that sickle there. Hum... black tar? That's strange. Wonder why anyone would need tar down here?"

He put the sickle down.

"My, my, gonna take a lot of work cleaning out this place if we ever want to use it for storage. Look at this old trough. It's full of dirt and, what's that? More tar? Why would anyone need tar ...."

He scratched his head and began looking around the room.

Honorable Intentions   199

Jeff went to the place where the shiny gold had been exposed.

"Look here, Uncle Jim. What's this?" he asked, shining his flashlight into the hole.

His uncle shined his own light at the spot. His eyes grew wider.

"What the? This column is shiny, like a shiny yellow surface... Oh my stars! C.S.A? Is that what I think it is? Gold? Gold! Jeff, lookee here! There's gold on the side of this column! Lands sakes, boy!"

Jim drew out a small pocketknife from his overalls and excitedly scraped the precious metal.

"This must've belonged to the Confederate States-". Jim stopped in mid-sentence as the knife and flashlight dropped from the old man's hands. Uncle Jim clutched at his heart and fell. Gasping for air he whispered, "Jeff, get my pills, they're in the kitchen. And best get Bessie too. Please hurry!"

Jeff panicked and grew angry at himself for not having foreseen Uncle Jim's strong reaction. He ran up the stairs and got Bessie who retrieved a heart pill from the bathroom and brought it to her husband.

"Jim, here's your nitroglycerin! Take this quick!"

Jim took the pill and was soon calm. Bessie and Jeff carefully helped him out of the chamber and up the stairs to the kitchen where he sat down and relaxed.

"Bessie, you'll never believe me," Jim gasped.

"Please settle down now, dear. Take your time," Bessie said as she sat down and wiped Jim's brow with a damp cloth.

He continued, "Jeff and I found gold underneath our own house. How in the world did it get there? Someone must have put it there for a reason."

Bessie began wiping her own brow with the cloth.

Jeff had to act quickly to come up with an explanation. "By the looks of it, it's been there for quite some time. I'm going to look underneath the house some more. Uncle Jim, are you going to be OK?"

Jim smiled as Jeff went out the front door, ran to his car, retrieved Fillmore's document, ran underneath the house again and dropped the document near the end of the trough.

"I found something!"

Bessie grabbed the large flashlight, came down the stairs and entered the small chamber.

Hands on her hips she declared, "Look at this filthy place!"

"Look at this piece of paper!"

"Let's go to the kitchen where we can read this more carefully," Bessie said as Jeff and she exited the dusty room.

"Lands sake! This is a document written to Mr. Thomas Carter, our relative who built this place. It's dated November 25, 1864. It seems to imply that a Mr. Fillmore was placing this gold into his care to guard it from Sherman's troops."

Bessie continued to read the document silently. She gasped in amazement as she dropped the paper.

"Lands sakes alive! It says that there are one hundred and twenty blocks of gold worth ... thirteen million six-hundred thousand dollars!!!"

Jeff caught Aunt Bessie who was about to swoon to the floor. He patted her face with the wet cloth. Jim's eyes looked as big as saucers.

"How much would that be worth in today's dollars?" Jeff asked.

After a few intense moments, the elderly couple recuperated from their shock and laughed.

Tears of joy welled up in Jim's face. Bessie grew quite pensive, her elbows resting on the table.

"My, oh, my. Now I understand it all."

"What, Mama?"

"Columns of gold; columns of gold. Remember Daddy, how we wondered for years what was written on Thomas' grave. Now, it all makes sense. Thank the Lord for a reprieve from the mystery!"

They were quiet until Uncle Jim chuckled, "Seems that since we're the owners of this place, the least we can do is keep the gold!"

Bessie looked down at the document and then at Jim with a foreboding gaze.

"Oh, no. We must give it back to our government. They would know what best to do with the money. Oh, no. This isn't ours at all. We didn't earn it. The South, well, I mean, our very own government needs this money. Remember what one of our presidents said years ago: that through our taxes, we are making our contribution to the welfare of our nation? Think of the poor babies that could be fed, the roads that we could rebuild for the sake of the children, the many lives that could be changed for the good. No, we mustn't keep this for ourselves. We must do the right thing."

"But Aunt Bessie, that gold belongs to the Confederacy which no longer exists," Jeff said. "So, it really belongs to the owners of the property, doesn't it?"

"We must return it to whatever government we are answerable to. If we don't do the right thing, we compromise our values. We would be robbing the rightful owners. I appreciate your concern, dear Jeffrey, but this belongs to others indeed," Bessie insisted.

"No. I must live by honorable intentions if I am to live at all, no matter what the cost. Integrity is not to be lost on me or your uncle here, right Jim?"

Uncle Jim sincerely nodded.

"So what do you plan to do?"

"Why, I will call the FBI right now. Perhaps they will tell us what we should do," she said as she folded the paper carefully and put it in a Bible on the kitchen counter.

"But the FBI building is closed, isn't it? I think all weekend..."

"Nevertheless, I'll call and leave a message," she said as she gave Jeff a hug and left the room.

"No use talking to her. You're talking to a woman who thinks the people in Washington are as honest as good ole Abe. Still, she's just thinking of doing what's right. We were blessed to inherit this farm and the land we enjoy. Doing anything else with that gold would be downright dishonest. It could jeopardize our whole lives. Besides, maybe there will be some reward for our finding it. You'll see."

There was nothing Jeff could do. An inner conflict raged within him. He decided to leave things as they were. He wouldn't risk a good relationship to sway his determined relatives.

Aunt Bessie re-entered the room and, getting some of the serving dishes, said, "Left a message. I'm sure we'll be hearing from them."

The threesome enjoyed a late supper of pork chops, corn, mashed potatoes, okra, rutabagas and homemade sweat tea. To celebrate, Aunt Bessie even had her traditional, crumbled-up corn bread in a glass of cold milk.

"I can't tell you what being here with you two means. I don't know what I would do without you."

Bessie squeezed Jeff's hand.

After cleaning the kitchen, Jeff and Uncle Jim relocated to the living room where they watched the news.

During a commercial Jeff looked over to his uncle and asked, "Don't you think we'd better take you to your doctor's for a checkup?"

Jim just laughed, "The only thing he'd do is fuss at me for not taking better care of myself. No, all I have to do is take my pills from time to time. I'll be fine."

After watching television they went to bed. For the first time in a long while, Jeff slept. The decision over the gold was final. Clean and comfortable sheets accompanied by a relatively worry-free world granted him a good night's rest. Dreams of an amazingly gorgeous and carefree Crystal filled his mind. At least time would not take those visions from him.

26

Jeff awoke, startled from a loud knock at the front door.

"Please come in."

"Thank you, ma'am."

Jeff got up, hastily dressed and went to see who could be visiting so early. Two men dressed in conservative black suits donned their badges.

"FBI, ma'am. This is agent Creel. I am agent Martin. We need to talk with you about the recent discovery in your basement," the taller of the two said.

"Certainly. Come into the kitchen and have a seat."

Uncle Jim was already sitting at the table sipping some orange juice.

"Care for some coffee?"

Both agents denied her offer cordially.

"It's such an honor to have men serving our government in our home."

Jeff stood nearby leaning against one of the counters yawning and rubbing his eyes.

Abruptly Mr. Creel opened the conversation, "You know that this gold you found just happens to be an issue of national security!"

Creel moved over to the kitchen table and slammed his black briefcase down. Mr. Martin closed his eyes and breathed with a look of disgust.

"Sorry, my partner gets carried away sometimes. This is an important issue, however. You told me over the phone that your nephew here found the gold?"

Jeff nodded.

"So, Mr. and Mrs. Carter, how long have you all been living on this farm?" Creel continued.

"All of our lives," Jim chimed in.

Creel glanced at Jeff searching for his answer.

"I don't live here. Just stay here on the weekends to help out."

"And you nor your aunt or uncle ever knew the gold was there?" asked Martin, whose gray hair, tall, thin, straight stature and self control granted him a certain respectability.

"No."

The shorter agent spoke up, "That's a little hard to believe. Sitting on a gold mine for some time. Nevertheless, how do you explain its being there?"

Bessie handed Agent Creel Fillmore's document.

The agents read the document with interest. Their eyebrows raised in astonishment.

"Well, it is clear that this gold belongs to the Federal Government," barked the shorter agent as he opened the briefcase and curtly inserted the document.

Uncle Jim, a look of disappointment on his face, asked, "Isn't it true that a finder's fee might be in order?"

"Not at all. It was merely under your house. All of it should go directly where it belongs. You really have no say in the matter. In fact, you should be grateful we are taking it off your hands without charging for removal and shipping costs."

Jim bolted out of his chair, "Sir, I can't believe how you are treating us! We are willing, of course, to give the government what is due. But we are respectable citizens!"

"I do apologize for Dave's behavior," Martin said as he gave Creel a hard look. "But I am forced to agree with part of his conclusion nevertheless, Mr. Carter."

"Sir, can you tell me how the Federal Government has anything to do with gold destined for the South, especially when it was found on private property?"

Creel responded, pointing his index finger in Jeff's face, "Young man, this document seems to infer that the gold subsidies were extracted from a federal facility, to be more specific, a bank, in the township of Charleston, South Carolina for the purpose of safeguarding them from compromising forces ..."

"Yeah, Sherman, who represented the aggressive northern forces! Remember what the battle was all about? State's rights!"

Jim Carter was boiling.

"There are no bank accounts or names mentioned on the document having to do with any private citizens, either. These funds belong to our government. Besides, sir, we have neither the time nor the interest to discuss such historically limited issues. I must warn you that any efforts on your part to circumvent the authority of the U.S. Government would be met with stiff penalties if not incarceration!" Creel exclaimed.

That did it. Uncle Jim lunged at the bald man, "Why you!"

In the scuffle, Jim grabbed his heart and fell to the floor in agony. Bessie let out a yell. Agent Martin tried to assist but Jeff asked both agents to leave.

"Young man, you will be hearing from us!" Creel exclaimed as he retrieved his briefcase and walked out the front door.

"Mr. Carter, again my apologies. Due to the law we will be sending a dispatch of agents to this farm to guard our interests. I hope you understand. Please emphasize to your family that they should do the right thing in order not to jeopardize their livelihood," agent Martin said as he exited the building.

"Aren't you sort of doing that to them already?" Jeff called after the agents.

Bessie gave her husband another pill. Both of them helped Jim to Bessie's car and Jeff drove the couple to the Roper Hospital Emergency Room where Jim was put in a wheelchair.

"I don't need all this, Mama. I am perfectly capable of walking under my own power."

They signed in at the front desk and waited for twenty minutes. After a brief examination, a nurse jotted some things down on a chart and called a physician.

"Hello, I am Dr. Sinclair. Heard you had an episode, Mr. Carter. You should stay here for a few days for observation and some tests. If any of your arteries are blocked, we may have to operate. Have you had heart problems in the past?"

"For some time now," Bessie responded. "He has been taking all his pills religiously, though. I'll be stayin' here the next few days with him, if that would be all right."

"Certainly. We'll be moving him into a room within the hour. I'll check on him from time to time," the physician said and then left down the busy hallway.

"Mama, we can't just sit around and let the F-B-I run host over our farm. I need to get back there and take care of business."

"You just sit right there, Papa! Things will be all right. Maybe Jeff here can housesit over the weekend. He can call us if there's any problem. Would you mind, honey?" Bessie asked as she rubbed Jeff's shoulder.

"Sure thing. I'm going now. Everything's gonna be OK. Give me a call if anything else happens here. Love you two."

Jeff drove to his Logan Street home to pick up some things for an overnight stay. He was surprised to see Patrick sitting on the porch swing. It was a beautiful early morning for it.

"Hey bro, what you know?" Jeff yelled as he exited his car and walked up the stairs to the porch.

"Where you been?" Patrick asked as he swatted some mosquitoes from his face.

"You wouldn't believe me if I told you. Really!"

"Whassup? You look a little preoccupied," Patrick said as he got up from the porch swing and high-fived his friend.

"Let's go inside for a sec and get away from these mosquitoes," Jeff said as he unlocked the door, and they walked up the stairs to the second floor.

They sat down in two chairs situated near the kitchenette.

"OK, I'm gonna tell you something no one else can ever hear. Promise you won't tell?"

"I've never seen you this serious before. What's happening?"

"My uncle found a load of ... of gold underneath his house last night."

"Shut-up, dog-"

"Patrick- Anyway, back during the Civil War the relatives who owned Aunt Bessie and Jim's plantation were given a shipment to guard underneath their house. They were afraid of the Northerners using it for their cause."

"No kidding?"

"No kidding."

"Have you or your relatives told anyone about it?"

"Unfortunately my aunt called the FBI!"

"Oh, maaan! They in heap big trouble kemosabe! What did they do, surround the place?"

"I don't know. I had to take my uncle to the hospital and haven't been back to the plantation yet. Can you ride with me out there, buddy?"

"Let's go," Patrick said as the two descended the stairs, went out on the porch, jumped in Jeff's car and spun out of the driveway headed for West Ashley.

"Gold, man. GOLD! You all got your own little Fort Knox thing going on. Man, that is a trip. I can't wait to tell-"

"No one! Remember?"

"Yup."

When Jeff and Patrick arrived at the plantation they couldn't believe their eyes. The place was crawling with SLED agents, the FBI, the County Sheriff and a small contingency of the National Guard.

As Jeff approached the main house he was stopped by a guardsman, "Sorry boys, this is private property."

"You bet it's private property. Mine! Well, I mean it belongs to my aunt and uncle. Let us through please."

"I'll have to check it out. Just a second." The man who was in his early 30's spoke into his walkie-talkie, "Yes sir. We have two young men who say they are related to the owners. Should I let them in? Yessir."

"What are your names?"

"Jeffrey Carter and Patrick Gold."

The guard gave them a strange look after hearing Patrick's last name and spoke again into the walkie-talkie, "Yessir, they seem to be legit. Yessir." The guard motioned them on.

Jeff parked his car as close to the house as possible. Patrick and he ran up the stairs and walked by a few men who were heavily armed. Entering the kitchen, Jeff and Patrick stood in the doorway looking at Agents Martin and Creel who were standing over the kitchen table looking at a map. Their side arms and badges could readily be seen.

"Mr. Creel, I agree that we need to locate all of the gold. That means combing the entire area in a mile wide radius. This might take some time."

"Yes, but we don't need to compensate the Carters for having to stay off their property while the investigation is under way. We are the United States Government and can do anything we want. Certainly they must understand this. I say let's confiscate the farm altogether so we won't have to worry about little trifles."

"Do you have to take the hard line every time? No, we will pay for their hotel bills until this issue is resolved. They did come to us voluntarily."

"Oh, hello Mr. Carter. Mr. Gold, is it? Just sorting out some details as to what we plan to do."

"It looks like a war zone out there! Why are so many people on our farmland?"

"Well, Mr. Carter, you're talking about a sizable amount of currency located within the confines of the property. Not only did we find some gold bullion around each of six columns underneath the house, but there may be more buried on other areas of the plantation. We must search diligently."

"You'll have plenty of time for that," a deep voice came from a short man in a gray suit just entering the kitchen.

"Mr. Schullery's the name. Zack Schullery ... IRS."

"Oh no," Patrick and Jeff echoed.

"Oh yes, we have an interest in this. Thank you for calling me, Dave," the IRS agent motioned to Mr. Creel.

Patrick whispered in Jeff's ear, "Can't find a cop for miles when you need them but everybody's here today..."

"We have surmised for a long time that some gold was lost during the Civil war. Now we have proof positive. We even suspect," the beady-eyed Schullery said, "that your relatives knew of its existence all along."

"They only learned of it just last night! That's why they called, v-o-l-u-n-t-a-r-i-l-y!" Jeff insisted.

"I suppose you're right. Nevertheless, this property, with the exception of the gold itself, now belongs to the IRS."

"The heck you say! How do you figure that?"

"Let's see. The gold has been here since 1864. George Sewall Boutwell was the first commissioner of the Internal Revenue Service from 1862-1863. That means that the gold and the holder thereof fall under the jurisdiction of U.S. Federal law and are subject to any interest thereunto."

"You mean to tell me that you are taking this plantation away from my aunt and uncle to pay for interest on the gold they knew nothing about?"

"That is correct. Possession will proceed posthaste. In fact, subject to federal law, it would not be out of the question to have your relatives incarcerated for unlawful possession of said federal property!"

"That's ludicrous!"

"Watch your tone, young man. Yes, it has been in your family line for the entire period!"

"That's a little harsh, isn't it Mr. Scullery?"

"That's the way it is, Mr. Martin."

Martin raised his eyebrows.

"Oh, yes. I know your name. We know everything about everyone involved."

"Well, I for one am not gonna let this happen. I can assure you of that!" Jeff said as he took Patrick by the arm and led him out of the house to the car.

"Was that a Glock?-"

"Patrick!" Jeff gritted his teeth.

"I can't believe that man! I can't believe this is happening. What a crock! It's my fault too. I could kick myself in the ..."

Patrick just looked at Jeff. He didn't understand.

Jeff swerved the car off the dirt road onto Highway 61 towards downtown Charleston.

"And where are we going?"

"I'm going to see a lawyer friend I know. Maybe he might help us out."

"How do you know a lawyer friend, especially one that's crazy enough to be awake so early on a Saturday morning? I don't hear any ambulances."

Jeff finally made it to an otherwise deserted Broad Street and parked in front of Lawson, Marshall, Graves, and Black.

To Patrick's amazement, a single car, a sharp black Lexus, was parked in front of the building.

Honorable Intentions

Jeff remembered ascending the stairs after he was summoned by the law firm concerning the inheritance he now didn't have. This was all too confusing.

He knocked on the door, which was locked. Peering in, he could see some lights. Someone was there. Finally Jeff saw Mr. Graves come to the door. The lawyer didn't want to open up to the strangers.

"Yes, Mr. Graves. I think you represent Jim and Bessie Carter West of the Ashley?"

"Uh, that's quite confidential. And who are you?"

"Their nephew, Jeff Carter."

"I recognize your name from documents I had prepared for them. Please come in. It's awful early, gentlemen. The office is closed. I'm merely doing some research for a Monday morning appointment. What may I help you with? Are the Carters OK?"

"Yes Mr. Graves, they're doing fine. However, I need you to help me sue the American Government. They are trying to take my aunt and uncle's land."

A big grin came on Graves' face, "Sir, it is not a viable option to bring any judicial action against the Federal Government. There is no recourse. I suggest that you try further arbitration with their associates. Strange though. Usually when commandeering private property from the common citizenry the government grants proper remuneration commensurate with current property values."

Jeff and Patrick looked confused.

Mr. Graves restated his response, "The government pays the owner for the land they are securing."

"Not in this case. You see, the IRS wants the land to pay interest."

"IRS?" Graves asked, glancing at his watch. "Gentlemen, I must begin preparations for my Monday morning meeting. So much to do. Don't worry. There will be no charge for this consultation."

"You mean, you're not going to help us at all?"

Chuckling to himself and peering at the two young men, Mr. Graves said, "I would find a good lawyer who regularly deals with them. I specialize in estates and wills. Good day, gentlemen," the casually dressed man said as he rose symbolizing that the brief, non-productive meeting had concluded.

"What the heck are we going to do now?"

"I'm with you, bud!" Patrick said as they descended the stairs towards Broad Street.

Jeff smiled, "It's so good to have at least one friend who really cares! Thanks."

They got into Jeff's car and decided to drive around town until they came up with some sort of plan.

"Well, there's just one thing I can do, and I'll have to do it by myself."

Looking a little offended, Patrick listened to Jeff's long tale of what Patrick and he had done together, Jeff's time travel, the girl, the war, the whole nine yards.

"So you're the original time traveler. OK, I guess I can live with that. Are you crazy! What are you saying? That I should believe you? Stop the car. Stop the dad-blamed car!"

Patrick exited the vehicle and started walking away.

"Buddy, you're just ... being weird, OK? Who hit you on the head, anyways? You've lost it, man!"

Jeff retrieved the two letters written by Morris and ran beside Patrick.

"OK, OK, you want proof, my skeptical friend? Look at this," Jeff grabbed Patrick's arm and pushed the two letters into his hands. Patrick read the correspondences.

"Cool. So you made up some letters, dated them so they would look old. It looks like they were written yesterday. It's a joke, right? There is no way I am going to believe this crap even if we are friends!"

"Can you keep your voice down, please? I thought you of all people would trust me. Guess not."

Jeff turned away and walked to his car.

Patrick followed suit and sat in the passenger seat rubbing his eyes.

"OK, let me show you something else then," Jeff said as he dug into his coat pocket and extracted the black jewelry case. "Here, look at this baby!"

Jeff opened the case revealing the exquisite diamond-studded ring Crystal had given him.

"K-Mart! I bought my mother one of those last year for her birthday," Patrick laughed. "Of course, she took it back and bought a better one at the mall. Women!"

Patrick could see that Jeff was a little put out.

"Look bro, you're asking me to believe that you were able to accomplish what has never been done since the inception of mankind! Cut me some slack, OK?"

"That's true. I know this is hard. I tell you what. Why don't we take this ring to a dealer and see what it's worth? Some of the jewelers are opened by now. If the ring is worth less than one hundred dollars, I'll drop the whole thing. OK?"

Patrick rolled his eyes, gave Jeff a thumbs-up, and said, "Whatever!"

Jeff drove to King Street and parked. Patrick and he walked down the sidewalk and finally entered one of the many nice jewelry stores along the way.

A short man who had long, thin eyebrows hidden behind his thick black glasses spoke up.

"May I be of assistance, uh, gentlemen?" the man asked in a high pitched voice as he looked judgmentally at the two jean-clad young men in front of him. The obtrusive mole on his nose almost made Jeff laugh, but he restrained himself.

"Yes, can you tell me how much this ring would be worth if I were to sell it today?" Jeff asked as he carefully handed the black box to the clerk.

"Let me get my manager, please. I'll be right back," the clerk said as he turned towards the back room.

"Uh, excuse me. Let me hold the ring, please. It's very old and I don't want it out of my sight. Thanks."

"Certainly," the clerk said, well offended at the request.

A very large man wearing thick suspenders, a white and gray striped shirt and black fancy slacks entered the room.

"Yes, I hear you have a ring you want appraised."

Jeff handed the black box to him. The man opened the box and his eyes widened.

"Why, uh, yes, I haven't seen one of these in some time. You say it's quite old?"

"Yes sir, but I'm not sure about the year."

"These types of rings were produced in the middle 1860's, particularly in the Savannah area. Where did you get such an exquisite item?"

"It was given to me by a dear friend. How much would you say it's worth?"

"I will do the appraisal right here. I know that with such a valuable piece of finery, you must be quite nervous about letting it out of your sight. Do you want an official appraisal, or verbal?"

"Verbal will do."

The jeweler grinned, carefully put a focus glass in his eye, and meticulously examined the ring.

"Part of the value of the stone is how the light passes through the gem and strikes the human eye. This is determined by the cut and proportion of the stone itself," the man hesitated a moment.

"You've heard of the four 'C's which determine the ring's value, have you not?"

"Just a little bit."

"Amazing. Stupendous. I've never seen such an example of high-grade quality. As to clarity, the center Ruby, an oval shape, has an 'F' rating as do the eight small diamonds surrounding it."

"Flunked again," Patrick laughed.

"Oh, on the contrary. No, an 'F' rating means flawless design indeed, which is rare. In fact, I would change that rating to be 'IF' for internal flawless construction. No clouds or splotches to hinder the passage of light. Sir, you literally have a gem on your hands! As to color, let me see."

The jeweler pulled out a large dusty book and compared the color of the stone with that of other examples.

"The Ruby itself is a pigeon blood red. In all probability it was selected with care. In my estimation the ring has a 'D' rating."

Patrick was about to speak but the man looked up again. "That means that it is simply and exquisitely colorless, through and through. Purity in manufacture."

Patrick glanced at Jeff, who himself was starting to beam from ear to ear.

"And as to cut, two factors come into play. Symmetry is very good. No imbalances in the placement of the facets. The stone's proportions have been well engineered, and it is well polished. Sometimes diamond cutters will try to gain profit by keeping the stone as large as they can. Therefore, the cut of the stone suffers. That is not the case in this instance. The cutter who did this work was well paid. The light is allowed to minimally pass through the stone on the oval edges, thus it is returned back to the viewer's eye which grants brilliance and lively play."

The old man took out an instrument and examined the gem further. "This is my leverage gauge. It measures the cut ratio of the stone's diameter to its depth. This is critical to the overall cut evaluation," he said as he looked at the gem closely. "Tolerance bracket is noted as being 61% which is high."

The jeweler smiled, "There is fire in this gem, sir, and in all likelihood fire is involved in the heart of the one who is its bestower!"

Jeff winked at Patrick.

"Finally, as to carat, the center Ruby is easily a magnificent 10 carat cut. The eight little cousins, or, diamonds, surrounding the center stone are one-quarter carat each. The band itself, let's see... yes, the band is made of 22 karat gold."

The jeweler, who had begun to sweat profusely, took off his focus glass, wiped his forehead with a nearby cloth, and paused to reflect on all of the information gathered.

"Well, given the cut, clarity, color and carat construction, and additionally with the added value per the antiquity of the precious item, this ring would be worth a fair market value of ... nine hundred thousand four hundred and fifty dollars."

Patrick's knees buckled. Jeff helped him up.

"And," very seriously the jeweler looked right into Jeff's eyes, "you should guard it with your life! This ring belongs on a queen's lovely hand, sir, I assure you. And who will be the princess who is destined to receive such a prize?"

"That I have to figure out. But I've got a good idea. Oh, do we owe you anything for the appraisal?"

"No sir. It was simply my joy in analyzing the item. What a pleasure! Do be careful, whatever you do, son."

Jeff and Patrick shook hands with the old man and exited the shop.

"Oh my..." Patrick said. "Oh, my..."

He appeared speechless for a few seconds as the two walked towards Jeff's car. They entered the vehicle and just sat.

"I am so sorry. But where else could you have gotten that thing. Geeze, you're almost a millionaire! So what are you going to do now? Did you say you had a plan?"

"I need to return to the past and straighten everything out."

"That's impossible. You can't do it again. What would I do? You're the best friend a guy ever had. Come on, Jeff. There must be another recourse. Look, you've got a life here, with me, er, with us. With Eppy Electronics!"

"And Mr. Singleton? Sure... There's no other way of saving my aunt and uncle from their problems. Gotta go back, that is, if I can. I don't even know if the professor will let me. We'll just have to wait and see. Look, are you getting hungry? Wanna stop at McD's drive thru for an Egg McMuffin?"

Patrick agreed. Jeff drove off towards the restaurant.

27

The men went to McDonalds where they got a late breakfast at the window, pulled into a parking space, and began to eat.

"There is simply no way I can make things right in this time. Besides, you and Cindy have been ganging up on me for the past eight years trying to help me find a girl. I've found my girl... back there. It's just that she will never have to program a microwave or nuke a roast or –"

"Or ride in this fancy automobile while listening to WTMA or a rock station. We got to think of something else," Patrick said as he turned up the radio and bobbed his head to the rap beat.

Just as Jeff was going to turn the radio down, there was a news flash.

"This is a special bulletin. Two young men, both wearing dungarees, are wanted for questioning concerning a robbery which occurred in the West Ashley area. They are driving a late model Chevette. One of the boys has brown hair, is 5 feet, 10 inches tall and has facial hair. His companion, standing about 6 feet tall, has blonde hair, and is in his early twenties. Please be on the lookout. These men are armed and considered extremely dangerous. The robbery, which occurred at the residence of James and Bessie Carter, has claimed the lives of the same. This concludes this public announcement."

"What in the name of – they're talking about us!"

"Did the authorities kill your aunt and uncle? I don't think so," Patrick said.

"No, but putting us on an all points bulletin isn't what I call playing around. Patrick, I'm going to see the professor," Jeff said as he started the car and drove towards the college.

"Don't gun the engine. It'll only attract attention. Just drive slower and I'll duck down in the seat. They'll be expecting two of us," Patrick said as he hid out of sight.

After driving down Lockwood Boulevard onto Broad Street, and down Logan past his apartment, Jeff finally reached the stop light at the grocery store at Beaufain. His heart stopped as he saw a policeman in a car sitting on the curve on the opposite corner scoping for speeders. Jeff looked in his rear view mirror and pretended to comb his hair with his fingers. "Don't even move," he said to Patrick without moving his lips.

The cop talked on his radio. He then looked down at something and peered in Jeff's direction.

"Here I go," Jeff said as he slowly pulled away at the green light.

The cop was preoccupied with something else.

Jeff breathed a sigh of relief. He drove onto Bull Street and parked. Patrick and he jumped out and walked calmly to the lab. The professor was in his office.

"Professor, nice to see you again," Patrick said as he shook hands with the older man.

"I've got to tell you something, but I want you to listen, please."

"Is this something that can wait, Jeff? I'm working on -"

"Professor, this is a matter of life and death. Can you help us?"

Professor Helm invited Patrick and Jeff to take a seat.

"There isn't time to argue or discuss. Suffice it to say that when I went back in time, to 1864-"

"Jeff-" the professor's hand went up. "Should we be discussing this in front of ... your friend? I thought we were to keep this whole thing to ourselves!"

"He knows, he knows. Just listen. It'll be OK. You said that it was important for the time traveler not to interact with people. I blew it! And as a result, things changed - drastically! I mean, some things are better, like my aunt and uncle are now alive. But the government wants their house and land. I don't know whether their lives are in jeopardy, and Patrick and I are now wanted for crimes we didn't commit."

"Settle down, my boy. Settle down. Now tell me, what's happened?"

Jeff disclosed details of his and Patrick's situation.

Surprisingly the professor understood the gist and gravity of the circumstance.

"So, it would follow that the only way to solve the problem would be to initiate a return to the past..." the professor smiled. Then he frowned.

"We are dealing with historic events, my boy. We can't play with time as if it were a rubber ball from the Five and Dime! People's lives are at stake here. Genealogies, successes, failures. These are not easily trifled with. We are not God!"

"Prof., I am the one who messed things up. I've got to be the one who fixes it. I've gotta try. You must understand. Lives have already been changed for the worse."

"All the more reason not to delve into the past!" Helm exclaimed.

The professor got up from his chair and paced around the room shaking his head. "Einstein and the others were right. One's lust for power, one's cravings for the intrusively inaccessible privileges, I mean, once you've tasted the fruit..."

"OK, OK. Patrick and I will go back to the plantation and disappear. My aunt and uncle who are both failing in health will be put behind bars to rot. The government will steal the plantation outright. Everything will be hunky dory!"

The professor raised his hand up in the air as if to call for a corporate reflective pause.

"I see your point. If you were to do this crazy thing... to take yet another journey back into the past, how long would it take you to aright things?"

A slight smirk appeared on Jeff's face as he said, "Well, that's the one thing I don't think you're gonna like. You see, I was kinda thinking about a one way ticket..."

"What? You can't stay back in the 1860's. That's out of the question!" the professor rose again and agitatedly paced around the room. He faced Jeff.

"Why should I let you settle down in another time? No other man has had the privilege. Of all of the qualified great men and women of the world, Jeffrey Carter is the one who has a chance at living in another time?"

"There's a girl."

"A girl, for Jeffrey Carter?" the professor's eyebrows went up and a chuckle came from his lips. Then a frown replaced the smile.

"That's impossible as well, isn't it? This is crazy! Will there be children? This is utterly unacceptable!"

"We'll adopt. I've already got someone in mind."

The professor plopped down in his chair and began shaking his head. He extracted a pipe from his white lab coat, stuck it in his mouth and peered at the ceiling.

"Is there a way to make a one way trip, anyway? I mean without the green belt?"

The professor walked over to a window, his hands resting on his hips.

"I knew the question would haunt me some day. I had not a premonition, but just thought of the possible need to develop a one-way scenario. What better way for me or another loved one to escape the annihilation of the world by nuclear forces than to venture back into safer times such as the settling of the early west, or ..."

Turning around Professor Helm said, "Yes, my boy. I developed an override switch and a round sensor akin to those on the green belt. One must only put the sensor in one's pocket. Upon arriving in the past the traveler would merely crush the small device and that would be that. Are you sure this is what you want to do with your life?"

"Absolutely," Jeff said as he looked at a dumbfounded Patrick.

"As impossible as it seems, as unethical as it is, I can see no other option," Professor Helm said as he ushered Patrick and Jeff into the laboratory.

"May I get ready?" Jeff asked as he walked over to retrieve the proper period clothing for his trip.

Patrick walked over to the money table and was flabbergasted to see the amount of clothing racks and authentic coinage. He went to the green belt which had been put on a chair near the command center and lifted it up to take a look.

"TIME RETRIVAL BELT ON STANDBY!" the belt screamed.

Patrick almost dropped the device on the floor. "Guess I'll just put this back," he said sheepishly and sat down.

"Things aren't going to be the same around here without you, my boy. You're one of my favorite students. I can't believe I'm actually doing this," the professor said as he started setting up the control panel. "Here's that small sensor I was telling you about. Go ahead and put it in your pocket."

"Thanks, Prof. Don't suppose you have any specs for a Model T Ford while we're at it?"

The professor gave Jeff a hard look.

With an approving nod from the professor, Jeff collected enough money, both southern and northern, to last him about two months. He was sure that he would be able to find suitable employment within that time.

In disbelief Patrick silently observed Jeff and the professor's activity.

"So what do I tell your aunt and uncle? They'll be losing their plantation and, according to you, their favorite nephew!"

Jeff abruptly walked over to his best friend, "No, no. You don't understand what I plan to do. You see-"

"Tell him nothing," the professor said as he continued to fool with the controls.

"The least he knows the better. What happens if someone gets wind of this operation and they start interrogating him?"

Jeff turned to Patrick, "Suffice it to say that whatever I plan to do will take care of them better than before. Who knows? I might send them a little-"

"I said not a word, please Jeffery!"

"Talk about abandoning someone who loves you," Patrick kidded.

Jeff threw off the coat he had just put on.

"Doggonit, Patrick. You're absolutely right! I knew I couldn't go through with this. How could I think about leaving them - and you!"

Jeff's friend felt guilty for having taken the joke too far.

"Jeff, Jeff. How old are your aunt and uncle?"

"They're in their seventies, Prof."

"And you're willing to give up the rest of your young life to spend not more than ten or twenty more years with them? Who knows how long they'll live if they're in jail? Think, boy, think. I don't believe they would want you to sacrifice your own happiness for their sakes."

"I see what you're saying." Jeff put the coat on again, got a cowboy hat and some boots and put them on as well.

Turning to Patrick, he extended his hand but Patrick gave him a big embrace instead.

"I can do this because none of the guys is lookin'."

"Don't suppose you'd like to come along? Lot of excitement ahead," Jeff said.

"Sorry... They don't have cable."

"Maybe in a few months..." Jeff grinned at the professor.

"Don't even think about it! To what time and date should I send you?"

"Can you set it for Thursday, December 1st, 1864 at 8:00 AM?"

The professor entered the information.

"By the way, Professor Helm, this time can you relocate my landing to the right about 100 feet? During the last reentry I nearly drowned in a pigsty, literally!"

Professor Helm made a few adjustments and said, "Done!"

He glanced at Jeff from the lighted control console and asked, "One way ticket, huh?" Sighing he mumbled, "First time for everything … Done. Have any questions?"

"Only one. When I arrived from the past the first time, I started coughing like all get out. What happened there?"

"Let's see. You reentered 2010 from the year 1864 after sojourning there for a week's period. Why would you have coughed?" The professor raised his head, beamed and stuck his index finger in the air.

"Oh, yes... pollution, my boy! There is little or no pollution especially from factories in the rural areas in 1864. The Industrial Revolution hasn't happened yet. Maybe I can make a reentry DNA adjustment module, er, not that this machine will ever be used in the future."

Jeff walked over to the professor.

The professor, a bit teary eyed at that point, embraced him and said, "I don't know if I'll ever see you again, my boy, but take care of yourself and give that girl of yours a big kiss!"

Jeff ascended into the octagonal chamber, winked at Patrick and mentally readied himself by closing his eyes.

"Ready, set, go," the professor said as he turned a dial, which initiated the time sequencing.

"Hey, what do I tell Mr. Brown, Cindy and the others?" Patrick yelled over the whir of the spinning top.

"Tell them I went to join the army. Just don't tell them which one! Tell Mr. Singleton that I know he'll miss me. And give Cindy a big fat hug!"

"Goggles! Goggles!" yelled the professor as he motioned Patrick to join him behind the control console.

"INITIATING PRIMARY DATASTREAM MANIPULATION SEQUENCE..." the computer began it's time travel flowchart prompts.

"PLEASE INPUT CLEARANCE PASSWORD:"

The professor input the requested information.

"PASSWORD ACCEPTED. INITIATING START-UP SEQUENCES, PROFESSOR. PLEASE ENTER DESTINATION DATE AT THIS TIME:"

Professor Helm complied.

"DATE OF CESSATION OF TIME TRAVEL EPISODE: RETURN MOTIF IS SET FOR THE DURATION OF ONE HOUR UNLESS OTHERWISE STIPULATED. PLEASE CONFIRM OR CHOOSE ALTERNATE RETURN DATEFRAME:"

The professor pressed the Enter key and waited.

"CONFIRMED: TRANSPORT MODE SECURE AND LOCKED."

The old man grinned and uttered a slight 'hurrah!'

The noise of the top was intense. The floor shook violently. It was a wonder that the whole room didn't collapse. Lights were going on and off.

"Bye, bro. May the force be..." Patrick looked at the professor and continued, "never mind. Bye!" Patrick screamed.

Within a few minutes, Jeff's body had been metamorphosed into a series of swirling dots of blue energy, which soon dissipated into thin air. Seconds later he was gone.

Soon thereafter the top decelerated, its noise replaced by a constant electric hum. To Patrick's relief, the room stopped shaking, and calm was restored.

Professor Helm and Patrick stood there for the longest time, gazing at the empty chamber. This had proved to be both an historic event and an emotional episode. For the both of them, the loss of a good friend to another era would never be forgotten. For the professor, the moment was a mark of successful accomplishment which could never be denied.

Without looking in Patrick's direction the professor said, "For your sake I wish I had a memory eraser like the one they used in the Men In Black, but I haven't invented one yet. Something about the displacement of fluid from one grouping of memory cells to another section of the brain, one would imagine."

"Professor, there is a practical reason for my not being able to mention any of this to anyone. I don't want them to send me to Bull Street in Columbia for a permanent stay! Can I come back from time to time to see how you're doing?"

"Certainly," the professor said as he shook Patrick's outstretched hand. Patrick took one last look around the lab, shook his head and exited the building.

Epilogue

Patrick never saw the professor again. The wiry old man was reported to have given an abrupt notice to the school weeks later. Something about taking an early retirement so as to visit 'historic places'.

Aunt Bessie and Uncle Jim never knew that ownership of their land had been in question. They were saddened to hear that Jeff had left for the army without saying goodbye, until one day Aunt Bessie found a small wooden box in the attic. It contained a letter of explanation from Jeff about his whereabouts and about all that had transpired. He pleaded with them not to tell others but to burn the note to safeguard his secret.

As proof of his escapades he enclosed in the package fifty thousand dollars of stock certificates he had purchased for them in 1925 at the ripe old age of ninety-three. A new company named Standard Oil had begun expanding. Due to the age of the documents and the time of investment and dividends over the years, the stock was worth more money than Jim and Bessie could spend in a lifetime.

Mr. Brown hired another, in his words, "less competent" employee to replace Jeff.

Mr. Singleton was thrilled that Jeff was gone but was himself fired two weeks later when it was found that he was the one who had been stealing merchandise from the shipping and receiving department. Apparently Singleton had been trying to replace Jeff with someone who could help him in his lucrative ventures.

Cindy was happy when Patrick reassured her that Jeff had finally found a mate. She kidded Patrick from time to time, asking him for proof that this was really so.

As for Patrick, he found himself waking up early one Sunday morning in a nostalgic mood.

He invited Sandy, his girlfriend, to accompany him to Rutledge Baptist Church.

It was funny that the preacher emphasized how a person could feel secure in a non-secure world by trusting a God who was not bound by time.

When they got out of the service, they enjoyed a nice meal at the Olive Garden after which Patrick took Sandy to her place so she could do some extra work.

As was his custom, Patrick drove downtown and parked at Marion Square. After walking a few blocks down Coming Street, he stopped dead in his tracks. There, standing before him on the right side of the road where a vacant lot once stood, was a brick, two-story building that had an old bronze plaque attached to the wall near the stairway. It read,

"The New Southerland Inn is dedicated to the memory of Rev. Jon Southerland for his tireless service for preserving young lives. Made possible by a gift from Mr. Jeffrey and Mrs. Crystal Carter and their son Stephen Warren Carter, of the Jerusalem Methodist Church this 31st day of July, 1872."

While tears flowed down his cheeks, Patrick reaffirmed his determination to keep Jeff's marvelous secrets to himself.

Amazing things can happen with time. Changes transpire which one might not think possible. Although Jeff was gone, swept away by endless threads of history, Patrick would never forget their friendship, its memories permeating his mind.

The next afternoon after work, Patrick picked up a copy of The Charleston Evening Post, brought it home, got a Coke from the fridge, and settled down in his living room. As he turned to page two of section 'A' he read,

"Mr. James M. Morris was arraigned in Federal Court in downtown Charleston today. The police had suspected Mr. Morris of a string of burglaries in the Charleston and West Ashley areas in recent months and upon a search of his residence not only found a room full of stolen electronic equipment but drugs and weapons as well. Upon looking for more merchandise and contraband, one of the officers searched underneath the house and found more than $183,000,000.00 of U.S. currency stored around the columnar supports.

According to the police, Mr. Morris claims to know nothing about the gold. If convicted, he could face up to one hundred and fifty years in Federal Prison. Further details are pending."

Honorable Mention

On September 3, 1843, Andrew Jackson Smith of Lyon County, Kentucky was born into slavery. The son of Elijah Smith, Andrew was determined not to live a life of human bondage. Rather, he ran away and joined the Union forces fighting for the emancipation of blacks throughout the nation.

On November 30, 1864, Smith was serving as a Corporal in the 55th Massachusetts Volunteer Infantry. On that clear Wednesday morning, the 55th participated in the "Battle of Honey Hill", South Carolina. The men in their unit, along with thousands of other Northerners advanced towards the southern mound known as Honey Hill. Incurring heavy fire while crossing a swamp in front of an elevated Confederate position, the unit suffered many losses. When the 55th's flag bearer was killed, Smith bravely took up his group's battle flags and carried them through the remainder of the fight. For his heroic action, he was posthumously nominated for the Medal of Honor in 1916, but the War Department would not award him the honor due to the lack of official documentation.

On January 16, 2001, one hundred and thirty seven years after the Battle of Honey Hill, President Bill Clinton presented the Medal of Honor to Andrew Jackson Smith which was received by two of his descendants, his daughter, Caruth Smith Washington and grandson, Andrew S Bowman on his behalf. At a ceremony at the White House, President Clinton said," Corporal Andrew Jackson Smith, of Clinton, Illinois, ... distinguished himself on 30 November 1864 by saving his regimental colors, after the color bearer was killed during a bloody charge .... Forced into a narrow gorge crossing a swamp in the face of the enemy position, the 55th's Color-Sergeant was killed by an exploding shell, and Corporal Smith took the Regimental Colors from his hand and carried them through heavy fire. Although half of the officers and a third of the enlisted men engaged in the fight were killed or wounded, Corporal Smith continued to expose himself to enemy fire by carrying the colors throughout the battle... Corporal Andrew Jackson Smith's extraordinary valor in the face of deadly enemy fire is in keeping with the highest traditions of military service and reflects great credit upon him, the 55th Regiment, and the United States Army."

This dedication is to all, both North and South, who fought for what they believed in on that horrendous day.

Don't miss

THE FACTORY
The financial world of 2026 collapses. Jobs are so scarce, work is made available only to those between 25 and 45. Jack, a former colonel, is lucky enough to find work in a furniture factory but soon discovers that his boss is a maniacal masochist. With no rights, Jack and his coworkers must decide between complacency and action against tyranny.

FULL DISCLOSURE
As John, a Vietnam Vet and survivor of Agent Red, scrounges in the streets of inner city Washington, the President's daughter and her Secret Service team encounter an explosion which exposes them to the biological chemical. The only known antidote to save their lives is available from John's blood. Unfortunately the war hero finds that he must battle not only the merciless elements of inner city squalor but those in Washington who have their own hidden agendas.

Made in the USA
Columbia, SC
18 September 2023

23000597R00126